The Future of Knowledge Management

The Future of Knowledge Management

Edited by Birgit Renzl, Kurt Matzler and Hans Hinterhuber

palgrave
macmillan

First published 2006 by
PALGRAVE MACMILLAN
Houndmills, Basingstoke, Hampshire RG21 6XS and
175 Fifth Avenue, New York, N.Y. 10010
Companies and representatives throughout the world

PALGRAVE MACMILLAN is the global academic imprint of the Palgrave
Macmillan division of St. Martin's Press, LLC and of Palgrave Macmillan Ltd.
Macmillan® is a registered trademark in the United States, United Kingdom
and other countries. Palgrave is a registered trademark in the European
Union and other countries.

ISBN 13: 978–1–4039–4760–4   hardback
ISBN 13: 978–1–4039–4760–0   hardback

This book is printed on paper suitable for recycling and made from fully
managed and sustained forest sources.

A catalogue record for this book is available from the British Library.

Library of Congress Cataloging-in-Publication Data
The future of knowledge management / edited by Birgit Renzl, Kurt Matzler
and Hans Hinterhuber.
      p. cm.
   Includes bibliographical references and index.
   ISBN 1–4039–4760–0 (cloth)
      1. Knowledge management. 2. Organizational learning. I Renzl, Birgit,
1974– II. Matzler, Kurt. III. Hinterhuber, Hans H., 1938–

HD30.2.F88 2005
658.4′038–dc22   2005051005

10   9   8   7   6   5   4   3   2   1
15   14   13   12   11   10   09   08   07   06

Printed and bound in Great Britain by
Antony Rowe Ltd, Chippenham and Eastbourne

Contents

List of Tables

List of Figures

Acknowledgements

We would not have been able to put together this book without the commitment and dedication of the OKLC (Organizational Knowledge, Learning and Capabilities) community, which gathered for their fifth conference at Innsbruck University in 2004. The OKLC audience provided a valuable forum for debating the issues presented in this book. We would like to acknowledge particularly, as the driving force behind this community, Jacky Swan, Harry Scarbrough, Haridimos Tsoukas, Sue Newell, Maxine Robertson, the organizers of all the previous conferences, the members of the Scientific Committee, and especially the conference participants, who have proven truly dedicated to our cause. Special thanks also to Reinhold Karner from KTW Software & Consulting in Kirchbichl/Tyrol, Austria, for his help. KTW supported the Innsbruck event considerably and extended its commitment to the OKLC community by sponsoring the Best Paper Award for the conferences that followed.

We would like to express our gratitude to the authors for their enthusiasm and patience in contributing to this book. We also want to acknowledge Sabine Uitz for her assistance with the preparation of the manuscript and her unfailing dedication. Thanks also to Nicole Morgenroth-Mann for assisting us with the proofreading and keeping an eye on language matters.

BIRGIT RENZL
KURT MATZLER
HANS HINTERHUBER
Innsbruck, 2005

Notes on Contributors

Elena P. Antonacopoulou is Professor of Organizational Behaviour at the University of Liverpool Management School and Director of GNOSIS, a dynamic management research initiative. She is also currently Senior Fellow of the Advanced Institute of Management Research. Her principal research interests include change and learning processes in organizations. At present is undertaking a series of research projects in organizational learning, social practice and dynamic capabilities and is focusing on the development of new methodologies for studying social complexity in organizations. She writes on all the above areas and her work is published in international journals such as *Organisation Studies, Journal of Management Studies, and Academy of Management Review.* She is currently Subject Editor for Organizational Learning and Knowledge for the *Emergence: Complexity and Organizational* journal and has just completed a five-year term as joint Editor-in-Chief of the international journal *Management Learning.* She serves on the editorial board of three journals: *Organization Science, Academy of Management Learning and Education* and *Society, Business and Organization.* She has served in numerous positions at board and executive levels at the Academy of Management, USA and is currently serving a second term on the Board of the European Group in Organisation Studies (EGOS). www.gnosisresearch.org

Albrecht Becker is Professor of Business Administration and Management Accounting at Innsbruck School of Management, University of Innsbruck. His research interests cover the social and organizational context of management accounting, particularly interpretative and comparative management accounting research, organization theory, and organizational learning and knowledge. Recent research and publications include foundations of management accounting theory, ethics and gender issues in management accounting, comparative management accounting, and work on organizational knowledge.

Irma Bogenrieder trained at a market research institute and is currently Associate Professor, Organizational Design and Organizational Processes at the Rotterdam School of Management, Erasmus University Rotterdam. Her current research focuses on (external) influences on learning in communities of practice, especially the issue of multimembership, and co-operation in teams. Dynamics of innovation in general is another field of interest. She has published in management learning and organization studies.

Manfred Bornemann was Assistant Professor at Karl Franzens University, Graz, where he lectured on general management, organizational theory and knowledge management. He has published several articles in the field of intellectual capital reporting and is active in several national and international IC communities. As a consultant, he was involved in developing and implementing the intellectual capital report for ARC, and developing the first regional intellectual capital statement for a research network in the field of nanotechnology. Recently he finished a guideline for intellectual capital reporting for SMEs, based on the experiences of 25 implementation projects.

Elisabeth Brauner is Associate Professor and Head of the PhD Program in Experimental Psychology at Brooklyn College and the Graduate Center of the City University of New York. Her publications and research interests range from basic social to applied organizational psychology and management theory. She is currently working on hypermnesia in groups, transactive memory assessment in small groups and organizations, and the influence of metaknowledge on the acquisition of transactive knowledge. Recent publications include work on knowledge management in organizations, information processing in groups, and argumentation structures in small group problem-solving discussions.

Paola Cillo is Assistant Professor of Management at Bocconi University, Milano, Italy Institute of Management and Business Economics, where she teaches courses on innovation and new product development. She earned her PhD from Bocconi University in 2001. She has been Visiting Scholar at Wharton School, 2000–2001. She teaches at the SDA Bocconi School of Management. Her research interests and publications relate to the exploration of the role of market knowledge in fostering innovations' success and the relationship between market orientation and innovation in symbol intensive industries.

Johann Füller is CEO of HYVE AG, a company specializing in virtual customer integration. He holds a degree in mechanical engineering, and in industrial engineering and management. Currently he is a PhD candidate in Marketing at Innsbruck University School of Management. His research interests are innovation creation in online communities and virtual consumer integration into new product development.

Daniel Geiger is a lecturer in the Department of Management, Freie Universität, Berlin. He recently completed his PhD thesis dealing with the epistemological foundations of knowledge-management. His current research interests are narrative-based knowledge sharing in communities of practice; the nature of knowledge in organizations, and organizational competences.

Stefan Güldenberg is Assistant Professor at the Department of Strategic Management, Management Control and Consulting at the Vienna University of Economics and Business Administration. He received his PhD in economics and social sciences from the Vienna University of Economics and Business Administration in 1996 and his Master degree in business mathematics from the University of Ulm in 1994. During 1998/99 Stefan Güldenberg was a Schumpeter research fellow at the John F. Kennedy School of Government, Harvard University. His main research interests are strategic management, leadership, knowledge management, organizational learning and management control.

Hans Hinterhuber is Professor of Strategic Management and Head of the Department of Management at the University of Innsbruck, Austria; he is also a visiting professor for International Management at Bocconi University, Milan, Italy. He is a member of the board in companies in a wide range of industries in Europe. He researches and teaches on issues of strategy, leadership, diversification and coherence in organizations. Hans H. Hinterhuber has authored or edited more than 30 books and published over 300 articles in a wide variety of scholarly and business journals.

Gregor Jawecki is a project manager for the company HYVE AG, whose expertise is in the virtual integration of end-consumers. He holds a degree in business administration with specialization in marketing from the Innsbruck University School of Management. His research focus comprises the analysis of innovative behaviour in online communities, particularly in the field of sports.

Heinz Konrath is Finance Director of Avaya, Mediterranean Europe, Middle East and Africa. He received his Master degree in knowledge management from Danube University, Krems in 2002. Over the last 15 years he has been in international leadership positions in the field of finance and operations of globally operating corporations. His main interests are leadership, change management, organizational culture, performance management and knowledge management, specifically in relation to restructuring, reorganization and re-engineering initiatives in a multinational and multicultural environment.

Kurt Matzler is Professor and Chair of the Department of International Management at the University of Linz, Austria. His primary research and teaching interests are customer value management, resource based view and knowledge management. In these areas he has published several books and a range of articles in the leading journals in this field. Kurt Matzler is

Academic Director of the Executive MBA-Program at the Management Center Innsbruck (MCI) and teaches at several MBA-Programs in Switzerland and Austria. He also serves as a consultant to companies in the public and private sector. He was Visiting Scholar at WHARTON SCHOOL, University of Pennsylvania in 1996. He was also Visiting Adjunct Professor for International Business at the School of Business of Fairfield University, Connecticut, USA in 1998 and at Southeast Missouri State University in 2000. In 2001 he received the Erwin-Schrödinger Research Award and was Visiting Scholar at Bocconi University, Milan.

Hans Mühlbacher is Professor of Business Administration at Innsbruck University School of Management. He has held visiting professor positions at universities in France and the USA. He is Associate Editor for International Business of the *Journal of Business Research* and member of several editorial boards of international journals. His major research interests are strategic marketing and multicultural branding. He has published a book on international marketing and a number of articles in major journals such as *International Journal of Research in Marketing, Journal of Business Research* and *European Journal of Marketing*.

Sue Newell is Cammarata Professor of Management at Bentley College, USA. She previously worked in the UK, at Aston University, Birmingham University, Warwick Business School and Nottingham Business School. Her last job in the UK was at Royal Holloway, University of London, where she remains a visiting professor. She was one of the founding members of the IKON (Innovation, Knowledge and Organizational Networking) research center, which is based at Warwick Business School. This reflects her main research interests, which focus on exploring innovation processes from a knowledge and networking perspective. She has published widely in both organization studies and information systems journals.

Emanuela Prandelli is an assistant professor of management and Senior Lecturer at SDA at Bocconi University in Milan, Italy. She was Research Assistant both at St Gallen University in 1998 and at the Kellogg School of Management in 1999, where she also attended as Visiting Professor in 2001. Her research focuses on marketing, e-business and the global market, and e-business and innovation management. She published several articles on the topic of marketing, innovation and e-business in top-ranked international journals (including *California Management Review* and *MIT Sloan Management Review*) and is author of two books: *Marketing in Rete* (McGraw Hill, 2002) and *Oltre la notizia. Economia e gestione delle imprese editrici di quotidiani* (Etas, 1999).

Birgit Renzl is Assistant Professor at the Innsbruck University School of Management. She is teaching courses in strategic management, knowledge management and management research at undergraduate, graduate and executive level (University of Innsbruck, Mining University of Leoben, Universidad de Alcalá, Madrid). She was Visiting Scholar both at the Graduate School of Business at the University of Strathclyde, Scotland in 2003 and at the Institute of Management at the University of St Gallen, Switzerland in 2004. Her current research focuses on knowledge sharing, communities of practice, knowledge-based organizations and innovation.

Maxine Robertson is a senior lecturer in organizational behaviour at Warwick Business School. She is a core member of IKON and co-author of *Managing Knowledge Work* (Palgrave, 2002). Her main research interests focus on the management of knowledge workers and knowledge-intensive firms; the management of interactive innovation processes; and knowledge management. She has published extensively in all of these areas, including articles in *Organization Studies, Journal of Management Studies, and Management Learning and Organization.*

Ron Sanchez is Profesor of Management at Copenhagen Busines School and Linden Visiting Profesor in Industrial Analysis at Lund University, Sweden. He has published several books on knowledge management, as well as numerous articles in leading management journals. His next book is *Modularity, Strategic Flexibility, and Knowledge Management*, to be published by Oxford University Press.

Mohanbir Sawhney is McCormick Tribune Professor of Technology, Chairperson of the Technology Industry Management Program and Director of the Center for Research in Technology and Innovation at the Kellogg School of Management, Northwestern University. Professor. Sawhney is a globally recognized scholar, teacher, consultant and speaker in strategic marketing, e-business and innovation. He has been widely recognized as a thought leader: *Business Week* named him as one of the 25 most influential people in e-business; Crain's *Chicago Business* named him a member of '40 under 40', a select group of young business leaders in the Chicago area. He is a fellow of the World Economic Forum.

Ursula Schneider heads the Institute of International Management at the University of Graz. She also teaches at the College of Europe in Bruges, at the University of St Gallen and in Brisbane, Bangkok, Kuala Lumpur and Delhi. Her research is focused on organizational networks, alliances and internationalization strategies of TNC, as well as on monitoring and measuring intangibles and on knowledge management. She has worked on research panels for OECD, the EU, the Austrian, Swiss and German governments and the Austrian and the European Academy of Sciences. Additionally, she is a member of the board of three academic management journals and has received two research awards. Her books on knowledge management include *The Knowledge Management Challenge* (1996), *The 7 Deadly Sins in KM* (2001) and *The Dark Side of Knowledge* (2005), all in the German language.

Georg Schreyögg is Professor of Management at the Faculty of Business and Economics, Freie Universität, Berlin. His current research interests include dynamic competences, organizational knowledge, and path-dependency in organizational decision-making. His work has been published in several books and journals such as *Academy of Management Review*, *Journal of Business Ethics*, *Managementforschung* and *Organization Studies*. Address: Freie Universität Berlin, Garystrasse 21, 14195 Berlin, Germany; e-mail: info@fu-schreyoegg.de

Christian Stadler is a research fellow at the University of Innsbruck. He holds a PhD in business history. His research interests include long-term success, innovation, organizational change and the resource-based view of the firm. Address: University of Innsbruck, Center for Strategy and Leadership, Universitätsstrasse 15, 6020 Innsbruck, Austria, email: christian.stadler@uibk.ac.at

Jacky Swan is Professor in Organizational Behaviour at Warwick Business School, University of Warwick. She completed her PhD in psychology at Cardiff University. She is a founding member of IKON and conducts her research in related areas. Her current interests are in linking innovation and networking to processes of managing knowledge across different industry sectors and national contexts. She has been responsible for a number of UK Research Council projects in innovation and is currently working on projects investigating 'Managing Knowledge in Project-Based Environments' and 'The Evolution of Biomedical Knowledge for Interactive Innovation in the UK and US'. She has published widely, including articles in organization Studies, organization and human relations and is co-author of the book *Managing Knowledge Work* (Palgrave, 2002).

Gianmario Verona is Associate Professor of Management at Bocconi University, where he is also Associate Director of PhD in business administration and management and Senior Lecturer at the School of Management. He has been Visiting Fellow both at the Center for Innovation and Product Development, MIT and at the Center for Strategy and Leadership, Innsbruck University. He teaches technology marketing, new product development and technology and innovation management; has published several articles in leading international journals; and is co-author of three books.

Salvatore Vicari is Professor of Management at Bocconi University, Milan, Italy Institute of Management and Business Economics, where he teaches courses on innovation and new product development both in the undergraduate programme and at the SDA Bocconi School of Management. He has been Director of the PhD programme in management at Bocconi University. He is now Prorector of Bocconi University for External Relations. His research interests focus on organizational creativity and knowledge management. He is author of many publications in leading academic outlets.

Introduction

Birgit Renzl, Kurt Matzler and Hans Hinterhuber

This book aims to provide a forum for leading scholars in knowledge management to engage in debate on current research and shed light on future prospects in this field. The papers in this issue are based upon the 'Fifth European Conference on Organizational Knowledge, Learning, and Capabilities [OKLC]', hosted by the Department of Management at the University of Innsbruck in April 2004. Following the previous conferences in Warwick (2000) Leicester (2001), Athens (2002) and Barcelona (2003), the conference has moved to the centre of Europe. This shift towards the centre is present also in a metaphorical way, in the sense of focusing on the core topics in knowledge management. The debate on organizational knowledge, learning and capabilities emphasizes the knowledge-based view of an organization, reflecting the current debate among academics and practitioners on the centrality of knowledge in organizations and the alignment of the multi-perspective views of knowledge. Over time the OKLC conference has continually evolved into a strong community of interest unifying various perspectives of knowledge in organizations, such as:

- knowledge-sharing;
- knowledge creation and innovation;
- the relationship between knowledge and value creation;
- communities of practice;
- the relationship between the management of knowledge and advances in communication and information technologies;
- evaluating knowledge and intellectual capital reporting;
- managing knowledge and competence;
- the knowledge-based view; and
- dynamic capabilities.

The aim of this book is to outline the 'Future of Knowledge Management'. Knowledge management evolved in the mid-1990s as a response to

1

the advance of the knowledge society. Demand for knowledge management technologies has shown two-digit growth rates in the last few years (Abrams et al., 2003). German management professors rank knowledge management first when asked what they consider to be the core issues in strategy research (Matzler et al., 2003). According to our study on the future of management tools and concepts among consultants in Germany, Austria and Switzerland, knowledge management is considered one of the hottest topics (Matzler et al., 2005). However, consultants are quite sceptical about the effectiveness. Companies' satisfaction with knowledge management initiatives is generally low and, from the 20 management concepts studied, knowledge management is the one with the highest need both for academic research and for development of practical tools.

We are living in a knowledge society that yields high returns on knowledge resources (Drucker, 1999). In the knowledge-based view (Grant, 1996), which was established in the mid-1990s, knowledge is regarded as the most important source of competitive advantages for firms.

While the knowledge-based view initiated the debate about epistemological issues such as what is knowledge and how do we generate new knowledge (Nonaka, 1991; Nonaka and Takeuchi, 1995; Tsoukas, 1996) in addition to issues of transferability (Szulanski, 1996; Kogut and Zander, 1992; Zander and Kogut, 1995), there has been, however, little development of methods and tools to implement knowledge management in firms. In the beginning of the knowledge management age the tools were highly driven by information and communication technology. However, their use is rather limited when it comes to knowledge. In contrast to information, knowledge is highly personal. Knowledge presupposes values and beliefs and is closely related to human action (Tsoukas and Vladimirou, 2001). Knowledge is based on personal judgements and tacit commitments. It is necessary to consider the following aspects when dealing with knowledge in firms (as Matzler et al., 2005; Renzl, 2004):

- *Tacit dimension of knowledge*: Apart from the explicit dimension there is always a highly individual tacit dimension of knowledge, which is difficult to articulate. Knowledge is considered as the process of knowing integrating the two complementary dimensions of tacit and explicit knowledge (Polanyi, 1966; Tsoukas, 2001). Therefore, it is not enough to capture solely the explicit part of knowledge. Methods and tools of knowledge management need to consider knowing as a process operating at different levels of consciousness.
- *Practice*: Knowing is intimately related to practice (Orlikowski, 2002; Argyris, 1993; Cook and Brown, 1999). Knowledge develops in the situation at hand. Action and practice are influencing thinking and knowing and vice versa. Thus, knowing reflects the highly dynamic process of thinking and acting among the participants involved.

• *Social aspect*: Since knowledge is considered as a process of knowing, interaction among the participants involved is crucial (Nonaka and Takeuchi, 1995). In organizations people share and create knowledge through social construction.

Based on the above definition of knowledge and knowing accordingly, developing knowledge management tools seems rather challenging. Compared to other tools in our study, knowledge management has to face a particularly challenging position (Matzler et al., 2005). Respondents perceived knowledge management as a highly important topic. However, they are not satisfied with the methods and tools applied. Future research in this area is required in order to sustain both a management debate and a set of practices, in addition to an academic field of research.

There was widespread diffusion of knowledge management literature during the late 1990s. knowledge management seemed to be 'en vogue'. The ABI Inform Index shows a total of over 4000 articles concerning knowledge management in 2002 (Serenko and Bontis, 2004, p. 185). The number of articles on knowledge management and intellectual capital increased at an average annual rate of 50 percent during 1995 to 2005. The question arises, is knowledge management just another management fad? Following Abrahamson's (1996) management fashion model Scarbrough and Swan (2001) analysed the role of fashion in knowledge management to explain its widespread diffusion from the mid-1990s onwards. They consider the ambiguity of the concept itself as a primary clue to the fashion-setting possibilities (Scarbrough and Swan, 2001, p. 3). The concept of knowledge management is multi-faceted and includes a variety of approaches such as epistemological issues, information technology, knowledge work, measuring and evaluating intangible assets, and soon. However, 'management fashions will only diffuse if they claim to be fundamental in their application and timeless in their scope – if they claim to offer solutions to real or perceived efficiency gaps' (Scarbrough and Swan, 2001, p. 9).

This book provides a selection of papers dealing with fundamental issues in knowledge management. In the first part of the book, new perspectives on knowledge and learning are discussed. The second part deals with emerging issues in knowledge and innovation, since the topic of innovation comprises a core area in knowledge management. Relevant issues in managing the knowledge-based company complete our synopsis on the future of knowledge management in the third part. We hope that the present book contributes to a better understanding of future issues in knowledge management.

References

Abrahamson, E. (1996) 'Management Fashion', *Academy of Management Review*, 21(1), 254–85.

Abrams, L. C., R. Cross, E. Lesser and D. Z. Levin (2003) 'Nurturing interpersonal trust in knowledge-sharing networks', *Academy of Management Executive*, 17(4), 64–77.

Argyris, C. (1993) *Knowledge for Action – A Guide to Overcoming Barriers to Organizational Change* (San Francisco: Jossey-Bass).

Cook, N. S. D. and J. S. Brown (1999) 'Bridging Epistemologies – The Generative Dance Between Organizational Knowledge and Organizational Knowing', *Organization Science*, 10(4), 381–400.

Drucker, P. F. (1999) 'Knowledge-Worker Productivity – The Biggest Challenge', *California Management Review*, 41(2), 79–94.

Grant, R. M. (1996) 'Toward a Knowledge-Based Theory of the Firm', *Strategic Management Journal*, 17 (Winter Special Issue), 109–22.

Kogut, B. and U. Zander (1992) 'Knowledge of the Firm, Combinative Capabilities and the Replication of Technology', *Organization Science*, 3(3), 383–398.

Matzler, K., H. H. Hinterhuber, S. A. Friedrich von den Eichen and H. K. Stahl (2003) 'Core Issues in German Strategic Management Research', *Problems and Perspectives in Management*, 1(1), 149–61.

Matzler, K., M. Rier, H. H. Hinterhuber, B. Renzl and C. Stadler (2005) 'Methods and Concepts in Management: Significance, Satisfaction and Suggestions for Further Research: Perspectives from Germany, Austria and Switzerland', *Strategic Change*, 14(1), 1–13.

Nonaka, I. (1991) 'The Knowledge-Creating Company', *Harvard Business Review*, 69(6), 96–104.

Nonaka, I. and H. Takeuchi (1995) *The Knowledge-Creating Company – How Japanese Companies Create the Dynamics of Innovation* (New York/Oxford: Oxford University Press).

Orlikowski, W. J. (2002) 'Knowing in Practice – Enacting a Collective Capability in Distributed Organizing', *Organization Science*, 13(3), 249–73.

Polanyi, M. (1966) *The Tacit Dimension* (London: Routledge and Kegan Paul).

Renzl, B. (2004) 'Seven Propositions on Knowing – Basic Principles for Organizing Knowledge in Firms', Paper presented at the 20th EGOS Colloquium, The Organization as a Set of Dynamic Relationships, Ljubljana University, Slovenia.

Scarbrough, H. and J. Swan (2001) 'Explaining the Diffusion of Knowledge Management: The Role of Fashion', *British Journal of Management*, 12, 3–12.

Serenko, A. and N. Bontis (2004) 'Meta-Review of Knowledge Management and Intellectual Capital Literature: Citation Impact and Research Productivity Rankings', *Knowledge and Process Management*, 11(3), 185–98.

Szulanski, G. (1996) 'Exploring Internal Stickiness: Impediments to the Transfer of Best Practice within the Firm', *Strategic Management Journal*, 17 (Winter), 27–43.

Tsoukas, H. (1996) 'The Firm as a Distributed Knowledge System – A Constructionist Approach', *Strategic Management Journal* (Winter Special Issue), 11–25.

Tsoukas, H. (2001) 'Do we really understand "tacit knowledge"?', in M. Easterby-Smith and M. A. Lyles (eds), *Handbook of Organizational Learning and Knowledge* (Malden MA: Blackwell), 410–427.

Tsoukas, H. and E. Vladimirou (2001) 'What is Organizational Knowledge?', *Journal of Management Studies*, 38(7), 973–93.

Zander, U. and B. Kogut (1995) 'Knowledge and the Speed of the Transfer and Imitation of Organizational Capabilities: An Empirical Test', *Organization Science*, 6(1), 76–92.

Part I

New Perspectives on Knowledge and Learning

1
Modes of Knowing in Practice: The Relationship between Knowledge and Learning Revisited

Elena P. Antonacopoulou

Introduction

The emphasis placed in recent years on knowledge and learning as the new sources of wealth (Badaracco, 1991; Drucker, 1993; Sveiby, 1997; Boisot, 1998) has led to a preoccupation with ways in which knowledge and learning can be 'managed' so that their contribution to organizational performance can be best predicted and achieved. This preoccupation has resulted in knowledge and learning's being treated like entities to be manipulated at will. Moreover, as a result of this preoccupation, the attention has shifted more towards the outcome of learning and knowledge, away from the process of learning and knowing itself. The ongoing challenge in knowledge management debates remains the need to identify ways we can better understand the dynamic nature of knowing in action. Although practice-based approaches (Bourdieu, 1980; Orlikowski, 1992; Turner, 1994; Gherardi, 2000) have enabled us to capture some of the forces which shape the nature of knowing, we have yet to fully understand how knowing is put into practice. This chapter contributes to this debate and argues that a better understanding of the relationship between learning and knowledge can provide valuable insights into knowing in practice.

Our understanding of the relationship between learning and knowledge appears on the one hand to treat learning and knowledge as distinct entities (Davenport and Prusak, 1998; Nonaka and Takeuchi, 1995) and on the other hand to assume implicitly that learning and knowledge are strongly connected and even interdependent (Kolb et al., 1991; Lave, 1993; Coulson-Thomas, 1997). Knowledge is presented as a product of learning and existing knowledge is perceived as a precursor of further learning (Juch, 1983; Gagné, 1983; Thomas and Harri-Augstein, 1985). There is limited research that examines the relationship between learning and knowledge. An examination of the relationship between learning and knowledge could shed light on the nature of their association by highlighting the factors which may determine both whether knowledge is a precursor of learning and whether knowledge is shaped by learning. Moreover, an examination of the relationship between learning and knowledge may also help clarify the connections between different aspects of learning and knowledge in the process of creating, sharing, disseminating and utilizing knowledge and learning. In other words, it can reveal different modes of knowing in practice.

Furthermore, such analysis may provide new insights into the nature of learning and knowledge at an organizational level. The lack of agreement in current literature as to whether learning and knowledge at an organizational level is the sum of individual or group learning and knowledge or an integral part of organizational functioning regardless of the people involved (Argyris and Schön, 1978; Brown and Duguid, 1991; Kim, 1993; Richter, 1998) necessitates a more careful examination of the interactions between different levels of analysis. Perhaps our preoccupation needs not to be whether learning and knowledge take place at an organizational, group or individual level, but how activities at each of these levels may shape the process of learning and knowing at every level. This chapter contributes to this debate by exploring the relationship between learning and knowledge as shaped by the interaction of individual (personal) and organizational (contextual) factors. The analysis is based on recent empirical findings from a study of managers in the financial services sector in the UK.

Therefore, this chapter reviews the relationship between learning and knowledge and presents different modes of knowing in practice, based on empirical findings. The analysis challenges existing assumptions about the relationship between learning and knowledge and provides new results showing the personal and contextual forces which shapes knowing in practice. The findings presented show how the interaction between personal and contextual factors shapes the role of knowledge in the learning process and the impact of different modes of knowing on the way knowledge is created and utilized. The analysis highlights seven modes of knowing. These modes of knowing, it is argued, reflect the dynamics which account for how knowledge and learning at an individual level find meaning and expression in the process of social interaction. The different modes of knowing also seek to reflect the indeterminate nature of knowledge and learning and the complexity underpinning their relationship.

The discussion unfolds in four sections. The main assumptions which underpin our current understanding of the relationship between learning and knowledge are presented first. The second section presents and discusses the empirical findings from the study, while the third section of the chapter distils the main issues and highlights the nature of the relationship between learning and knowledge in the various modes of knowing in practice. The discussion concludes by reviewing some of the implications of future research in organizational knowledge and learning.

Learning and knowledge: Their relationship

Early notions about the role of learning and knowledge as fundamental elements in political and social activity can be traced back to the philosophy of the ancient Greeks. The views of Socrates, Plato and Aristotle about the nature of knowledge have played an important role in the history of learning theory and the way it has developed to this day (Hergenhahn, 1982). These early theories about learning have given rise to the need to understand questions such as, what knowledge is; what are the origins of knowledge; what does it mean to know; and even, how do we know what we know? These questions are concerned with the nature and evolution of knowledge (epistemology) and are central to the philosopher's quest to understand knowledge in relation to education and learning (Antonacopoulou, 2000). Early notions about knowledge indicate the variety of forms that learning takes and the difficulty of measuring how much exists at any one time or establishing accurately the level of transferability across boundaries (Machlup, 1962; Haynes and Allinson, 1988). They also indicate the diversity of learning forms (conscious and unconscious) and resources (structured and unstructured) in the social context.

These ideas have shaped many of the definitions that are to be found for learning and knowledge, and the way their relationship is understood. For example, existing definitions of learning present knowledge as one of the outcomes of learning or one of the elements which constitute the learning experience (see Bass and Vaughan, 1969; Walker, 1975; Thomas and Harri-Augstein, 1985). Knowledge is also seen as an important part of the learning process because, as some commentators argue, the recognition of one's own need to learn, the search for the new knowledge, the test of that new knowledge in practical action, and the consolidation of the whole exercise within the memory are all essential to complete learning (Revans, 1971; Klatt et al., 1985).

The relationship between learning and knowledge has also affected our understanding of knowing. Two the dominant positions appear to inform our understanding of knowledge: the 'cognitive' and the 'constructionist' perspectives (Fiddis, 1998) or what Venzin et al. (1998) call the 'cognitivistic' and the 'connectionistic' profiles. Both perspectives or profiles can be traced in Ryles' (1949) argument against Cartesian dualism and the differentiation between 'knowing how' (that is, procedural, skill-based knowledge) from 'knowing that' (that is, declarative knowledge). Put differently, this distinction is what more recent writers have termed as 'explicit' and 'tacit' knowledge respectively (Polanyi, 1966; Nonaka and Takeuchi, 1995). These distinctions have created more room for encapsulating the importance of knowing what Cook and Brown (1999) refer to as the 'epistemology of practice' which draws attention to the role of inquiry, implying that the action has the sense of a query, like a problem or a question. Knowing also draws attention to the interaction between the social and physical world. We act within this world and our actions either give shape to something in the physical world or affect the social field. Hence knowing, since it is about our actions, relies on this interaction. Therefore, knowing is about the interaction between the knower and the world.

In recent years the recognition of the fluidity of learning and knowledge has sought to be addressed by researchers who have accounted for the unpredictability and complexity of learning and knowing within organizations (Boland and Tenkasi, 1995; Choo, 1998; Von Krogh et al., 1998; Antonacopoulou, 1998; Gherardi, 1999). Recognizing the contextual nature of learning and knowing, these contributions invite us to explore the relationship between learning and knowledge through the culturally located systems which shape learning and knowledge within organizations (Engestrom, 1993, Blackler, 1993, 1995). In other words, the relationship between learning and knowledge must be sensitive both to implicit and explicit social rules, sensitive to the role of language and symbols as well as to power and the political dynamics that underpin the process of learning and knowing. Indeed, sensitivity to these issues could extend further our analysis of the qualitative nature of learning and knowledge as 'first order' or 'second order' (Walzlawick et al., 1974), what Antonacopoulou (1999a) describes as '*learning by knowing the same*' versus '*learning by knowing differently*'. Extending this analysis and exploring the relationship between learning and knowledge could explicate the contested, temporal and multifaceted nature of learning and knowledge as reflected in different modes of knowing.

It is therefore both necessary and timely that as we explore the future of knowledge management we investigate how learning and knowledge interact and identify the contributing factors, at individual and organizational level, which may shape their interaction. Moreover, there is a need to consider in more depth whether knowledge is created through learning or utilized after learning and, indeed, if knowledge is a precursor of further learning. Furthermore, in the light of the currently unidirectional representation of the relationship between learning and knowledge, there is a need to explore the multiplicity of factors which shape how and why learning and knowledge may or may not coexist.

The relationship between learning and knowledge across three retail banks

The questions raised in the previous section formed part of the focus of a recent study which sought to examine individual managers' learning and changing across three retail banks. This study examined the interaction between individual and organizational factors and the impact on the nature of the interrelationships between processes such as change, learning, training, self-development and career development (Antonacopoulou, 1996). Choosing from the emerging findings of the study, the paragraphs which follow present evidence which highlights the relationship between learning and knowledge from the perspective of the individual manager. Using the individual as the unit of analysis allows a better understanding of the interaction between personal (psychological) and contextual (social) factors shaping the relationship between processes. The findings are discussed in relation to the organization- and industry-specific characteristics. A brief overview of the research setting and the methods is provided first, before the main findings are presented, discussed and analysed.

The research setting

The retail banking sector provides an interesting example of an industry which has undergone a process of reconstruction that demanded fast responsiveness to change and a high need for learning. Triggered by a series of external forces (for example, trends in the world economy) and internal forces (for example, changes in the market, the intensification of competition and soon), the recent changes have forced a new orientation towards the basic principles of banking (Cappon, 1994). No longer are banks purely money-laundering organizations; instead they are diversifying into new businesses and have become increasingly sensitized to the importance of valuing the customer.

In response to these changes banks are moving away from former paternalistic approaches to developing the skills of their employees. Traditionally, banks tended to recruit school-leavers whom they trained internally through a formal disciplined classroom approach that provided job-specific skills. Professional development, particularly for those aspiring to managerial roles, was mainly focused on gaining professional qualifications such as the Association of Charter Institute of Banking Diploma (ACIBD). In the light of uncertainties in the market at the time of writing, banks are no longer willing to invest in the traditional training and development approaches. The new training and development policies are orientated towards a more learner-centred approach with an emphasis on personal responsibility for development. A common assumption, which underpins the introduction of self-development, is that by transferring the responsibility for learning and development to the individual this would enable them to be better placed in responding to the rate of change in the sector. This philosophy is reflected in the practices of the three banks in the study and is seen to significantly affect individual and collective learning practices (see Antonacopoulou, 1998, 2001, 2005 for more detailed discussion). The characteristics of the industry and the way these characteristics are reflected in the philosophy and practices of the three banks in the study are also seen to shape the perceptions of individual managers in terms of the role attributed to knowledge and learning in responding to the new requirements. More importantly, they provide insights into the way learning and knowledge are associated.

Methods

The relationship between learning and knowledge is captured in the complex interactions between organizational or contextual and individual or personal factors. The study sought to capture this interaction by reviewing organizational practices supporting learning and knowledge and to examine the impact of these practices on individuals' perceptions and actions. The way personal and contextual factors are negotiated is reflected by individuals' perceptions of learning and knowledge, the way knowledge is employed in the process of learning, the perceived role of knowledge in identifying and pursuing learning goals; and the utilization and longevity of knowledge from learning.

In pursuing these issues the study adopted a case study approach for contextualizing the analysis of the findings. The data was collected using a variety of methods, which allowed both for the necessary depth of discussion to be developed and subsequent triangulation. The qualitative interview (semi-structured) was the main data collection method, while questionnaires and observation were supplementary data collection methods also employed. The managerial sample was selected by the researcher, so that it would be representative of the employee population in each bank; would consist of a broad spread of regions, seniority, years of service in the bank, education and qualifications and age; and would include both genders. Twenty-six managers from each organization participated in the study, making a total sample of 78 managers across the three retail banks.

The interviews with individual managers sought to examine their perceptions of the nature and role of learning and knowledge in the light of the ongoing organizational changes. Some of the questions managers were asked concerned the perceived relevance of their existing knowledge to their current job, the extent to which their current knowledge is in excess of or below job requirements; and the implications on the utilization of knowledge and the need for learning. Additional questions sought to examine managers' perceptions of the learning process and to establish the factors affecting learning.

A longitudinal approach also formed part of the research methodology in an attempt to trace the process of learning. Exploring individuals' learning goals is one way of tapping into the multiplicity of issues which shape the nature of learning and the role of knowledge, as well as the nature of knowledge in the process of learning. As part of the longitudinal analysis, managers were asked to identify and describe a learning goal and to explain what knowledge they perceived as relevant in fulfilling the specific learning goal. The development of this learning goal was followed up with a second interview, which was scheduled to take place six to eight months after the initial interview. The objective of the second interview was to trace the way managers pursued their learning goal and to identify the actions managers took in fulfilling the learning goal. Moreover, this approach sought to examine whether these actions influenced managers' learning and the utilization of knowledge. The perceived longevity of knowledge was also discussed with participating managers. The empirical findings, which follow, raise some interesting issues about the way managers in the study perceive knowledge, learning and their relationship.

Findings and analysis

This section selectively presents the study's findings, which show the relationship between learning and knowledge as perceived and acted upon by managers across three retail banks. The discussion will focus primarily on those findings which illustrate how existing knowledge is developed and utilized by managers and how the changing circumstances in the bank affect knowledge and learning. Individual managers' learning goals will also be discussed in relation to the perceived knowledge requirements. Finally, the longitudinal findings will provide further insights into the process of learning and the implications for knowledge creation and utilization and the perceived longevity of knowledge.

It is important to place these findings in the context of other findings with regard to managerial learning in the three banks (discussed elsewhere in more detail – see Antonacopoulou, 1998, 1999b, 2000, 2001) and to summarize the following key observations.

Firstly, findings across the three banks show consistently that managers perceive learning in very narrow terms, primarily equating it with attending training events provided within the bank. Learning is frequently defined by managers as the acquisition of information and skills relevant to their current job.

Secondly, the findings show a multiplicity of personal and organizational factors affecting learning both positively and negatively. Personal factors include the perceived need to learn, the perceived ability to learn and the expected benefits from learning. Organizational factors include the rigidity of the current structural and cultural arrangements, the implicit and explicit messages of the organization, the gap between rhetoric and reality, the perceived encouragement of the organization for learning and development, opportunities to be creative and so on.

Thirdly, the findings indicate the political nature of learning in organizations as reflected in the tendency of individuals to pursue learning goals which are in line with organizational requirements (for example, relevant to their job) and through methods approved by the organization (for example, attend a formal training event). Using these observations as a backdrop, the

findings which follow explore in more depth the nature of learning in relation to knowledge and the nature of knowledge in relation to learning.

Current job requirements, existing knowledge and the nature of learning

There are a number of noticeable similarities in the characteristics of
managers across the three banks. One such similarity is that the vast majority of managers in the sample are holders of the Association of Chartered
Institute of Banking Diploma. This is the main qualification many bring to
their current job and managers in the sample appear to have studied for
this diploma because it was seen as '*a passport to a career in banking*'. Despite
the length of time on the job, the majority of the managers in the sample
have not acquired any additional qualifications. Overall, the view that
managers appear to be taking is that '*the job requirements will determine the
need to learn something new*'. Therefore, many would tend to rely on their
existing knowledge to perform their job and would take a rather passive
approach towards learning. In describing their current knowledge managers
draw a distinction between '*technical knowledge*' (acquired through professional qualifications and structured training programmes) and '*management
knowledge*' (developed through day-to-day experiences and interacting with
others in the workplace).

What is noticeable in managers' descriptions is reference to the corresponding skills of the technical or management knowledge described as a
way of capturing the actions that would reflect that knowledge. In fact,
managers tended to avoid referring to knowledge as a term, because '*it is
too vague*' or '*abstract*'. Therefore, many would refer to presentation skills,
organizational skills, motivational skills, interpersonal skills and so on. to
describe management knowledge, while tending to refer to lending skills,
computer skills, taxation skills and so on to describe their technical
knowledge.

Managers across the three banks on the whole feel that they are much
better equipped with technical knowledge rather than management knowledge. The technical knowledge corresponds to the specialist roles that are
characteristic of their career in banking to date, and this is what the organization provides through its training programmes and encourages through
the professional qualification. Therefore, according to a large proportion of
managers, acquiring the technical knowledge has been '*a matter of credibility*' rather than development and learning. However, although useful, technical knowledge is perceived by most managers as increasingly less relevant
and out of date. When asked to reflect on the relationship between their
existing knowledge and their current job, a significant proportion of managers in each bank (Bank A: 54 per cent; Bank B: 58 per cent; Bank C:
35 per cent) recognize that their existing knowledge bears limited relevance
to their job requirements. With over 25 years of service in the bank in
some cases, managers in the study qualified for the ACIBD a long time ago

(in some instances as far back as 20 years ago). One manager explained: *'Professional knowledge is quite useful in the job I do, but you start to do it at junior level and by the time you finish it you are senior and you don't practice it'.* (Manager, Bank C)

According to managers, recent changes in the market have shifted the focus from technical to management knowledge. In the light of the emphasis placed by the three banks on customer service and sales and the less structured nature of their job, managers feel that the technical knowledge is very unlikely to secure their career progression in the future. In relation to this point, a manager said: *'The shifting emphasis of the bank away from 'traditional skills' to centralized decision-making and sales orientation makes technical knowledge less relevant.'* (Manager, Bank B) Overall, the new requirements of their job are posing new challenges that some managers find frustrating because it necessitates *'relearning'* and *'starting from scratch'.*

However, the perceived imbalance between job requirements and their current knowledge does not only result from the changes in the organization and the market but also depends on the level of utilization of the current knowledge. When asked whether their present job utilizes their existing knowledge and the extent to which their knowledge is in excess of or below present job requirements, a significant and consistent proportion of managers across the three banks (Bank A: 57 per cent; Bank B: 50 per cent; Bank C: 50 per cent) argue that their current knowledge is in excess of the present job requirements.

This apparent contradiction in managers' responses raises an interesting point about the nature of knowledge in relation to its utilization. Managers who perceive that the existing knowledge is in excess of job requirements pointed out the presence of additional knowledge in their possession which is not being utilized. The knowledge which is under-utilized tends to be mainly management knowledge (for example, team-building, leadership, marketing), although a small proportion of managers also referred to technical knowledge (for example, computer programming and legal issues). Managers' explanations of the reasons for the under-utilization of knowledge raise further interesting issues.

Some managers explained that this knowledge was not utilized because the scope of the present job did not permit it. Some managers referred to the nature of the job as more technically orientated. Others highlighted the increasing use of technology as a factor limiting the use of their knowledge. Others still pointed to the limited resources (for example, staff) which in greater numbers would have provided them with opportunities to develop and utilize their knowledge (for example, leadership). As one manager pointed out: *'I cannot practise my leadership skills, because I no longer have staff to manage'.*

Another factor which managers describe as contributing to the under-utilization of knowledge is the restrictions imposed by the rigidity of the banking system and the regulations and procedures that managers must follow. These restrictions are said to limit managers' initiative and to not fully allow for stretching of their abilities. A manager in Bank A said: '*I am not allowed to use all the abilities I have. I do not have the control.*' A manager in Bank C echoed this view, saying: '*The knowledge may be there, but is of little use, because I feel I am often dictated to in what I can and cannot do. I feel closely monitored and controlled.*' A manager in Bank B shares this view, pointing out: '*There are more things I can do given the right environment. The set-up is completely wrong. There is no sense of direction either for the individual or the organization. Everything is too short-sighted.*'

Both the under-utilization of knowledge and the factors that managers provide to explain this raise awareness of some of the conditions which shape the perceived nature of knowledge, its creation and its utilization. One finds that while technical knowledge may be acquired and stored in order to be used when the job requires it, management knowledge is created *in situ* as individuals interact with others and discover issues that they need to explore and respond to. This observation is further exemplified in managers' perceptions of the relative importance of technical over management knowledge.

Managers in all three banks appear to value both technical and management knowledge. When asked to describe the core skills in their job, they described technical and management knowledge as equally significant. However, when asked to rate management knowledge in relation to technical knowledge, the majority of managers in each bank (Bank A: 73 per cent; Bank B: 61 per cent; Bank C: 69 per cent) rated management knowledge as more important than technical knowledge. Management knowledge is perceived as more important than technical knowledge primarily because it is perceived to complement and advance technical knowledge. Managers made the following remarks:

- '*Technical knowledge shows you what you need to do, but management knowledge enables you to adapt the technical knowledge to different situations.*' (Manager, Bank C)
- '*Management knowledge transcends across organizations, whereas technical knowledge is only relevant and specific to the job and the organization which requires it.*' (Manager, Bank A).
- '*Management knowledge gives you direction. Technical knowledge was lost in the mist of time, and overtaken by the need to focus on management knowledge – making the best use of your resources within and outside the organization.*' (Manager Bank B)

Overall, what is noticeable in managers' perceptions of the importance of management knowledge in relation to technical knowledge is the perceived difficulty of acquiring the former in relation to the latter. This point brings to light another important issue, namely how management and technical knowledge are perceived to be created and learnt.

Managers attribute the difficulty of acquiring management knowledge to the relatively greater dependency on people as opposed to technical knowledge, which is supported by manuals and books. As one manager pointed out: '*You can always learn the technical knowledge, whereas if you can't manage people you can't do the job. Everything at the end counts to people. It's a matter of interpersonal relations.*' (Manager, Bank C) Another manager said: '*Management knowledge is the hardest to learn. The technical knowledge is easier to find out. You can find it out from a book.*' (Manager, Bank A) A manager further points out: '*Management knowledge is very valuable. It can make or break a situation. It gives guidance and enables you to pass on knowledge to others. Management knowledge ensures that various complex tasks are fully completed through others. Technical knowledge enables you to know what you are talking about and to have credibility in the eyes of others.*' (Manager, Bank B)

What can be distilled from these findings is that whereas technical knowledge on the one hand may be acquired, management knowledge on the other hand is created through experiences and day-to-day interactions with others. And whereas the former is already available, the latter must be discovered. This observation suggests that the distinction between technical and management knowledge reflects different kinds of learning.

Borrowing Gherardi's (1999) distinction between 'learning in the face of problems' and 'learning in the face of mystery', it could be argued that technical knowledge reflects learning as problem-solving, whereas management knowledge reflects learning as a mystery. Put differently, if knowledge is to be seen as a product of learning then the predefined nature of that knowledge locates it in specific activities and for particular purposes. This is the case with technical knowledge. However, the findings of the study also indicate that there is a type of knowledge which is discovered when existing situations require different responses and when the existing knowledge cannot provide the answers. This describes management knowledge. Therefore, technical knowledge is acquired to serve a specific purpose , for example deal with lending requests or apply the appropriate procedures in financial transactions. Management knowledge, however, emerges when the current technical knowledge is not sufficient to respond fully to a particular situation. In short, it could be argued that management knowledge reflects the process of discovering new ways in which the technical knowledge may be utilized. Unlike technical knowledge, which could be planned and arranged, management knowledge cannot be predicted or predetermined; it tends to be discovered. These findings show that different forms of learning may lead to different types of knowledge and different types of knowledge depending on how they are utilized may spark different modes of knowing which may be employed accordingly as individuals seek to respond to different circumstances.

This analysis raises several important points that need to be further exemplified. Firstly, it is interesting to note the way knowledge is articulated in terms of skills. The difficulty of articulating knowledge and its distinction into technical and management knowledge captures the limitation of expressing value for something that cannot easily be measured or quantified. This limitation is particularly prominent in the three banks, where the dominant language is 'quantitative'. The number-orientated culture of banking has favoured this quantification of knowledge, with the emphasis placed in the past on technical expertise and competence. These principles encourage the distinction between technical and management knowledge, akin to a distinction between 'hard' and 'soft' issues respectively.

The distinction between management (soft) and technical (hard) knowledge, as reflected in the findings, is not intended to create another dualism between tacit and explicit knowledge. The point about these types of knowledge is not so much what they are, but what their implications are. The distinction between hard and soft knowledge is significant, because it shows how the interaction between the personal (psychological) and contextual (social) factors shapes the nature of knowledge and its relevance to different circumstances. In other words, organizational and industry-specific characteristics and practices interact with the characteristics of individuals to produce responses which shape how knowledge is created and utilized in one's practice. These observations emphasize that knowledge in its various forms is created through the choices individuals make in their attempts to make sense of the requirements placed on them and in their efforts to respond to what is expected of them. This point is further exemplified in the longitudinal findings from the study, which show how different types of knowledge depending on how they are utilized, define the nature of learning and its outcomes.

Identifying and pursuing learning goals and the knowledge dimension

The longitudinal approach adopted in this study examined managers' learning goals, tracking down the role of knowledge both in defining the learning goal as well as the nature of knowledge in relation to the learning process. The learning goals described by managers varied significantly, as expected. The learning goals that managers across the three banks identified included, among others, '*understanding lending, product availability and lending policies*', '*to improve management skills in delegation, team-building and decision-making*', '*the role of marketing in tax issues and personal financial markets*', and '*to manage information better to provide a better training approach, to quantify results and meet internal competition*'.

Managers' descriptions of their identified learning goals show that on the whole managers tend to be primarily concerned with acquiring further knowledge and developing skills which are both relevant to their present role within the bank and in line with the bank's expectations. The focus on organizational priorities has been found to shape the nature of the learning goals that managers seek to pursue. Indeed, due to the focus on organizational priorities and the uncertainty in the light of the organizational changes, one finds that managers' learning goals tend not to be very ambitious. Managers' learning goals would be best described as relatively incremental and evolutionary, building on their existing knowledge rather than revolutionary and transformational, seeking to depart from their current platform of understanding. The incremental nature of managers' learning goals is found to have an impact on the perceived role of knowledge in pursuing the identified learning goal.

Overall, the findings show that the majority of managers in the three banks perceive that existing knowledge, past experiences and current skills are the foundation for building new knowledge. Existing knowledge and experiences are a way of defining the focus and orientation of their learning. For example, a manager in Bank C who identified credit procedures as the focus of her learning goal said, '*previous technical knowledge from the ACIBD is useful to understand credit procedures in the bank*'. Similarly, a manager in Bank B whose learning goal was to understand insurance practices said, '*I can call on existing product knowledge and the complaints manual to find out more about insurance regulations and policies*'. A manager in Bank A whose learning goals were to improve the management of staff and to increase sales ability said, '*knowledge of the bank's products is important, as well as my current interpersonal skills in assessing staff abilities and requirements and developing their needs. The experience I have gained over the years in dealing with customers will help me in improving sales ability.*'

Therefore, aligning existing technical and management knowledge to the learning process is intended to make the learning goal more meaningful and the experience of learning potentially less threatening. The degree of familiarity with what is to be learnt generates a different degree of exposure, which shapes the role of knowledge in the learning process. For example, the findings suggest that in instances where the learning goal is intended to build on existing technical knowledge, that knowledge will be used as a mechanism for classifying and storing the new knowledge. However, if the learning goal entails greater unfamiliarity, as is the case when pursuing learning goals which seek to advance management knowledge, then the existing technical knowledge can mainly be used as a benchmark for making sense of the implications of the new experiences. Acknowledging that the learning process entails uncertainty and an element of surprise, as discussed in the previous section, helps explain the reliance of the majority of managers in the study on their existing knowledge in defining the focus of their learning.

Therefore, the role of knowledge in the learning process comprises drawing connections between what is already known and what may be discovered. However, the synthesizing role of knowledge in the learning process is dependent on the outcomes of learning, which themselves cannot be fully predicted or accounted for. Some of the outcomes from learning are reflected in the benefits that managers anticipate will result from the learning goal they pursue. Among the benefits managers across the three banks referred to include: '*increased knowledge and skills*', '*improved job performance*', '*becoming a better manager*', '*increased promotion opportunities*', '*greater employability internally and externally*'. However, there is no guarantee that these expectations will be met by the learning goals that have been set. The findings of the present study show that in some instances organizational and personal factors may lead either to a reluctance to learn or to a learning goal to be abandoned (Antonacopoulou, 1998, 2005). These findings show that unanticipated difficulties and obstacles to learning are as difficult to account for as the expected benefits from learning.

The unpredictability of the outcomes from the learning process has implications for the role of knowledge. A small proportion of managers across the three banks, who acknowledge the mystery that learning sometimes entails, point out that accepting their ignorance – their not knowing – would be as important as attempting to connect what they learnt with what they already know. These managers point out the need for '*humility*', '*a questioning mind*', '*personal enthusiasm and commitment*', and '*willingness to learn*' as equally essential in pursuing a learning goal. A manager in Bank C said, '*Humility, confessing that I don't know and getting someone to help me, is what I will need in order to fulfil my learning goal*'. A manager in Bank B said, '*knowledge of self and recognition of my strengths and weaknesses, honesty with others and myself as opposed to being defensive are going to be important ingredients*'. Finally, another manager in Bank A said, '*My self-motivation, believing in myself and my goals and a willingness to work hard will see me through*'.

Managers' comments emphasize that the nature and role of learning for an individual's development is not just shaped by knowledge. Motivation, humility and the willingness to commit one self to the learning process are equally significant, a point that also finds support in the current learning theories (Revans, 1971; Argyris, 1982). This point is supported by longitudinal findings from the study, which show the widespread impact of learning extending beyond the generation of new knowledge, as the current literature frequently promotes (Gagné, 1983; Thomas and Harri-Augstein, 1985). This point raises some interesting issues in relation to knowledge as a product of learning.

The longitudinal findings from the present study show that learning has an impact on managers' motivation, attitudes and perceptions about learning and shapes their self-confidence (see Antonacopoulou, 1998, 1999a). The words of a manager in Bank B sum up these issues: '*There is a certain degree of pleasure when you really want to do something you enjoy rather than being forced to do it. If you can get through difficulties, you can deal with additional ones more easily.*' A manager in Bank A echoes this view, saying,

'*I proved I can do it. I can see a way forward now. Success breeds success*'. These outcomes are far more wide-reaching than the benefits anticipated by managers. Moreover, the benefits from learning are perceived by managers to extend beyond a personal level and to reflect benefits for the organization. The comment of a manager in Bank C demonstrates the point aptly: '*I want the bank to be successful and ensure that the confidence they placed in me is not misplaced. My success is also the bank's success.*'

In short, these findings show that knowledge is not the only outcome from learning. Moreover, the impact of learning on self-confidence, personal satisfaction and motivation may determine whether knowledge results from learning, as well as whether learning is likely to take place in the first instance. Therefore, the presence of knowledge is no guarantee that learning will take place and, equally, there is no guarantee that learning will result in new knowledge. As the findings of the study show, in some instances the unpredictability of the learning outcomes makes more relevant the appreciation of one's ignorance as a basis for supporting the learning process. These points clarify that while the role of knowledge in the learning process may comprise integrating what is currently known with what can be discovered, knowledge also plays a key role in transforming understanding and making learning meaningful. This point is reflected in the longitudinal findings from the present study in relation to managers' attitudes towards learning and the longevity of knowledge resulting from the learning goals that managers fulfilled.

Managers who fulfilled their identified learning goal were asked a series of reflective questions about the factors influencing their decision to set the specific learning goal, the relevance and utilization of the knowledge from the learning goal in their present job and future development, and the perceived longevity of the knowledge resulting from the learning goal they fulfilled. The similarity and consistency in the responses of managers to these questions across the three banks is startling.

In relation to the factors which influenced their decision to set the specific learning goal, managers' responses reveal on the one hand the impact of the changing circumstances in their organization, and on the other hand the choices they made in response to these changing circumstances. The majority of managers across the three banks argue that the decision to set the specific learning goal was based both on the recognition of the need to learn and the willingness to improve, as well as the awareness of job and business requirements. The words of a manager in Bank A make the point aptly: '*It was the realization that if I was to play a part in the organization in the future, I needed to change*'.

The emphasis on balancing personal and organizational priorities also leads the majority of managers across the three banks to argue that in pursuing the identified learning goal they were seeking to address both present and future needs. It is interesting to note that although initially the nature of the learning goal was incremental, focusing primarily on specific job requirements, the way the learning goal unfolded in the course of the learning process served to extend its focus and orientation and subsequently reveal the potential for utilization of the emerging knowledge. The majority of managers in the three banks argue that the identified learning goal was intended to address both present and future development needs and consequently the knowledge can be utilized in both their present and future roles. A manager in Bank C made the following comment: '*There are innumerable aspects that I can apply to my job now and in the future. It's like a circle, a comfort zone that expands*'. A manager in Bank B added: '*I intend to utilize the knowledge from the learning goal, both now and in the future, because I would like to remain in the branch network. As the organization's expectations change, I can remain a step ahead*'.

Managers attribute the expected future utilization of the knowledge acquired to two main factors: the perceived '*transferability of knowledge*' and '*the confidence that learning provides to deal with new requirements and unfamiliar situations*'. It appears that the confidence resulting from learning raises the willingness of managers to explore ways in which knowledge can be further extended. The experience of pursuing the identified learning goal has transformed the way they perceive knowledge and their willingness to improvise ways in which it may be utilized in the future. This point is particularly evident in managers' perceptions of the longevity of knowledge emerging from the learning goal they pursued.

Managers were asked for how long, in their view, the knowledge acquired from the learning goal is likely to last and when they believe they are likely to need new knowledge. The managers' responses reveal the paradoxical nature of knowledge in the process of learning. The paradox is reflected in the view that managers across the three banks share consistently, namely that knowledge has a limited life span yet at the same time it can last forever. Some examples of managers' responses to the question of how long will the knowledge last reflect the point more clearly:

- '*The knowledge will remain useful, but the emphasis will vary over time, depending on the set-up of the bank in the future and the demands of the future job.*' (Manager, Bank A)
- '*The core of what you learn stays with you all the time, but it needs to be topped up with additional knowledge as the needs keep changing*' (Manager, Bank B)
- '*Forever and a day the knowledge will help me, but it will keep developing, because the job won't stand still. It's an on-going thing, not something you learn once.*' (Manager, Bank C)

Similarly, managers in all three banks recognize that the need for new or additional knowledge will be ongoing, but at the same time dependent on the requirements of the job and the changes in the organization, which will also determine the speed of response. Managers' responses to the question of when will new or additional knowledge be necessary reflect these observations.

- *'With so much change going on it is hard to specify the time. There is always room for improvement. No manager can say they know everything to do their job. They can get by, but they should do more.'* (Manager, Bank A)
- *'How long is a piece of string? Anything you learn is useful even if you don't use it immediately. If you want to develop, you must learn all the time.'* (Manager, Bank B)
- *'I need additional knowledge very much like now! Knowing what you are trying to achieve is important before deciding how.'* (Manager, Bank C)

These findings reflect once again the way the interaction between personal and contextual factors shapes the nature of learning by determining the role of knowledge when engaging with different familiar and unfamiliar experiences. The analysis of the findings indicates that learning extends existing knowledge through new experiences as much as it provides opportunities to generate new experiences by involving an element of surprise. The perceived utilization of knowledge both in their current and future job as well as the perceived longevity of knowledge reflect a marked change in managers' attitudes towards learning and their perceptions of the role of knowledge. Knowledge in relation to the learning process both synthesizes existing knowledge with new knowledge and transforms understanding by identifying the need to learn. Integrating the process of learning with the process of knowing helps make the experience more meaningful. The nature of knowledge in the process of learning, as well as the nature of learning in the process of knowing, is determined by the choices individuals make in their efforts to balance organizational and personal priorities and maintain some sense of stability in the light of organizational changes. In essence, the analysis reveals the dynamic interaction between learning and knowledge and, in particular, how the indeterminate nature of learning shapes the role of knowledge and how the indeterminate nature of knowledge shapes the learning process. This point captures a central characteristic of the relationship between learning and knowledge.

Different modes of knowing in the relationship between learning and knowledge

The findings presented and the analysis developed in the previous sections suggest that the relationship between learning and knowledge is dynamic and at times paradoxical. The reciprocal interaction between learning and knowledge as discussed in the previous sections reveals the nature of learning in relation to knowledge and the nature of knowledge in relation to the learning process. This reciprocal interaction reflects the various personal and organizational conditions which shape the relationship between learning and knowledge. The various factors shaping the way learning and knowledge are associated by individuals in the study suggests on the one hand that learning and knowledge may be interdependent, but on the other hand that they do not necessarily coexist.

The paradoxical nature of the relationship between learning and knowledge is reflected in the findings of the study, which show that knowledge *per se* is not a precursor of further learning, despite the various roles that knowledge performs in the learning process. On the basis of the findings, it could be argued that accepting ignorance is as important in the learning process as knowledge itself and may determine whether or not learning takes place. Moreover, the way knowledge can be utilized appears to play a further determining role in shaping the nature of learning and the role of knowledge in the process of growth.

Therefore, learning is not just a process triggered by the need to know, but a journey into the unknown. The motives and expectations from the learning process may determine the forms of knowing that may result. For example, if learning is intended to enhance existing understanding to improve the performance of a specific task, then the emphasis may be on acquiring and *storing* relevant knowledge and *repeating* it in similar tasks when familiar problems present themselves. However, if learning is intended to transform understanding, then the emphasis may be on *reflecting* upon and *questioning* current knowledge and its applicability to different situations. Therefore, the way knowledge is utilized may shape the purpose and focus of the learning process, which may also define the role of knowledge and its impact on different forms of knowing. Based on the analysis of the findings, seven different forms of knowing result from the relationship between knowledge and learning. Depending on the nature of learning (for example, learning as problem-solving or learning as a mystery) and the nature of knowledge (hard/technical versus soft/management), their interaction may be reflected into different modes of knowing including:

- *Knowing by storing* – when the emphasis is placed on collecting relevant knowledge for a specific task.
- *Knowing by repeating* – when the emphasis is placed on applying specific knowledge to similar situations.
- *Knowing by improvising* – when the emphasis is placed on exploring ways in which knowledge may be utilized in unfamiliar situations.
- *Knowing by reflecting* – when the emphasis is placed on the search for new meaning in relation to what is currently known.

- *Knowing by questioning* – when the emphasis is placed on assessing the relevance and applicability of knowledge in new situations and accepting ignorance.
- *Knowing by synthesizing* – when the emphasis is placed on integrating what is known with what is discovered.
- *Knowing by transforming* – when the emphasis is placed on on searching for a new platform of understanding.

The seven modes of knowing proposed in this chapter seek to reflect the process of learning and the way knowledge is employed and not to suggest a particular outcome. Moreover, these modes of knowing are dependent on personal and contextual factors, which will shape how knowledge may be utilized and how accessible it may be both to the individual (as a carrier of knowledge), and to those with whom the individual interacts (that is, with other organization members, by sharing the knowledge and learning together). The different modes of knowing presented in this chapter also reflect the socio-political dynamics which shape how knowledge at the individual level finds meaning and expression in the process of social interaction. This process of social interaction also provides learning with meaning and purpose. The different modes of knowing reflect the indeterminate nature of knowledge and learning and the complexity underpinning their dynamic interaction.

Conclusion

This chapter has provided new insights into the nature of the relationship between learning and knowledge by identifying different forms of knowing. Using recent empirical findings, the discussion has explored the indeterminate nature of learning and knowledge and some of the conditions which shape the role of learning in relation to knowledge, as well as the role of knowledge in relation to learning. The contribution of this analysis marks the first steps in our efforts to integrate the concepts of knowledge and learning by exploring their relationship. Essentially, learning and knowledge come to life when different modes of knowing support a connection between the knowledge and learning that lies within (the individual) and the knowledge and learning that lies outside (among other organizational or group members) in the field of action and interaction with the world.

The chapter has proposed seven modes of knowing, which reflect various types of knowledge and forms of learning shaped by the interaction of personal and contextual factors. The interaction between personal and contextual factors provides insights with regard to implicit and explicit social rules and the role of language and symbols, as well as the power and political dynamics that underpin the process of learning and knowing. The focus of the present study on the retail banking sector provides strong indications of the impact of industry-specific characteristics on managers' perceptions and actions. Moreover, the focus of the present study on the individual as the unit of analysis reveals the nature and impact of power and political dynamics on the choices individuals make when responding to organizational expectations and requirements. Perhaps even more importantly, the findings provide indications of the language that is being used and the symbols that are employed to quantify and add value to processes which are not possible to measure or predict with any certainty. These observations clearly highlight the need for further research to extend these issues in different contexts and levels of analysis.

Moreover, the analysis developed in this chapter also highlights the need for more research into the language that currently informs the way we seek to articulate learning and knowledge. The difficulty of describing the multiple forms of learning reflects the limits of our language in capturing in simple terms the underlying complexity of the phenomena that we seek to study. This point emphasizes the need for further research which seeks to unearth the complexity of knowing, in relation to the order which appears at the surface of what we currently describe as learning and knowledge.

References

Antonacopoulou, E. P. (1996) 'A Study of Interrelationships: The Way Individual Managers Learn And adapt and the Contribution of Training towards this Process', unpublished PhD thesis, Warwick Business School, University of Warwick, UK.

Antonacopoulou, E. P. (1998) 'Developing Learning Managers within Learning Organizations', in M. Easterby-Smith, L. Araujo and J. Burgoyne (eds), *Organizational Learning: Developments in Theory and Practice* (London: Sage), pp. 214–242.

Antonacopoulou, E. P. (1999a) 'Individuals' Responses to Change: The Relationship between Learning and Knowledge', *Creativity and Innovation Management*, 8(2) 130–9.

Antonacopoulou, E. P. (1999b) 'Training does not imply Learning: The Individual's Perspective", *International Journal of Training and Development*, 3(1), 14–33.

Antonacopoulou, E. P. (2000) 'Reconnecting Education, Training and Development through Learning: A Holographic Perspective', *Education + Training*, special issue on 'Vocational Education and Training in SMEs', 42(4/5), 255–63.

Antonacopoulou, E. P. (2001) 'The Paradoxical Nature of the Relationship between Learning and Training', *Journal of Management Studies*, 38(3), 327–50.

Antonacopoulou, E. P. (2005) 'The Relationship between Individual and Organizational Learning: New Evidence from Managerial Learning Practices', *Management Learning*, under review.

Argyris, C. (1982), Reasoning, Learning and Action, USA: Jossey-Bass.

Argyris, C. and D. A. Schön (1978) *Organizational Learning: A Theory in Action Perspective* (Reading, MA: Addisson Wesley).

Badaracco, J. L. (1991) *The Knowledge Link: How Firms Compete through Strategic Alliances*, (Boston, MA: Harvard Business School Press).

Bass, B. M. and J. A. Vaughan (1969) *Training in Industry: The Management of Learning*, 2nd edn (London: Tavistock).

Blackler, F. (1993) 'Knowledge and the Theory of Organizations: Organizations as Activity Systems and the Reframing of Management', *Journal of Management Studies*, 30, 863–84.

Blackler, F. (1995) 'Knowledge, Knowledge Work and Organizations: An Overview and Interpretation', *Organisation Studies*, 16(6), 1021–46.

Boisot, M. (1998), Knowledge Assets: Securing Competitive Advantage in the Information Economy (New York: Oxford University Press).

Boland, R. J. and Tenkasi, R. V. (1995), "Perspective Making and Perspective Taking in Communities of Knowing," Organization Science, 6, 4, 350-372.

Bourdieu, P. (1980) The Logic of Practice (Stanford, CA: Stanford University Press).

Brown, R. and P. Duguid (1991) 'Organizational Learning and Communities of Practice: Towards a Unifying View of Working, Learning, and Innovation', *Organization Science*, 2(1), 40–57.

Cappon, A. (1994) 'A Life-Cycle View of Banking', *Journal of Retail Banking*, 16(1), 33–37.

Choo, C. W. (1998) *The Knowing Organisation: How Organizations Use Information to Construct Meaning, Create Knowledge and Make Decisions*, (Oxford: Oxford University Press).

Cook, S. D. N. and J. S. Brown (1999) 'Bridging epistemologies: The Generative Dance between Organizational Knowledge and Organizational Knowing', *Organization Science* 10(4), 381–400.

Coulson-Thomas, C. J. (1997) 'The Future of the Organisation: Selected Knowledge Management Issues', *The Journal of Knowledge Management*, 1 (1), 15–26.

Davenport, T. H. and L. Prusak (1998) *Working Knowledge*, (Boston, MA: Harvard Business School Press).

Drucker, P. F. (1993) *Post-Capitalist Society*, (London: Butterworth-Heinemann).

Engestrom, Y. (1993) 'Work as a Testbed of Activity Theory', in S. Chaiklin and J. Lave (Eds), *Understanding practice: Perspectives on Activity and Context*, (Cambridge: Cambridge University Press), PP. 64–103.

Fiddis, C. (1998) *Managing Knowledge in the Supply Chain: The Key to Competitive Advantage* (London: Financial Times Retail and Consumer Publishing).

Gagné, R. M. (1983) *The Conditions of Learning*, 3rd edn (New York: Holt, Reinhart and Winston).

Garvin, D. A. (1993) 'Building a Learning Organisation', *Harvard Business Review*, July/August, 78–91.

Gherardi, S. (1999) 'Learning as Problem-Driven or Learning in the Face of Mystery?', *Organisation Studies*, 20(1), 101–124.

Gherardi, S. (2000) 'Practice-Based Theorizing on Learning and Knowing in Organizations', *Organization*, 7(2),211–23.

Haynes, J. and C. W. Allinson (1988) 'Cultural Differences in the Learning Styles of Managers', *Management International Review*, 28(3), 75–80.

Hergenhahn, B. R. (1982) *An Introduction to Theories of Learning*, 2nd ed, (London: Gower).

Juch, B. (1983) *Personal Development Theory and Practice in Management Training*, (Chichester: Wiley).

Kim, D. H. (1993) 'The Link between Individual and Organizational Learning', *Sloan Management Review*, Fall, 37–49.

Klatt, L. A., R. G. Murdick and F. E. Schuster (1985) *Human Resource Management*, (Florida: Bell and Howell).

Kolb, D. A., S. Lublin J. Spoth and R. Baker (1991) 'Strategic Management Development: Experiential Learning and Managerial Competencies', in J. Henry and D. Walker (eds), *Creative Management* (London: Sage and The Open University), pp. 221–231.

Lave, J. (1993) 'The Practice of Learning', in S. Chaiklin and J. Lave (eds), *Understanding Practice: Perspectives on Activity and Context*, (Cambridge: Cambridge University Press), pp. 3–34.

Machlup, F. (1962) *The Production and Distribution of Knowledge in the US*, (New York: Princeton University Press).

Nonaka, I. and H. Takeuchi (1995) *The Knowledge Creating Company: How Japanese Companies Create the Dynamics of Innovation* (New York: Oxford University Press).

Orlikowski, W. J. (1992) 'The Duality of Technology: Rethinking the Concept of Technology in Organizations', *Organization Science*, 3(3), 398–427.

Polanyi, M. (1966) *The Tacit Dimension*, (New York: Doubleday).

Revans, R. W. (1971) *Developing Effective Managers: A New Approach to Business*, (London: Longman).

Richter, I. (1998) 'Individual and Organizational Learning at the Executive Level', *Management Learning*, 29(3), 299–346.

Ryles, G. (1949) *The Concept of Mind* (London: Hutchinson & Company).

Sveiby, K. E. (1997) 'The New Organizational Wealth: Managing and Measuring Knowledge-Based Assets (San Francisco: Berret Koehler Inc).

Thomas, L. F. and E. S. Harri-Augstein (1985) *Self-Organised Learning: Foundation of a Conversational Science for Psychology* (London: McGraw-Hill).

Turner, S. (1994) *The Social Theory of Practices: Tradition, Tacit Knowledge and Presupposition* (Cambridge: Polity).

Venzin, M., von G. Krogh and J. Roos (1998) 'Future Research into Knowledge Management', in G. von Krogh, J. Roos and D. Kleine (eds), *Knowing in Firms: Understanding, Managing and Measuring Knowledge* (London: Sage), pp. 26–66.

Von Krogh, G., J. Roos and D. Kleine (1998), *Knowing in Firms: Understanding, Managing and Measuring Knowledge* (London: Sage).

Walker, S. (1975) *Learning and Reinforcement* (London: Methuen).

Walzlawick, P., J. H. Weakland and R. Fish (1974) *Change: Principles of Problem Formation and Problem Resolution* (New York: Norton).

Zande, U. and B. Kogut (1995) 'Knowledge and the Speed of the Transfer and Imitation of Organizational Capabilities: An Empirical Test', *Organization Science*, 6(1), 76–92.

2
Knowledge Management and Organizational Learning: Fundamental Concepts for Theory and Practice

Ron Sanchez

This chapter investigates several issues regarding the nature, domain, conceptual foundations and practical challenges of knowledge management and organizational learning. The chapter first identifies and contrasts two fundamental philosophical orientations to knowledge management – the *personal knowledge* orientation and the *organizational knowledge* orientation – and illustrates the distinctive kinds of knowledge management practices that result from the two orientations. It then summarizes three essential organizational processes in knowledge management: (1) maintaining learning loops in all organizational processes; (2) systematically disseminating knowledge throughout an organization; and (3) applying knowledge wherever it can be used in an organization. A general model of organizational learning – the Five Learning Cycles model – is introduced to represent how individuals, groups and the overall organization are linked in an organizational learning process. Key challenges in managing each of the five learning cycles are discussed, and examples of appropriate managerial interventions are proposed for each learning cycle. Concluding comments suggest how knowledge management processes reflect a fundamental shift in management thinking and practice from traditional concepts of command and control to more contemporary concepts of facilitation and empowerment.

Introduction

As a growing focus of concern within management, knowledge management is an area of research and practice that is still searching for a stable set of core concepts and practical applications. This chapter undertakes to contribute to this search by addressing some fundamental questions about the nature, domain, conceptual foundations and practical challenges of knowledge management and organizational learning.

The first section of the chapter considers two fundamental philosophical orientations to knowledge management – the 'tacit' or *personal knowledge* orientation versus the 'explicit' or *organizational knowledge* orientation. I describe the deep assumptions underlying each orientation, and the resulting differing emphases in knowledge management concepts and practices to which each orientation leads. Examples drawn from current practice in several companies illustrate the distinctive kinds of knowledge management practices that result from the two orientations.

The second section proposes that there are three essential organizational processes that must be functioning well for any knowledge management system to be effective: (1) maintaining learning loops in all organizational processes; (2) systematically disseminating new and existing knowledge throughout an organization; and (3) applying knowledge wherever it can be used in an organization. I also argue that an organization that can carry out these processes effectively must develop processes for converting personal knowledge into organizational knowledge, and vice versa, on an ongoing basis.

The third section presents the Five Learning Cycles model of organizational learning. In this general model of learning processes in an organization, five kinds of learning cycles are identified that link individuals, groups, and the overall organization in an organizational learning process. The model makes clear how new knowledge developed by individuals in an organization must navigate each of the five learning cycles to become accepted by other people in the organization, and then how new knowledge becomes embedded in the organization and its way of working. In effect, the model shows at the macro level how personal knowledge is converted into organizational knowledge, and vice versa, in processes for active and continuous organizational learning.

The fourth section discusses some key challenges in managing each of the five learning cycles so that active learning processes can be maintained at the individual, group or organizational levels. I also suggest some ways in which managers can help to prevent breakdowns and dysfunctions from occurring in each of the five learning cycles, thereby helping to sustain overall organizational learning processes. Examples drawn from recent research into knowledge management practices help to illustrate the nature of such managerial interventions.

I conclude with some comments on the ways in which the knowledge management processes discussed here reflect a fundamental shift in management thinking and practice from traditional concepts of command and control to more contemporary concepts of facilitation and empowerment.

1.   Basic philosophical orientations to knowledge management

The growing stream of articles on and consulting approaches to knowledge management practice today reveals a wide range of recommended processes and techniques. Unfortunately – especially for managers looking for

Table 2.1 **Basic assumptions in personal *versus* organizational knowledge management approaches**

Personal Knowledge Approach	Organizational Knowledge Approach
Knowledge is personal in nature and very difficult to extract from people.	*Knowledge can be articulated and codified* to create organizational knowledge assets.
Knowledge must be transferred by *moving people* within or between organizations.	Knowledge can be *disseminated (using information technologies)* in the form of documents, drawings, best practice models and so on.
Learning can only be encouraged by *bringing the right people together* under the right circumstances.	Learning processes can be designed to remedy knowledge deficiencies through *structured, managed, scientific processes.*

Source: R. Sanchez (forthcoming), 'Personal Knowledge versus Organizational Knowledge Approaches to Knowledge Management Practice', in D. Rooney, G. Hearn, and A. Ninan (eds), *The Knowledge Economy Handbook*, (Oxford: Routledge).

insights to guide knowledge management practices – many of these recommendations often seem disconnected from each other, and in the worst cases various recommended approaches even seem to be contradicting each other. Analysis of current recommendations, however, suggests that the many ideas for knowledge management being advanced today can be grouped into one of two fundamentally different views of the nature of knowledge itself and of the resulting possibilities for managing knowledge in organizations. These two views are characterized here as the *personal knowledge* approach and the *organizational knowledge* approach. The basic premises and the possibilities for knowledge management practice implied by each of these two approaches are discussed below.[1] See Table 2.1 for a summary of the fundamental differences in the assumptions underlying the two approaches. Some important advantages and disadvantages of the two approaches to knowledge management are then discussed.

The personal knowledge approach

The personal knowledge approach to knowledge management derives from the fundamental assumptions that knowledge is essentially personal in nature and that it is therefore very difficult (perhaps impracticably so) to extract from the minds of individuals. In effect, this approach to knowledge management assumes, often implicitly, that the knowledge within an organization essentially consists of 'tacit' *personal knowledge* in the minds of individuals in the organization.[2]

Working from the premise that knowledge is inherently personal in nature and will therefore largely remain tacit in the minds of individuals, the personal knowledge approach generally offers recommendations for knowledge management practice that focus on managing people as individual generators and carriers of knowledge. To manage the personal knowledge of individuals, managers are typically urged to identify the kinds of knowledge possessed by various people in an organization and then to arrange appropriate interactions between knowledgeable individuals. For example, the personal knowledge approach views the dissemination of knowledge in an organization as a task that can best be accomplished by transferring people as 'knowledge carriers' from one part of an organization to another. Further, in this approach, a usual recommendation for stimulating organizational learning is to bring knowledgeable individuals together under circumstances that encourage them to share their ideas. These interactions are intended to encourage knowledgeable individuals to apply their knowledge constructively together; to share their knowledge with each other in order to move knowledge from one part of the organization to another; and hopefully through their interactions to create new knowledge that may be useful to the organization.

Some examples illustrate how the personal knowledge approach to knowledge management may be applied in practice.

Most managers of organizations today do not have a clear view of the specific kinds of knowledge that individuals in their organization possess. This common state of affairs is reflected in the comment usually attributed to executives of Hewlett-Packard in the 1980s: 'If we only knew what we know, we could conquer the world.' As firms become larger, more knowledge-intensive and more globally dispersed, the need for managers to 'know what we know' is becoming acute. A common kind of initiative within the personal knowledge approach is therefore an effort to improve understanding of *who* knows about *what* in an organization. The creation within Philips, the global electronics company, of an intranet-based 'yellow pages' listing experts with different kinds of technical knowledge within Philips's many business units is an example of such an effort. Philips employees can type in key words for a specific knowledge domain – say, for example, knowledge about the 'design of optical pickup units' for CD or DVD players and recorders – and the yellow pages will retrieve a listing of the people within Philips's worldwide business units who claim to have such knowledge. Contact information is also provided for each person listed, so that anyone in Philips who needs the kind of knowledge that an individual claims to have can get in touch with any one of those individuals.

Toyota provides an example of a personal knowledge approach to transferring knowledge within a global organization. When Toyota builds a new factory and wants to transfer knowledge about its production system to the new employees in the factory, Toyota typically selects a core group of two hundred to three hundred new employees and sends them for several months of training and working on the assembly line in one of Toyota's existing factories. After several months of studying the production system and working alongside experienced Toyota assembly line-workers, these trained workers are sent back to their new factory site to become the core of production teams formed with other new employees. When they are repatriated, these trained workers are also accompanied by two hundred or so long-term, highly experienced Toyota production workers, who then work alongside all the new employees in the new factory to assure that knowledge of how Toyota's production process works is fully transferred to all employees in the new factory.

Toyota's use of Quality Circles also illustrates a personal knowledge approach to creating new knowledge. At the end of each work week, groups of Toyota production workers spend one to two hours analyzing the performance of their stage in the production system to identify actual or potential problems in quality, productivity, safety and so on. Through their discussions, each group proposes 'countermeasures' to correct identified problems, and discusses the results of countermeasures taken during the previous week to address problems identified in earlier Quality Circle discussions. Through such interactions, Toyota employees share their ideas for improvement, devise steps to test new ideas and assess the results of their tests. This knowledge management practice, which is repeated weekly as an integral part of the Toyota production system, progressively identifies, eliminates and even prevents sources of process errors. Improvements developed and implemented by Quality Circles over many years have transformed Toyota's production system into one of the highest quality production processes in the world (Spear and Bowen, 1999).

The organizational knowledge approach

In contrast to the personal knowledge approach, the organizational knowledge approach assumes that knowledge is something that can be made explicit – that is, it can be articulated and explained by individuals who have knowledge, even though some effort and assistance may sometimes be required to help individuals articulate what they know. As a result, the organizational knowledge approach fundamentally assumes that much, if not all, of the knowledge of individuals that is useful to an organization can be articulated and thereby made explicit and available to others.

Working from this premise, the organizational knowledge approach generally advocates the creation and use of formal organizational processes to encourage and help individuals articulate the important knowledge they have, and thereby to create *organizational knowledge assets*. The organizational knowledge approach also addresses ways that organizational knowledge assets can be disseminated within an organization, usually through documents, drawings, standard operating procedures, manuals of best practice and the like. In this regard, information systems are seen as providing a critical means to disseminate organizational knowledge assets over company intranets or between organizations via the Internet.

Along with the assumption that knowledge can be made explicit and managed explicitly goes the belief that new knowledge can be created through definable, manageable learning processes. The organizational knowledge approach generally suggests that experiments and other forms of structured, targeted learning processes can be used to remedy important organizational knowledge deficiencies, or that market transactions or strategic partnering may be used to obtain specific forms of needed knowledge or to improve an organization's existing knowledge assets.

Given these assumptions, the recommendations for knowledge management practice proposed by researchers and consultants working within the organizational knowledge approach typically focus on designing organizational processes for *generating, articulating, categorizing,* and *systematically leveraging* organizational knowledge assets.

Some examples may help to illustrate the organizational knowledge management approach.

In the 1990s, Motorola was the global market leader for pagers (also known as 'beepers'). To maintain its leadership position, Motorola introduced new generations of pager designs every 12–15 months. Each new pager generation was designed to offer more advanced features and options for customization than the preceding generation.[3] To produce its rapidly evolving lines of pagers, Motorola also designed and built a new factory with higher-speed, more flexible assembly lines for each new generation of pager. To sustain this high rate of product and process development, Motorola formed teams of product and factory designers to co-develop each new generation of pager and the factory for producing the new generation of pager. At the beginning of each project, each new team of designers received a manual of development methods and techniques from the team that had developed the previous generation of pager and its factory. The new development team would then have three deliverables at the end of their project: (1) an improved and more highly configurable next-generation pager design; (2) the design of a more efficient and more flexible assembly line for the factory that would produce the new pager; and (3) an improved design manual that extended the development methods provided to the team in the manual it received by including improved development methods that the team had developed to meet the more demanding product and production goals for its project. This improved development manual would then be passed on to the next development team given the task of developing the next generation pager and its factory. In this way, Motorola sought to make explicit and disseminate the knowledge developed by its engineers during each project, and thereby to systematically leverage that knowledge in launching the work of the next project team.

In addition to Toyota's personal knowledge management approach that transfers employees around its factories to transfer knowledge about its production system, Toyota also follows highly disciplined organizational knowledge management practices that document in detail the tasks that each team of workers and each individual worker are asked to perform on its assembly lines. These documents provide a detailed description of the content, timing, sequence and output of each task: how each task is to be performed, how long each task should take, the sequence of steps to be followed in performing each task and the steps to be taken by each worker in checking his or her own work (Spear and Bowen, 1999). As problems arise and are analyzed on the assembly line or in employees' weekly Quality Circle meetings, suggestions for improving Toyota's processes are evaluated by Toyota's production engineers and then formally incorporated in revised task description documents.

In addition to documenting process descriptions for repetitive tasks like factory work, some organizations have also created organizational knowledge management approaches to support more creative tasks, such as developing new products. For example, Chrysler's 'platform teams' of development engineers have responsibility for creating the next generation platforms[4] on which Chrysler's families of automobiles will be based. Each platform team is free to evaluate and select its own design solutions for the many different technical aspects of its vehicle platform. However, each platform team is also required to place its design solutions in a 'Book of Knowledge' on Chrysler's intranet. All platform teams can then consult this catalogue of developed design solutions as they carry out their development processes, so that good design solutions developed by one platform team can be located, evaluated and possibly used by other platform teams.

Other firms have taken an organizational knowledge management approach in product development processes even further. For example, GE Fanuc Automation, one of the world's leading industrial automation firms, develops detailed, company-specific design methodologies for the design of new kinds of components for their factory automation systems. In effect, instead of letting each engineer use his or her own personal knowledge to create new component designs, GE Fanuc's engineers must work together to define standard design methodologies for each type of component the firm uses. Many of these design methodologies are then programmed so that the design of new component variations can be automated, and GE Fanuc's computers then automatically generate design solutions for new components. In this way, GE Fanuc tries to make explicit the best design knowledge of all its engineers, and then to systematically re-use that knowledge by automating new component design tasks.

2.   Advantages and disadvantages of personal versus organizational knowledge approaches

Both personal and organizational knowledge management approaches have some significant advantages and disadvantages, as summarized briefly below.

Advantages and disadvantages of the personal knowledge approach

A main advantage of the personal knowledge approach is that it offers some relatively simple steps to begin managing knowledge. A basic first step is to identify what each individual in the organization believes is the specific kind of knowledge that he or she possesses. Such statements of claimed expertise can help managers do a better job of matching individuals' knowledge with the knowledge requirements of various tasks in the organization – for example, making more effective assignments of individuals to specific tasks that they will be good at performing or composing teams with appropriate sets of knowledge to carry out a project. As Philips found with its intranet-based 'yellow pages', the relatively little effort needed to create a database listing the expertise claimed by individuals in the organization may greatly facilitate knowledge-sharing among individuals. These easy-to-implement personal knowledge management practices may also avoid some of the practical and motivational challenges that may arise when an organization asks individuals to make their knowledge explicit, a challenge that is discussed further below.

Although relatively easy to begin, the personal knowledge approach, if used exclusively by an organization, has some important long-term limitations and disadvantages. One disadvantage is that individuals in an organization may claim to have personal knowledge that they do not actually have (Stein and Ridderstråle, 2001). Moreover, if knowledge only remains tacit in the minds of individuals in an organization, then the *only* way to move critical knowledge within the organization is to move people who claim to have such knowledge. Moving people is often costly and time-consuming, and some individuals may resist moves that would disrupt their current work or family life. Even when knowledgeable individuals are willing to be moved, an individual can only be moved one place at a time and can only work so many hours per day, thereby limiting the reach and the speed with which an organization can practically hope to transfer an individual's knowledge. Further, people in other parts of the organization may not accept the knowledge of a newly transferred person or may otherwise fail to establish sufficient rapport with transferred individuals to allow the desired knowledge transfer to take place.

Perhaps an even more serious concern in many organizations is that leaving knowledge in tacit form in the minds of key individuals creates a risk that the organization may lose important knowledge if an individual becomes incapacitated, leaves the organization or joins a competing organization.[5]

Advantages and disadvantages of the organizational knowledge approach

In many key respects, the advantages and disadvantages of the organizational knowledge approach present a 'mirror image' of the advantages and disadvantages of the personal knowledge approach. The organizational knowledge approach is usually much more challenging to start, but may offer significantly greater benefits in the long term. I first consider some important potential advantages of the organizational knowledge management approach and then address some key challenges in starting and sustaining organizational knowledge management approaches in an organization.

The most fundamental advantage of organizational knowledge approaches is that once an individual's knowledge is articulated in an explicit form (a document, drawing, process description or other kind of organizational knowledge asset), information systems can usually be used to quickly disseminate that knowledge throughout an organization. In effect, converting personal knowledge into organizational knowledge creates a knowledge asset that can be made available anytime and anywhere it is needed in an organization – in effect freeing an organization from the limitations of time and space that constrain the dissemination of personal knowledge by moving individuals.

Moreover, once important forms of knowledge are made explicit within an organization, they can be codified and thereby made easier to leverage than knowledge left in tacit personal form. To *codify knowledge* is to place knowledge in categories that allow important interrelationships between different kinds of knowledge within an organization to be identified. For example, forms of knowledge in an organization that share similar theoretical or practical knowledge bases can be identified so that networks for knowledge-sharing can be organized among people working with similar kinds of knowledge. Once important forms of an organization's knowledge are articulated and codified, knowledge created in one part of an organization can also be proactively delivered through information systems to people in other parts of the organization that can benefit from having such knowledge. For example, in the late 1990s AT+T created an IT-based global knowledge network linking common processes in its factories worldwide. New knowledge developed in one factory that would be useful in improving similar processes in other factories could be entered into AT+T's IT system and proactively sent to all other AT+T factories that had similar processes.

A further advantage of the organizational knowledge approach is that once organizational knowledge is made explicit and disseminated to other individuals who have expertise in the same knowledge domain, an organization's organizational knowledge becomes 'visible' and can be discussed, debated, tested further and improved, thereby stimulating organizational learning processes. (Such processes may also help to identify which individuals in the organization who claim to have important knowledge are actually capable of making significant contributions to the organization's knowledge base, and which are not.)

By systematically making its current knowledge base more visible and analyzable, an organization can greatly improve its ability to identify deficiencies in its knowledge base. In effect, by making what it knows explicit, an organization can begin to see more clearly what it does not know and then take steps to develop or acquire important forms of knowledge that it does not have or that are not developed to a sufficient level within the organization.

Finally, an organization that articulates, codifies and disseminates its important knowledge assets may thereby minimize the risk that vital knowledge of key individuals may become unavailable if those individuals were to become incapacitated or leave the organization.

A number of significant organizational challenges must be overcome, however, to obtain these potential benefits of an organizational knowledge management approach. These challenges primarily arise in managing processes for articulating, evaluating, applying and protecting organizational knowledge.

Not uncommonly, some individuals in an organization may lack the skill or motivation to *articulate* their useful knowledge. Individuals may vary greatly in their abilities to articulate their knowledge, and significant organizational support and facilitation may be required to help some individuals with important knowledge to adequately impart their knowledge and contribute to the creation of organizational knowledge assets. Providing organizational support to individuals who have difficulty articulating their knowledge may involve significant time and financial cost.[6]

An even more fundamental challenge arises when an individual resists articulating his or her knowledge, even though requested by his or her organization to do so. Such resistance may commonly occur if an individual believes that his or her job security depends on the personal knowledge that he or she has that is important to the organization. Individuals may fear that revealing such knowledge would lead to dismissal or loss of influence in an organization, usually because they believe they would subsequently be less necessary or important to the organization. Overcoming such fears may call for a redefinition of the employment relationship within an organization, especially with regard to its key knowledge workers. New employment relationships and incentives may have to be defined to encourage key knowledge workers to engage in continuous learning, to make their knowledge explicit and to help disseminate their knowledge to others in the organization.

Organizations must also find ways to systematically *evaluate* knowledge that has been made explicit by various individuals. For example, individuals with different educational backgrounds and professional experience may have come to different conclusions about the most effective way to do something. Such differences will usually be revealed in the process of making their individual knowledge explicit. Organizational processes must be established for evaluating the knowledge that individuals have made explicit and for resolving conflicting knowledge beliefs of individuals. The people involved in making such evaluations must be respected within the organization for their expertise, objectivity and impartiality; in most organizations, such people are usually in short supply and their time is difficult to obtain. Involving such people in processes for evaluating organizational knowledge may impose significant costs on an organization, although the resulting benefits may far outweigh the costs. For example, some consulting firms today have panels of senior experts in various practice areas who review post-project recommendations from project teams and define 'best demonstrated practice' models for various practice areas.

Since knowledge is useful to an organization only when it is *applied* in action, a further challenge in implementing organizational knowledge management approaches is ensuring that knowledge articulated in one part of the organization is not rejected or ignored by other parts of the organization because of an intra-organizational 'not invented here' syndrome. One organizational knowledge management approach to this concern is requiring that 'best practice models' (such as those defined by panels of experts) be followed throughout an organization. As various groups within the organization apply current best practice models, they may develop new knowledge about ways to improve the current best practice and can then report their findings to a panel of experts for their process area so that their findings can be evaluated and possibly lead to modification of the organization's current best practice models. Implementing such an organizational knowledge management process, however, requires a high degree of organizational motivation and discipline in systematically contributing to and applying an organization's current best knowledge and best practice models.

Finally, to assure that organizational knowledge assets remain within the boundaries of the organization and do not 'leak' to competitors, security measures of the type most organizations now routinely use to secure their databases must also be extended to *protecting* an organization's explicit knowledge assets.

Combining personal and organizational knowledge management approaches

Personal and organizational knowledge management approaches involve quite different emphases and practices, but both kinds of knowledge management processes are likely to be needed in any organization. Each approach has important advantages, and in many respects the advantages of one approach can be used to help offset the disadvantages of the other.

The objective for knowledge managers is therefore to create knowledge management processes that synthesize the 'right' combination and balance of the personal and organizational knowledge management practices. What the 'right' combination and balance may consist of will vary with a number of factors specific to each organization and the way it tries to compete in its markets. However, some basic guidelines can be suggested.

As a rule, personal knowledge management initiatives that bring key knowledge workers face to face are likely to be necessary to build a climate of personal trust and respect among individuals who have important knowledge. Face-to-face meetings may also stimulate exchanges of ideas and speculations that people may be reluctant to contribute through more formalized, IT-based knowledge management processes. Thus, personal knowledge management practices are likely to be vital for *generating* significantly new ideas and thereby introducing new knowledge to an organization. By contrast, a key advantage of organizational knowledge practices is their capacity for more efficient, faster dissemination of knowledge, especially through IT systems. In addition, an organizational knowledge approach to disciplined use of best practices and common processes can create 'learning platforms' that enable the systematic sharing of new learning that can be used throughout an organization.

Organizations that have not previously implemented systematic knowledge management approaches should in most cases begin with relatively inexpensive, fast to implement and less challenging personal knowledge management practices, such as those discussed above. Such practices often create surprising organizational interest in and energy for developing more extensive knowledge management practices. Personal knowledge management practices should evolve to include organizational knowledge management approaches in the long run, however, because organizations that implement effective organizational knowledge management approaches are likely to be much more effective at leveraging their knowledge and may also become better at systematically generating organizational learning. The first few steps in implementing personal knowledge management practices within an organization should therefore be communicated as only the first step in an evolving knowledge management process that will eventually include more formal and systematic organizational knowledge management practices.

When the respective advantages of personal and organizational knowledge management practices can be combined, an organization should be able to develop and apply new knowledge considerably faster and more extensively than organizations that do not try to manage knowledge or that use only personal knowledge management practices or only organizational knowledge management practices. Thus, the eventual goal for knowledge management practice in organizations is to craft hybrid, organization-specific knowledge management processes in which organizational knowledge management practices can complement and extend active personal knowledge practices, as I suggest below.

3. Three essential processes in knowledge management

Whether personal or organizational knowledge management practices are used, there are three basic and essential organizational processes that must function well in order for knowledge management to be effective: (1) maintaining learning loops in all organizational processes; (2) systematically disseminating new and existing knowledge throughout an organization; and (3) applying knowledge wherever it can be used in an organization. Let us consider each of these processes.

A *learning loop* is any learning process that tries to improve another process, whether incrementally or radically. Quality Circles are an example of an incremental learning loop designed to steadily raise the quality of a production process. More radical learning loops are possible, however, such as regular efforts to 'think outside the box' in re-conceptualizing how a firm competes in its markets. Whether incremental or radical in intent, learning loops should be designed into *all* organizational processes. The reasoning behind this prescription has much to do with the current emphasis on the 'lean organization'. In today's competitive world, only lean organizations that are focused on and excel at key value-adding activities (and that outsource other necessary processes) are likely to meet rising demands for higher performance and lower price. Every process in a lean organization is therefore important and worthy of continuous improvement through organizational learning processes – that is, learning loops.

Once learning loops are in place in an organization, the next challenge is to *systematically disseminate* existing knowledge and new knowledge generated through learning loops throughout an organization. Whether accomplished by moving people with personal knowledge or by disseminating new explicit knowledge over IT systems, new knowledge must find its way to other locations in the organization where it can be used. Such dissemination processes can be either need-driven or proactive. Need-driven dissemination processes use passive systems (like the Philips internal 'yellow pages') to help individuals find explicit knowledge or other knowledgeable individuals when they feel the need for further knowledge. Proactive dissemination systems classify organizational knowledge and the kinds of people and processes that would benefit from various kinds of knowledge and then proactively direct new knowledge to people and processes that can benefit from that kind of knowledge.

Knowledge has value to organizations only when it is applied in action within an organization's processes. Thus, the basic goals of knowledge management practice are not just generating new knowledge, but also ensuring that new and existing knowledge is actually applied in all processes where the knowledge can be used throughout an organization. Achieving this objective is likely to require new incentives and new monitoring processes to assure that new knowledge created elsewhere does not fall victim to a 'not invented here' syndrome in which new knowledge is rejected or ignored by groups in whose processes the new knowledge would actually be useful. As a general rule, achieving high performing processes for knowledge generation, dissemination and application will require substantial redesign of both incentives and monitoring systems in most organizations.

Carrying out these three basic processes of knowledge management will require an organization to become adept at stimulating development of new knowledge by individuals and then converting the personal knowledge of individuals into explicit organizational knowledge and new actions based on new knowledge. In the next section, I discuss a general model of how the generation and application of new knowledge happens in organizations.

4.   A general model of organizational learning: The five learning cycles of the learning organization

In this section I develop a general model of the way in which a learning organization generates, disseminates and applies knowledge. I first define some key concepts and terms that are central to the analysis of organizational learning. Using these concepts, I then develop a general model of how an organization learns. The model identifies and explains *five learning cycles*[7] that drive an organization's learning processes and that knowledge management practices must therefore support, as shown in Figure 2.1.

The five learning cycles represent the processes through which

- individuals in organizations create new knowledge;
- individuals and the groups they interact with share, test and accept or reject new knowledge developed by individuals;
- groups interact with other groups to determine whether new knowledge developed by a given group will be accepted within the overall organization;
- new knowledge accepted at the organizational level is embedded in new processes, systems and the culture of an organization;
- new knowledge embedded in new processes, systems and organizational culture leads to new patterns of action by groups and individuals.

The five learning cycles represent organizational learning as a collective sensemaking process that follows an identifiable progression of cognitive activities. The progression begins with individuals noticing events of potential significance for the organization, then seeking to understand and derive meaning from those events by applying their current interpretive

New Organizational Knowledge Becomes Embedded in Organization's
Interpretive Framework(s) -- Its Culture, Systems, and Processes

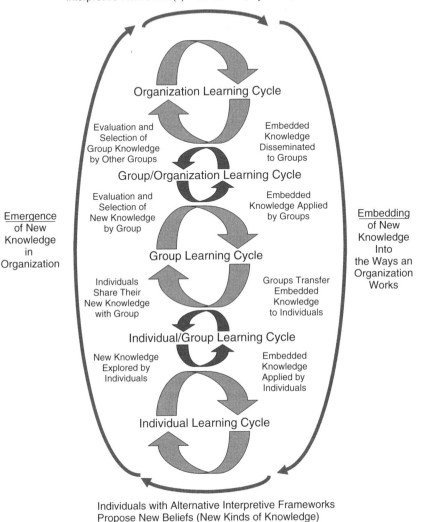

Figure 2.1   The five learning cycles of a learning organization
Source: Sanchez, 2001

frameworks and finally reacting to any meaning extracted from events by
forming new or modified sets of beliefs about the world and the situation
of the organization in the world.

To describe this process more adequately, however, we need to use a set of well-defined concepts that refer to specific aspects of this sensemaking process. I therefore next define several terms that represent the essential conceptual building blocks of organizational sensemaking and learning processes: data, information, knowledge, learning, sensemaking and interpretive frameworks.

Essential concepts and terms in analyzing organizational learning

In our analysis of the five learning cycles in a learning organization, *data* are representations of events that someone wishes to bring to the attention of other people in the organization. Data may include both qualitative and quantitative descriptions of events. As descriptions, data are always incomplete representations of events. Some aspects of an event may be noticed and reported, while other aspects are not noticed or reported. The aspects of events represented in an organization's data depend on what aspects of events observers both notice and consider of significance for the organization. Thus, all data are selective representations of events, implicit in which are some presumptions by individual observers about which events and which aspects of those events are likely to have significance for the organization. Thus, the data gathered within and considered by an organization are greatly influenced by the interpretive frameworks (defined below) of individuals that determine which events they notice and how individuals describe those events to an organization.

Information is the significance – or, more precisely, the *meaning* – that is derived from some data when the data are evaluated by an individual using his or her personal interpretive framework. People derive meaning from data through processes of comparison of data with other data, and the interpretive framework that an individual uses to derive meaning from data will determine the kinds of comparisons that the individual thinks are relevant for interpreting different kinds of data. When comparisons of some data suggest a significant change in the state of the world or an organization, that perceived change is the meaning or 'information content' derived from an individual's process of interpreting (comparing) data. Of course, comparisons of data that suggest that the state of the world or an organization has *not* changed may provide information that tends to reinforce belief in continuation of the *status quo*.

In our analysis, *knowledge* is a set of beliefs that individuals hold about cause-and-effect relationships in the world and within an organization. This pragmatic concept of knowledge, which treats knowledge as some variant of an individual's belief that 'A causes B', is fundamental to the notion of knowledge management. Because the basic objective of management is to help organizations *do things better*, knowledge management as a management process is inevitably concerned with forms of knowledge that can be used to cause things to happen more effectively and efficiently in an organization and its markets.[8] Thus, our theoretical conception of knowledge is one that is rooted in the action-oriented world of managers.

Further, although knowledge ultimately exists as a set of beliefs in the minds of individuals in an organization, I will use the term *organizational knowledge* to refer to a set of cause-and-effect beliefs that is sufficiently widely shared among individuals in an organization to enable them to act on those beliefs and to work together in doing something that is useful to the organization.

Learning is the process that results in a change in knowledge. Learning thus leads to change in an individual's beliefs about causal relationships in the world and within an organization. Learning changes the *content* of a belief about cause-and-effect relationships (adding or deleting specific causal relationships from an individual's set of beliefs), the *conditionality* of a belief (something thought to be a general principle is seen to have limits to its applicability, or vice versa) or the *degree* to which a specific belief is held (a strongly held belief becomes less certain, or vice versa). Because learning changes to some extent the web of interrelated causal relationships that makes up an individual's knowledge base, learning modifies an individual's interpretive framework (defined below) for making sense of the world and taking action in it.

Organizational learning can be said to occur when there is a change in the content, conditionality or degree of belief of the beliefs shared by individuals who jointly act on those beliefs within an organization.

Sensemaking is the process in which an individual perceives events, looks for similarities or differences between current events and past events and forms expectations about the significance of current events based on their similarities or differences with past events. In this way, sensemaking may lead to learning that changes the content, conditionality or degree of an individual's beliefs.

An *interpretive framework* is an individual's current set of beliefs about cause-and-effect relationships, against which he or she continuously compares current events in his or her sensemaking process. If the events that an individual currently observes appear inconsistent with the cause-and-effect beliefs that comprise his or her current interpretive framework, such inconsistencies may precipitate changes in the beliefs that make up the interpretive framework, thereby restoring consistency between current events and the individual's interpretive framework. In this regard, interpretive frameworks are both the *means* for individual sensemaking and the *result* of individual sensemaking.[9]

From a knowledge management perspective, the sensemaking processes of individuals are not a goal *per se* for an organization, but rather a means to achieve the broad objectives of the organization. To help an organization achieve its goals, managers must be able to integrate the sensemaking activities of its individual participants into effective organizational processes for learning and taking action.

The Five Learning Cycles model of organizational learning

Our discussion of the role of knowledge management in organizational learning begins with the presumption that no one can manage a process that is not adequately defined and analyzed. The first step in developing a useful model of organizational knowledge and learning must therefore be to define and analyze the forms of knowledge and learning in an organization and the ways in which both can be interrelated and integrated in an organization's various processes.

Perhaps the most fundamental distinction in forms of knowledge involved in organizational learning is whether some knowledge (1) exists only as a belief in the mind of an individual, (2) is shared among participants in a work group or (3) is accepted and used at the level of the overall organization. These three distinctions are represented by the Individual, Group and Organizational Learning Cycles in the Five Learning Cycles model shown in Figure 2.1. Two other learning cycles – the Individual/Group Learning Cycle and the Group/Organization Learning Cycle – link the Individual, Group and Organizational Learning Cycles. Let us consider each of these cycles in an organizational learning process.

Individual Learning Cycle

The Individual Learning Cycle at the bottom of Figure 2.1 indicates that the ultimate source of organizational knowledge is the knowledge (beliefs about causal relationships) that individuals in an organization develop through their own personal sensemaking processes. Of course, organizations develop and apply various kinds of frameworks for sensemaking, such as frameworks for gathering and interpreting data about markets and the like. In any organization, however, at least some individuals will usually have the critical capacity and imagination to develop their own interpretive frameworks that complement or even challenge existing organizational frameworks for sensemaking. Ultimately, the meanings that can be derived from data within an organization depend on the kinds of interpretations that each individual in the organization makes, which in turn depends on the deductive and inferential powers that each individual uses in interpreting data available to them within their own interpretive framework.

Thus, the wellsprings of organizational sensemaking – and the learning that sensemaking leads to – are the dual capacities of individuals in an organization both to apply existing interpretive frameworks and to generate new interpretive frameworks that improve or extend the sensemaking capabilities of existing frameworks. The Individual Learning Cycle represents the reservoir of individual interpretive frameworks that individuals in an organization use in their individual sensemaking processes.

Individual/Group Learning Cycle

Learning that results from an individual's personal sensemaking process may sometimes be applied directly in performing his or her task within the organization, but the work of most individuals is done in some group, team, network of peers or other context for interacting with other people in the organization. Thus, before an individual's learning can become the basis for taking action in an organization, the individual's knowledge must be shared with the other individuals in a work group, so they can consider whether that individual's learning (that is, his or her new beliefs) should be accepted as valid and become the basis for group action.

A critical step in an organization's learning is therefore the process through which individuals share knowledge with other people that they work with. This critical link between individuals and the groups they work with is represented by the Individual/Group Learning Cycle in Figure 2.1. The Individual/Group Learning Cycle includes the repertoire of interactions through which individuals within an organization's various groups share (or may fail to share) their individual knowledge and learning with others in their group.

Group Learning Cycle

For individuals in a work group to perform their group tasks in a coherent, co-ordinated manner, they must share some core set of beliefs (that is, knowledge) about how to get their task done. In performing individual and group tasks, people may learn by doing or by analyzing. Learning while doing a task can lead to practical, hands-on, 'know-how' knowledge (Sanchez, 1997) of how to perform a given task well or better – the kind of learning that creates 'repeatable patterns of action' that are the essence of an organization's capabilities (Sanchez, Heene and Thomas, 1996). Know-how knowledge developed by a group usually becomes embedded in a repertoire of routines that the group can perform on demand (Nelson and Winter, 1982). Learning by analyzing a task, on the other hand, helps to develop more theoretical 'know-why' insights into why a given task can be accomplished by taking certain kinds of co-ordinated actions (Sanchez, 1997). Groups that are capable of performing analyses that lead to new know-why knowledge, however, may establish 'double-loop' learning routines that enable them to redesign how they do their work process (Argyris and Schoen, 1978).

The Group Learning Cycle in Figure 2.1 therefore represents both the repertoire of know-how routines that a work group has developed for executing tasks assigned to it, as well as any know-how and know-why learning capabilities a group has developed for improving the group's current routines for performing its tasks.

Group/Organization Learning Cycle

The outputs of the Group Learning Cycle may include three forms of learning. Groups may learn how to perform their own task better, such as the process improvement learning that emanates from Quality Circles and other forms of continuous process improvement. This form of know-how learning may often be applied directly by the group to its own processes, but may sometimes involve process improvements that require support and resources from other groups in the organization (including groups of managers who allocate resources). Groups may also generate know-why learning that identifies new kinds of capabilities the group could develop and apply to its task. Implementing this form of learning may require new resources to build new capabilities and develop new routines, and these new resource requirements must be communicated to and accepted by the organization. Groups may also generate ideas for new kinds of tasks they could perform with current or new capabilities. This form of 'know-what' learning (Sanchez, 1997) must usually be shared with the organization in order to gather support for the group to undertake new kinds of activities.

The Group/Organization Learning Cycle in Figure 2.1 therefore represents the processes by which groups communicate their new know-how, know-why or know-what knowledge to the larger organization (that is, to other groups in the organization) in efforts to acquire the resources to put such knowledge into action. The Group/Organization Learning Cycle includes the repertoire of processes that groups in an organization can use in communicating their knowledge to other groups in the organization in efforts to gather organizational resources needed to implement their new knowledge.

Organization Learning Cycle

At the top of the five learning cycles is the Organization Learning Cycle. In this cycle, the groups that interact in an organization (including, but not limited to, groups of managers) exchange group knowledge and learning in an effort to have each group's knowledge accepted as valid and become a basis for taking action in the organization. Note, however, that the position of this learning cycle at the top of the Five Learning Cycles does not imply that this form of learning is the exclusive concern of top managers in an organization, as I clarify below. Rather, the Organization Learning Cycle represents the processes in an organization through which groups compete to influence and, if possible, to determine the sensemaking processes used in an organization. In principle, all groups within an organization may potentially play a role in this process.

Management's role in the five learning cycles

It is important to emphasize that the vertical arrangement of the five learning cycles in Figure 2.1 does not represent an authority hierarchy, with the ideas of front-line workers at the bottom and the ideas of top management at the top. As noted earlier, the critical distinction being made in this model is whether some knowledge is a belief that is held by an individual, that is shared by a group within an organization or that is accepted and used widely by groups within an organization. Thus, in this model of organizational learning, the beliefs of the factory-floor worker and the beliefs of the CEO of an organization are fundamentally in the same position: they are beliefs in the mind of an individual. Though a CEO may have certain advantages not available to the factory-floor worker, the ideas of both individuals must navigate the same organizational learning process and overcome essentially the same challenges if either individual wants to have his or her beliefs accepted by their work group and, ultimately, by the organization at large. In effect, all individuals with beliefs that they want to propagate as a basis for action within an organization must find a way to clear the cognitive hurdles of group and organizational acceptance in order to manage those beliefs 'into good currency' within the organization (van de Ven 1986), as suggested by the upward arrow 'Emergence of New Knowledge in Organization' in Figure 2.1.

In effect, the Five Learning Cycles model presumes that managers cannot dictate the beliefs that 'knowledge workers' will genuinely accept and commit to act on in an organization. Nevertheless, even though individual managers cannot impose their beliefs on others in the organization by fiat as it were, they do have an important source of influence on the knowledge base and learning processes of an organization, because top managers can usually decide which interpretive frameworks will be institutionalized as the 'official' or 'established' frameworks for sensemaking in the various systems and processes of the organization. For example, top management may decide to adopt a customer-relationship management (CRM) software system that will determine, at least in part, how customers are described, categorized, communicated with and otherwise managed by groups and individuals in the organization. In this way, certain interpretive frameworks and the knowledge on which they are based may be cascaded down from the organizational to the group and ultimately to the individual level in the model, as suggested by the downward arrow 'Embedding of New Knowledge Into the Ways an Organization Works' in Figure 2.1.

Although establishing interpretive frameworks selected by top management by no means assures that all groups and individuals in the organization will accept and use those frameworks, such frameworks in effect establish the orthodoxy against which alternative interpretive frameworks will be evaluated and against which they must sometimes compete.

In a learning organization, managers will understand the dynamics that drive all five learning cycles and will adopt knowledge management practices that assure that the five learning cycles function effectively and sustain the overall 'learning loop' of continuous organizational learning suggested by the four arrows surrounding the Five Learning Cycles in Figure 2.1. Managers must support and stimulate the generation of new ideas by individuals (the bottom horizontal arrow), the progression of new ideas upwards to group and organization levels (the left upward arrow), the adoption of new ideas by embedding them in the organization's systems and processes (the top horizontal arrow) and the implementation and testing of new knowledge in the systems and processes an organization uses.

I next suggest a number of fundamental issues and practical challenges that managers must understand and manage well in order for the five learning cycles to function well in driving the learning dynamics of an organization.

5.   Issues and challenges in managing the five learning cycles

Both through academic research into the psychological and social dimensions of the Five Learning Cycles model and through practical applications of the model by managers seeking to improve learning processes in their organizations, a number of important issues and challenges in managing the five learning cycles in organizational learning have been identified. I next consider some of the most important (by effect and frequency of occurrence) of the issues and challenges likely to arise in each of the five cycles.

Managing the Individual Learning Cycle

How an individual *learns* – how a person manages to move beyond the beliefs that form his or her current interpretive framework to form new beliefs that modify that interpretive framework – is a question that will no doubt be studied for decades to come. Yet today we do understand some things about individual learning processes that managers who want to stimulate and sustain processes of organizational learning should attend to.

We know, for example, that learning fundamentally occurs in the minds of individuals as they evolve their personal interpretive frameworks for making sense of the world. As Stein and Ridderstråle (2001) describe it, learning begins with a process of 'internal simulation' that causes a person to draw on past experience in trying to interpret and assess the significance of current events and thereby to be better prepared to understand and even anticipate future events and circumstances. This internal simulation is precipitated by events and situations that do not neatly fit within the understandings that comprise a person's current interpretive framework and that thereby invite or sometimes 'force' an individual to *imagine* possibilities that lie beyond the current content and limits of his or her interpretive framework.

Stimulating individual learning processes in this mode raises two key issues for managers. The first is the need to stimulate *metaphorical learning*, and the second is the need to build an organization's capacity for encouraging the emergence of *divergent interpretive frameworks* within an organization. The two issues are interrelated in important ways, as I now explain.

To understand what metaphorical learning means in a managerial context, it is useful to distinguish it from basic education and from training. For the purposes of this analysis, let us say that *education* is the acquisition of a base of facts and concepts and a set of skills in logical analysis and reasoning that together form the foundation for the interpretive frameworks of 'educated people' in a given society. Similarly, let us characterize *training* as processes for improving an individual's skills in the performance of specific kinds of tasks. When managers offer employees (including themselves) opportunities to pursue further education, they are in effect offering people the chance to acquire additional familiarity with and understanding of the 'conventional wisdom' that is regarded as 'knowledge' in a given society. Training programmes deepen specific skills that are regarded as useful within the conventional wisdom of a society and its business culture. Both of these forms of learning, however, are fundamentally *convergent* in nature; they lead individuals to develop personal interpretive frameworks that share deep, fundamental assumptions about 'how the world works' in general and in some specific aspects.

By contrast, metaphorical learning is learning that challenges and eventually changes the deep assumptions of individuals in a given social setting about how the world works, or could work. Metaphorical learning presents individuals with situations that have some deep structural similarity or fundamental points of relevance to the kinds of situations they have been educated and trained to interpret in certain ways, but then analyzes those situations with concepts and rationales that are different from those that currently form an individual's interpretive framework. In effect, metaphorical learning opportunities offer new conceptual frameworks and ways of reasoning about situations that demand that individuals 'stretch' beyond their current understanding to see and interpret even familiar things in a new way.

An example of metaphorical learning is the use of cases in executive development programs that lie outside the industries with which participants have experience or that introduce examples of atypical firm strategies and tactics within familiar industries. The new concepts and ways of reasoning introduced in such cases are intended to help program participants develop new ways of representing and thinking about their own familiar business situations. This intent is also evident in 'best in world' benchmarking processes. For example, when Chrysler decided to fundamentally rethink the way the company conceives of and designs customer service strategies, it did not just look to excellent customer service firms in the automobile industry. Instead, Chrysler benchmarked its customer service concepts and strategies against Federal Express, a firm recognized as a world leader in creating and maintaining very high levels of customer service and satisfaction. To benefit from this benchmarking, Chrysler managers had to engage in metaphorical learning by recognizing how Federal Express's ways of conceptualizing and designing customer service in its express package business could be applied in fundamentally rethinking how Chrysler conceptualizes, designs and delivers customer service in the automotive industry.

When metaphorical learning happens in the minds of individuals in an organization, it is likely to lead them to recognize and question the deep assumptions and ingrained practices of their organization and to propose new ideas that lie outside of their organization's current interpretive frameworks for determining what the organization should do and how to do it. Therein lies the second managerial challenge in stimulating the Individual Learning Cycle. Once some individuals do succeed in going beyond their current interpretive frameworks to imagine new possibilities for taking action in the world, they may try to suggest these new possibilities to their peers in the organization, as I discussed above in the Individual/Group Learning Cycle. If their ideas begin to gather support from their own group and other groups in the organization, this process adds diversity to the interpretive frameworks in the organization and thereby begins to compete against the established orthodoxy of interpretive frameworks in the organization.

The emergence of diverse interpretive frameworks in an organization should expand the sensemaking capacity of an organization, enabling it to sense new kinds of opportunities and threats and to imagine new ways of responding. At the same time, taking organizational action requires that individuals have a 'critical mass' of shared beliefs in their interpretive frameworks sufficient to serve as the basis for coherent collective action. Too much diversity in the interpretive frameworks of an organization may make it difficult or impossible for the organization to take effective action. Thus, managers must try to maintain a *dynamic balance* between generating new interpretive frameworks to expand sensemaking capacity and achieving sufficient convergence in interpretive frameworks to form a basis for effective collective action. While no simple rule exists to help managers determine what the optimal dynamic balance would be in their organization, it is essential to understand that metaphorical learning and the diversity in sensemaking that it generates are the wellsprings of organizational learning and thus must be systematically supported even while seeking sufficient convergence to achieve collective action.

Managing the Individual/Group Learning Cycle

The essential concern in managing the Individual/Group Learning Cycle is maintaining the willingness of individuals to share their knowledge with other people in their work group or peer network in an organization. Understanding how to maintain the willingness of individuals to share their knowledge in an organization starts with the recognition that individuals may perceive significant disincentives for sharing their knowledge. Individuals may decide not to communicate what they know to their peers and work group because they fear that fully disclosing and explaining what they know may diminish their perceived value and importance in an organization. In the extreme case, an individual may even fear being replaced by a less experienced person (or even a computer!) if they fully explain how they do analyses, prepare designs, organize a work process, make decisions and so on.

Ericsson and many other companies have experimented with the creation of specific incentives for individual knowledge-sharing and with the use of various socialization processes to encourage individuals to communicate what they know more freely to their co-workers (Stein and Ridderstråle, 2001). Other companies have undertaken to fundamentally redefine the employment relationship with their key knowledge workers in ways that would allay any fears of negative consequences that such workers would have if they were to share their individual knowledge. An example may illustrate why such a fundamental rethinking of the employment relationship may be needed.

In the mid-1990s I was helping a global electronics firm define and document the way one of its product divisions creates new product designs. A key part of this design process was defining the architecture of the next generation product – that is, the kind of components to be used in the product and the way the components would be interrelated in the product design. One senior designer was always given this critical task, because his architectures always seemed to work well. When I met with the designer and explained that I had been asked by the product division management to document the 'design rules' that he followed in creating new architectures, he at first appeared to be quite flattered that his skill in this area was recognized at such a high level in the organization, and he was very co-operative.

As we proceeded to discuss and write down the design rules that he followed, however, his attitude began to change, and soon he asked me to explain again exactly why management wanted to document the design rules he had developed. I explained again what his management had asked me to do, but soon thereafter he said that he had already told me everything that he could explain, even though he had earlier mentioned several other design rules that we had put on a list to discuss. It became clear that the designer was beginning to worry that if all the design rules he knew and followed were made explicit, perhaps he would be replaced by a junior designer or even a computerized design program. Eventually, only personal assurances by top management that they had no intention of replacing him – and a widely publicized redefinition of his role in the organization as leader of the division's architecture development and improvement process – persuaded him that there was nothing to fear in revealing his current knowledge and much for him and the organization to gain by continuously developing and building on that knowledge.

As more organizations recognize the fundamental importance to organizational learning of converting the tacit personal knowledge of their key knowledge workers into explicit organizational knowledge, organizations will increasingly have to rethink, redefine and clearly communicate employment relationships with their key knowledge workers to ensure that those individuals will not withhold knowledge that is vital to the organization.

Managing the Group Learning Cycle

The essential concern in managing the Group Learning Cycle is assuring that work groups will generate and apply new knowledge in an effective way. Effective management of this learning cycle requires recognizing the inherently social nature of individual learning processes, and the resulting potential for individuals in a work group to fall into the cognitive trap of 'group think'.

The ongoing formation of a person's interpretive framework for sensemaking is significantly influenced by the social interactions an individual experiences. In work processes within an organization, an individual is likely to seek a measure of 'cognitive congruence' with the co-workers and peers he or she interacts with frequently (Merali, 2001). Individuals evaluate the effects of their actions on the people in their social context and tend to adopt patterns of thought and norms of behaviour that are compatible with the ways of thinking and acting of other people in their social context. Thus, each individual's interpretive framework is co-evolving with a social context and seeks to achieve cognitive congruence that leads to a cognitive equilibrium with that context.[10] The social impulse to seek cognitive equilibria in the evolution of human interpretive frameworks has important practical implications for managing individual/group learning interactions.

First, left to their own devices, the individuals in a work group are likely sooner or later to converge towards a set of beliefs that are compatible, at least to the extent that they affect work processes the group must perform. While this may be helpful and even essential in achieving efficient co-ordinated action, the desire of individuals to achieve and maintain cognitive equilibrium can lead a work group into cognitive rigidity and 'group think' that is resistant to change in ideas once an equilibrium is attained. Stimulating the learning processes of individuals and the flow of new ideas from individuals into work groups is therefore likely to require managerial interventions to upset established cognitive equilibria at the work group level.

Various managerial interventions may help to overcome group think and expand the sensemaking capacity of a work group. The composition of a work group may be changed, for example, by assigning new individuals to the group who will bring new interpretive frameworks that will destabilize and eventually shift the group's current cognitive equilibrium. A group may also be given a task that would be impossible to perform while staying within its current cognitive equilibrium. For example, in the 1980s Honda's management wanted to reinvigorate its product development department, which was efficient in performing its basic development task but was showing signs of deepening group think by developing a succession of new car designs that were increasingly similar and familiar. To upset the cognitive equilibrium in its development department, Honda management launched a new development project for a 'City' car whose requirements for roomy interior space, compact external dimensions, exciting driving performance, outstanding fuel efficiency and other design objectives simply could not be met through the current approaches of its designers. Setting this challenging goal forced Honda designers to 'think outside the box', to abandon familiar design concepts and methods and to seek a new set of design concepts and processes outside its current cognitive congruence. The result was a bold and innovative design that quickly became an icon for the young generation of urban Japanese.

Cognitive congruence helps the individuals in a group work together in a coherent way and thereby become efficient in performing a familiar task, but it is also likely to prevent a group from seriously considering the potential gains that could result from exploring alternative ways to perform a current task or from imagining new tasks it could perform that could increase the group's contribution to the organization. Thus, ironically, the potential gains from managerial interventions to disturb cognitive equilibria are likely to be greatest in work groups that are performing their current tasks most efficiently, because such groups will probably have achieved the greatest degree of cognitive congruence in their cognitive equilibrium. Like Honda's managers, managers must therefore carefully evaluate whether the benefits derived from the efficiency with which a group is performing its current task (that is, 'doing things right') outweigh the potential gains in effectiveness ('doing the right things') that disturbing an efficient group's cognitive equilibrium might bring to an organization.

Managing the Group/Organization Learning Cycle

The central issue in managing the Group/Organization Learning Cycle is encouraging and maintaining interactions between work groups in an organization that can benefit from sharing their knowledge with each other and that have the potential to build new organizational knowledge (shared beliefs) through such interactions.

Virtually any approach to allocating tasks within an organization design – whether based on functional, product, regional or other divisions of labor – will to some extent create 'silos' within an organization by focusing various groups on their own specific tasks. As groups perform their tasks, however, they may develop knowledge that would be useful to other groups in the organization. Although groups may be connected organizationally by basic material and information flows necessary to maintain co-ordination among tasks, exchanges of knowledge among groups are unlikely to occur in any systematic way unless managers overtly cause such interactions to happen. The formation of multifunctional project teams is becoming an increasingly important way of fostering knowledge exchanges among groups within an organization, as the following example illustrates.

Raub (2001) studied how a large Swiss retailer used project teams to develop new organizational knowledge that enabled the firm to achieve new forms and levels of environmental performance. Raub describes the process as a set of interactions between the firm's top managers and several groups, undertaken in three phases. In the first phase, the firm's managers determined that rising customer expectations about the environmental performance of firms made it strategically necessary for the firm to improve its environmental performance, but the managers also understood that they did not know enough about the detailed operations of the firm to identify the specific operational areas with the greatest potential for improving environmental performance. The managers therefore formed several expert groups to help the managers define specific strategic options for environmental performance improvement in the major areas of the firm's operations. Each group had the detailed knowledge of an operational area needed to define specific environmental issues in each major area of the firm's operations, to propose ways of dealing with those issues and to identify specific forms of knowledge within and external to the organization that could be brought to bear on those issues.

In the second phase, a 'coordination team' was formed to promote exchanges of knowledge and information between the expert groups. Working with the expert groups, the co-ordination team allocated specific areas of activity and responsibility to the groups, categorized what each group identified as its relevant knowledge and established organizational structures and processes for systematically making this knowledge visible and accessible by the groups to promote the transfer of relevant knowledge among the groups.

The third phase involved intensive interactions among top managers, the co-ordination team and the expert groups to decide how the new knowledge developed by the groups would be put into action. Improvement projects identified by the expert groups were evaluated in detail, selected for action and prioritized. Plans for co-ordinating capability development initiatives recommended by the groups were drawn up and a top management monitoring process was established to assure that development and deployment of the new capabilities proceeded on schedule.

Raub's study suggests that building new organizational knowledge involves two basic kinds of group-based managerial initiatives. First, managers may be able to generate new organizational knowledge simply by creating opportunities for groups in their organization to interact in new ways that allow their current group knowledge to be shared, evaluated, integrated and then applied more widely in the organization. Second, managers may also stimulate the formation of new organizational knowledge by creating multi-functional groups that are given the task of working together in (and sharing joint responsibility for) creating new organizational knowledge that becomes the basis for building new organizational capabilities.

The Organization Learning Cycle

In the Five Learning Cycles model, the creation of organizational knowledge occurs when the knowledge of one or more groups in an organization is accepted as valid and adopted sufficiently widely within an organization to become the basis for organizational action. In becoming the basis for organizational action, knowledge may become embedded in an organization in a number of ways that profoundly affect the way groups and individuals in the organization work. Of particular importance in terms of its significant and long-lasting impact on the way an organization works is the knowledge embedded in the accounting and control systems of an organization, because these systems embody knowledge that is the basis for defining and measuring performance in the various tasks carried out in an organization. A key task of managers in managing the Organization Learning Cycle, therefore, is assuring that the control systems used in their organization are based on knowledge that is the most appropriate type of knowledge for meeting the demands of their organization's current competitive environment.

Control systems include all formalized processes for co-ordinating an organization's activities and for monitoring, measuring and assessing those activities. Control systems gather the data that are generated by an organization and define how those data are interpreted formally within an organization to create information that is 'officially' recognized within an organization as relevant in managing an organization. Control systems are therefore *de facto* interpretive frameworks that shape managers' and other employees' perceptions of how their organization is performing in its environment. Control systems take considerable time and effort to develop and put in place and organizations therefore are often reluctant to adopt significant changes in their control systems, even when their competitive environments are undergoing major changes. Managers must therefore continually question whether the control systems put in place yesterday – based on knowledge of how to compete effectively in yesterday's competitive environment – are still effective in helping an organization compete in today's competitive environment.

In his study of Groupe Bulle, a leading French computer company in the 1980s, Lorino (2001) documents the profound impact of control systems on organizational sensemaking and managerial decision-making. In the 1970s and early 1980s, competition in the computer industry was driven by hardware performance, quality and cost. Competitive success went to those firms that could develop high-performing computers (measured by calculations per second, for example) and cost-efficiently manufacture computers with high quality levels (measured by low defect rates, for example). To monitor its organizational performance in this competitive environment, Groupe Bulle developed a sophisticated set of cost measures used in managing hardware development, production of components and assembly of mainframe computers. Management processes were defined to achieve continuous improvements in those cost measures and advancement in the company went to those managers who could deliver performance in continuous cost reductions and efficiency improvements, as determined by the measures provided by the cost control system.

By the mid-1980s, however, the competitive environment in the computer industry had changed and there were many capable producers offering high-quality, high-performing computers at competitive prices. In an industry in which hardware had largely become a commodity, offering customized 'turn key' software solutions for individual customer needs became the key to competitive success. Nevertheless, Groupe Bulle continued to rely primarily on its established hardware-focused cost control systems to guide and monitor performance within the organization. The result was that the firm's management processes continued to focus on managing cost reductions in hardware development and production, while the primary source of competitive advantage had shifted to superior knowledge of how to create customized software solutions quickly and efficiently.

Of course, some managers within Groupe Bulle recognized the growing gap between what its control system was measuring and what mattered in the firm's competitive environment. But as Lorino points out, embedding organizational knowledge in the form of an official, institutionalized interpretive framework like an important management control system pressures individuals to adjust their personal interpretive frameworks to conform to the view of 'reality' embedded in the institutionalized framework. This pressure not only constrains the sensemaking processes of individuals and groups within the organization, but also shifts 'the burden of proof' in arguing for new or modified interpretive frameworks onto those seeking change. Thus, institutionalizing knowledge and related interpretive frameworks in an organization's control systems helps an organization to apply and extend that knowledge, but also tends to discourage development of new kinds of organizational knowledge and interpretive frameworks.

Managers must therefore be alert to the need to create and sustain a dynamic cognitive equilibrium between processes for applying and extending yesterday's knowledge (for example, through use of established control systems) and adapting the knowledge base of the organization to meet today's and tomorrow's competitive conditions. To this end, along with their use of current control systems, managers should implement what Lorino calls an 'inquiry procedure', a periodic process for open questioning of an organization's current control systems and the usually implicit knowledge that underlies them, to assure that an organization's interpretive frameworks are effective in monitoring an organization's performance in its current competitive environment.

Concluding comments

The fundamental knowledge management concepts and processes discussed here reflect a profound and growing shift in management thinking and practice today. This shift represents a clear evolution away from traditional management concepts based on command and control to concepts of management in which managers are more importantly concerned with developing, supporting, connecting and empowering an organization's employees as knowledge workers. In effect, knowledge management theory and practice today is part of a broad movement away from the presumption that management is the sole 'brain' of the organization to the assumption that building a broadly based *collective intelligence* among all participants in an organization (including, but not limited to, managers) is the essential task of management.

This shift, and knowledge management's central role within it, implies a profound change in the way managers lead organizations. Knowledge management presumes that managers are not the only people who can have useful ideas in an organization. Managers must therefore create broadly based knowledge-sharing and learning processes that stimulate and draw on the learning of all individuals and groups in generating the best possible flow of new ideas for their organizations. In the knowledge economy, therefore, managers cannot lead by the power of their formal authority, but rather must lead by stimulating and harnessing the power of ideas generated by learning processes throughout their organization. Moreover, in an economy in which knowledge workers have mobility, managers cannot lead by 'dictating' belief in a given idea or set of ideas. Rather, to create real commitment and motivation in organizational action, managers must first create active organizational learning processes in which all knowledgeable employees can become involved and contribute their ideas.

What this means in practice is that managers must increasingly take responsibility for committing their organizations to action not on the basis of their own personal ideas, but on the basis of the best ideas generated by the learning processes of their organization. For managers schooled in the traditional command and control concepts of management and derived concepts of leadership, acting on ideas generated by others in the organization may seem inappropriate and inordinately risky. For managers who understand what it means to lead by the power of ideas, however, acting on the ideas that their organization generates through its learning processes is not only the best way to try to achieve competitive success – it may well be the only way.

Notes

1   See also Ron Sanchez (forthcoming), 'Personal Knowledge versus Organizational Knowledge Approaches to Knowledge Management Practice', in D. Rooney, G. Hearn and A. Ninan (eds), *The Knowledge Economy Handbook* (Oxford: Routledge).

2   Some writers and consultants have even gone so far as to argue that *all* knowledge is tacit in nature. The irony inherent in trying to transmit to others the 'knowledge' that all knowledge is tacit, however, should be obvious.

3   By using modular product architectures to create increasingly configurable product designs, Motorola was able to increase the number of customizable product variations it could offer to customers from a few thousand variations in the late 1980s to more than 120 million variations by the late 1990s.

4   A platform includes a system of standard component types and standardized interfaces between component types that enable 'plugging and playing' different component variations in the platform design to configure different product variations (see Sanchez, 2004).

5   Patent, copyright and trade secrecy laws may give an organization *intellectual property rights* in the personal knowledge developed by individuals working in the organization. Such rights may of course discourage – though not entirely prevent – individuals from sharing their personal knowledge with other organizations.

6   The greater the extent to which an organization employs 'knowledge workers' with advanced education and training in formally communicating their ideas, however, the less intellectually difficult the articulation of organizational knowledge within the organization should be.

7   See Ron Sanchez (2001), 'Managing Knowledge into Competence: The Five Learning Cycles of the Competent Organization', R. Sanchez (ed), *Knowledge Management and Organizational Competence* (Oxford: Oxford University Press), pp. 3–37.

8   This concept of knowledge also helps to make an important distinction between simply being aware of something, which means having data or information in our framework, and having knowledge, which implies actually knowing how to do something or how to cause something to happen.

9   Because modifying interpretive frameworks can require significant cognitive effort, sometimes people may prefer to ignore current events that are inconsistent with their current beliefs; to focus on other events that tend to corroborate current beliefs; or simply not to worry about the inconsistencies of current events with current beliefs.

10   The extent to which an individual will seek a cognitive equilibrium with his or her social context in an organization may of course vary significantly with the personality of each individual, as well as with the tolerance for conflict within the culture of an organization.

References

Argyris, C. and D. Schoen (1978) *Organizational Learning: A Theory of Action Perspective* (Reading, MA: Addison-Wesley).

Lorino, P. (2001) 'A Pragmatic Analysis of the Role of Management Systems in Organizational Learning', in R. Sanchez (ed), *Knowledge Management and Organizational Competence* (Oxford: Oxford University Press), pp. 177–209.

Merali, Y. (2001) 'Building and Developing Capabilities: A Cognitive Congruence Framework', in R. Sanchez (ed), *Knowledge Management and Organizational Competence* (Oxford: Oxford University Press), pp. 41–62.

Nelson, R. and S. Winter (1982) *An Evolutionary Theory of Economic Change* (Cambridge, MA: Harvard University Press).

Raub, S. P. (2001) 'Towards a Knowledge-Based Framework of Competence Development', in R. Sanchez (ed), *Knowledge Management and Organizational Competence* (Oxford: Oxford University Press), pp. 97–113.

Sanchez, R. (1997) 'Managing Articulated Knowledge in Competence-Based Competition', in R. Sanchez and A. Heene (eds), *Strategic Learning and Knowledge Management* (Chichester: John Wiley & Sons), pp. 163–87.

Sanchez, R. (2001) 'Managing Knowledge into Competences: The Five Learning Cycles of the Competent Organization', in R. Sanchez (ed), *Knowledge Management and Organizational Competence* (Oxford: Oxford University Press), pp. 3–37.

Sanchez, R. (2004) 'Creating Modular Platforms for Strategic Flexibility', *Design Management Review*, Winter 2004, 58–67.

Sanchez, R., A. Heene and H. Thomas (eds) (1996) *Dynamics of Competence-Based Competition: Theory and Practice in the New Strategic Management* (Oxford: Elsevier Pergamon).

Spear, S. and H. K. Bowen (1999) 'Decoding the DNA of the Toyota Production System', *Harvard Business Review*, September/October 1999, 97–106.

Stein, J. and J. Ridderstråle (2001) 'Managing the dissemination of competences', in R. Sanchez (ed), *Knowledge Management and Organizational Competence* (Oxford: Oxford University Press), pp. 63–76.

Van de Ven, A. (1986) 'Central Problems in the Management of Innovation', *Management Science*, 32(5), 590–607.

3

Knowledge Management in Interaction: Transactive Knowledge Systems and the Management of Knowledge

Elisabeth Brauner and Albrecht Becker

The rationale behind the existence of organizations may be seen – among other reasons – in the advantages of the division of labour (Crozier and Friedberg, 1980). At the same time, size and structure of organizations require a subdivision among members along functions, tasks and duties. The larger an organization, the more departments and members will have to be co-ordinated. In order to ensure disparate parts and divisions are able to pool their efforts and their expertise, actions as well as knowledge need to be synchronized and co-ordinated. Knowledge management is a means to co-ordinate what is known in an organization, whereas organizational learning describes the change of that organizational knowledge. In a globalized environment characterized by hypercompetition and knowledge-intensive processes (D'Aveni, 1994) knowledge management and reflection on organizational learning become increasingly a necessity in organizations because they may be generators of competitive advantages (Penrose, 1995; Spender, 1996; cf. Becker et al., 2002).

The analysis of knowledge management presented here uses an interdisciplinary approach. We employ concepts originating from fields as diverse as business administration and management, organizational theory, human resource management, psychology and information technology. Thus, our own attempt to delineate a future of knowledge management constitutes a perspective that can itself be seen as knowledge management and learning across disciplines. In a first step, we will derive our main definitions from the current state of the art in the field. Then, we will present three propositions that describe our approach to knowledge management and organizational learning. We will discuss the consequences that follow from these propositions in the light of insights from the above-mentioned disciplines. We will conclude our analysis by reflecting on several desiderata that, in our view, should be taken into consideration with respect to the future of knowledge management.

On knowledge management and organizational learning

At first sight, it would seem almost self-evident to assume that knowledge management and organizational learning are closely interrelated because learning should involve change of knowledge. Nevertheless, the two fields have been rather divided, basically due to institutional reasons. Knowledge management research originates mainly from the field of information technology and business information systems (cf. Lehner, 2000). The main concerns are the techniques and technologies that deal with storing and processing information in organizations. Studying organizational learning has its roots in social science, specifically in organizational theory, human resource management and business administration, and management (cf. Easterby-Smith et al., 2000). Foci of interest are the social processes of learning by and in organizations (Easterby-Smith and Araujo, 1999).

Current definitions of knowledge management and organizational learning are equally diverse. One of the main issues under discussion is the nature and location of knowledge. Gherardi (2000) and Brown and Duguid (2001) criticize the view that knowledge is stored in individual memories because they claim that this point of view cannot explain the social character of knowledge particularly at the level of groups, communities of practice, and organizations (cf. Cook and Brown, 1999). Other approaches argue that knowledge is inseparable from practice (Lave and Wenger, 1991; Tsoukas, 1996; Wenger, 1998). They locate knowledge, or rather knowing, not in a person's head but in the actions he or she engages in, that is, in social practices. Practice is understood here as comprising co-ordinated activities that ground on knowledge, which resides in groups rather than in individuals. However, at the same time, knowing is defined as something that 'would be recognized as competent participation in the practice' (Wenger, 1998, p. 137), which implies that knowing is linked to individual actors. Thus, this approach contains a contradiction: knowledge is seen as being located in practices and/or groups on the one hand and as being located in individuals on the other. Like previous views, which have located knowledge in various organizational storages, namely people, routines or databases (Walsh and Ungson, 1991), this approach makes it difficult to deal with organizational learning.

As a result of this displacement of knowledge from an individual mind to a social level, organizational learning is often understood as the change of observable behaviour rather than a change of knowledge (Argyris and Schön, 1996; Daft and Weick, 1984; Fiol and Lyles, 1985; Levitt and March, 1999; March and Olsen, 1976). However, this does not take into consideration that one possible result of learning could be that the original behaviour was appropriate and should therefore be retained. External circumstances might otherwise be factors that prevent an individual or an organization from initiating new behaviour, although it might well be learned that the old behaviour is outdated. More sensible, therefore, is the view that organizational learning is the change in the potential for action (Huber, 1991). Specifically, this change can be interpreted as a change in the knowledge base. Thus, the question whether to locate knowledge in an individual, in a group or in an organization is crucial for understanding learning in organizations. It is also essential to resolve this problem if research is to result in concrete suggestions as to how knowledge management and organizational learning can be used for improving the performance of a company or organization.

Understanding organizational learning as the change of knowledge and thus of the organization's potential of behaviour, we define knowledge as information that has been interpreted into a context and stored in an individual's memory (Brauner and Becker, 2001, 2004). We then need a model for the transformation of individuals' knowledge to more aggregate social levels. The lack of such a sensible model, which could explain how the transformation of knowledge from the level of individual cognition to the social level of groups and organizations can be mastered theoretically as well as empirically, also constitutes the main conceptual problem for the approaches described above. If we assume that knowledge is always to be understood as individual knowledge and that learning should be understood as individual learning, such a model is important for several reasons. First, without such a model it will be difficult if not impossible to explain how individual knowledge can be made available to an organization. If an individual possesses knowledge, how can 'the organization' draw upon it? How can the process of sharing information be pictured if knowledge, even after sharing, continues to reside within the individual, as opposed to 'floating around' in the organization? Second, without such a model it will also be difficult to explain what exactly organizational learning is. How can an organization benefit if it is only and exclusively the individual who learns? How can the result of individual learning, namely a changed and expanded knowledge base, be made available to the organization? Third, without such a model it will be almost impossible to conceive specific recommendations for knowledge management. How exactly should knowledge management systems be designed? Which concrete recommendations can be given to organizations to foster sensible processes of organizational learning? The third issue in particular has created problems in organizations because the technical and technological solutions implemented over the past years have not been successful in the long term (cf. Spies, 2001).

Before we continue our analysis of knowledge management and organizational learning, we therefore introduce a model of knowledge in groups and organizations that has been developed in social psychology and adapted to organizational psychology. It has been useful for explaining the relationship between the individual level and the social or organizational level with regard to knowledge and learning.

Transactive knowledge systems in groups and organizations

For most organizations to be efficient it is necessary, if not indispensable, to be composed of diverse expertise. Diverse expertise ensures that knowledge is available to the organization. This diverse expertise will enable it to face and tackle distinct problems that can occur within the environment. However, to make use of this diversity, in addition to unshared knowledge, the existence of shared knowledge among participating individuals is a prerequisite. Unshared knowledge preserves diversity of expertise, whereas shared knowledge is necessary in order to bring about mutual understanding in the first place. Shared knowledge comprises basic knowledge necessary for interaction in day-to-day activities. Disparate expertise, however, cannot be integrated by all members sharing all knowledge. First, this would exceed the information-processing capacities of individual organizational members (Simon, 1951). Second, the advantages and benefits resulting from diversity would be eliminated. Acquiring knowledge *about* each others' knowledge is a much more economic way of integrating diversity. Thus, a person learns, and thereafter knows, *that* a co-worker has expertise in a specific area without acquiring all that expert knowledge him- or herself. If the need arises, he or she can then ask this co-worker to help answering questions or solving problems if they fall in the co-worker's expertise area. Knowledge about other people's knowledge is called transactive knowledge or metaknowledge (Wegner, 1987, 1995). Transactive knowledge is knowledge that is generated between or among people through transactions, such as communication and interaction. Exchange of information of any kind, be it verbal, non-verbal or even physical, can lead to the acquisition and storage of knowledge about the other person.

As soon as people start acquiring knowledge about other people's knowledge in transactive processes, particularly if transactive knowledge is mutual, that is, at least partly shared among the participating individuals, transactive knowledge systems start to develop (Brauner, 2002, 2003; Moreland, 1999; Wegner, 1987, 1995). Transactive knowledge systems are defined as on the one hand knowledge about other people's knowledge and on the other hand the transactive, knowledge-relevant processes that arise between and among participating individuals (Wegner, 1987, 1995). Various advantages are associated with transactive knowledge systems. As in the example above, the person acquiring knowledge about a co-worker's knowledge can gain access to the co-worker's knowledge through asking her about her expertise area. Thus, not only a person's own knowledge is available to them, but also other people's knowledge. They can draw on a much broader knowledge base than they actually possess themselves. More information can be stored in a transactive knowledge system because information can be disseminated among more people and expertise areas assigned to each of them. That way, the time required to gain new information and acquire new knowledge can be reduced considerably if the entire transactive knowledge system is involved.

Along with these benefits, transactive knowledge systems also bring forth disadvantages. Acquisition of knowledge is always time-consuming. Getting to know all co-workers in a department or an organization can take a considerable amount of time. Even a small group of experts in a project team or task force who are assembled to solve specific problems will need time to explore each other's expertise and mutually find out strengths and weaknesses. Unfortunately, work groups are mostly thrown into tasks without sufficient training in task-related issues or in working efficiently as a team. Specifically, teams would need to be trained in learning about each other's expertise in order to be able to acquire transactive knowledge that will be crucial for team success and effectiveness. Without such training, team members will not be aware of each other's expertise, or lack of expertise. Unawareness of lack of expertise in particular can result in misunderstandings about responsibilities. Unawareness of available expertise can lead to an expensive search for that knowledge outside of the group or organization (Brauner, 2002). The latter will, of course, be more likely in larger than in smaller organizations. Voluntary and involuntary turnover and change of membership can furthermore be intricate. Turnover is associated with memory or knowledge loss for a transactive knowledge system. If the member leaving was central to the group's goals and tasks, the knowledge loss can be critical to the group unless the group had been able to take preventive measures and replace the expertise or train another member in that expertise area. If, for instance, the webmaster of an organization decides to accept the job offer from a different employer, the organization can either try to train her assistant to be able to assume the responsibilities of the webmaster or try to hire a new person to take over the administration of the websites. However, even if it is possible to hire a formally adequately qualified replacement of the webmaster, critical idiosyncratic expert knowledge will be lost with the turnover because the new webmaster has to gain specific knowledge of the idiosyncrasies of that specific web design along with knowledge about other team members' knowledge. New members will always face difficulties in finding the right expert as long as they have not yet acquired knowledge about other members' knowledge. For this reason, training new members in trainee programmes or through job rotation can not just be helpful, but even critical to performance. Metaknowledge can thereby be acquired not only by the new member, but also by current members of the organization. Thus, a new member can be more easily integrated into the transactive knowledge system of an organization.

Nevertheless, the advantages of transactive knowledge systems outnumber and outperform the disadvantages by far. After all, transactive knowledge systems in groups and organizations develop unintentionally. That organizational members learn about each others' knowledge cannot be avoided. However, since research has shown that transactive knowledge systems lead to better performance in groups (Liang et al., 1995; Moreland, et al., 1998; Moreland, 1999; Wegner et al., 1985), the critical question is whether organizations develop preventive strategies to deal appropriately with turnover.

Three propositions

Transactive knowledge systems are the means by which individual knowledge can be integrated and incorporated into, and utilized by, organizations. Thus, we can now introduce the first proposition of our theoretical approach, which deals with the properties and characteristics of organizational knowledge.

Proposition (1)
Organizational knowledge is individual knowledge embedded in transactive knowledge systems

We pinpointed knowledge earlier as residing and being stored exclusively within an individual's memory. Such assumptions have been criticized as cognitivistic, assuming 'mentalistic processes' (Gherardi, 2000, p. 212) and being unable to explain the social character of knowledge as well as the process of knowing (Cook and Brown, 1999). However, through transactive knowledge systems individual knowledge is embedded into a social system in which individuals not only know what they know themselves, but also know and learn what other individuals within the social system know. Individual metaknowledge bridges the gap between disparate individual cognitions. This metaknowledge, or transactive knowledge, facilitates the access to knowledge available in the entire organization. Individuals use their knowledge about others' knowledge to connect to others through transactive knowledge systems. Transactive knowledge systems thus describe the social organization of individual knowledge. Hence, organizational knowledge can be understood as transactive knowledge systems, in which individuals are interconnected through metaknowledge that they ideally share to a large degree or are at least able to access remotely.

This proposition yields some further explanations for malfunctions of knowledge exchange in organizations. First, during the early 2000s the saying was circulated within the company Siemens, 'If only Siemens knew what Siemens knows'. If there existed something like organizational knowledge on the organizational level, then Siemens would, without doubt, know what it knows, that is, possess metaknowledge on its own knowledge. However, since according to our proposition knowledge is always individual knowledge launched into the organization by the individual upon request or upon necessity, Siemens as a company can only *be aware of* knowledge available to the company inasmuch as individual members of the organization are aware of their organizational transactive knowledge and utilize their transactive knowledge system through accessing each others' knowledge in communication and transactive processes. Because Siemens as a company is not capable of owning knowledge or metaknowledge and because knowledge is not located on the organizational level, Siemens will never know what its employees know.

Second, some researchers (for example, Nonaka and Takeuchi, 1995; Spender, 1996) assume that organizations possess implicit knowledge, which is knowledge that might be explicit to individuals but not shared with the organization. Therefore, this knowledge remains inaccessible to the organization. They furthermore claim that the organization should try to access this knowledge if it is in the organization's interest to possess this knowledge. This claim can well be incorporated into the theoretical model proposed here, though we would not subsume it under the original term of implicit or tacit knowledge (cf. Polanyi, 1966/1983; Ryle, 1962; see also Reber, 1989, 1993). Knowledge held by individual members will become transactive knowledge as soon as these members share this knowledge with other members of the organization, or, more specifically, as soon as they share the *fact that* they possess this knowledge. Individual knowledge then becomes part of a transactive knowledge system and at the same time it becomes organizational knowledge. Organizational knowledge is knowledge about which members possess metaknowledge and are therefore able to access it within other members.

Third, in their analysis of a reorganization project, Anand, Manz and Glick (1998) describe the case of an employee who was assigned to a different department by a decision of the company's board. After the board was completely exchanged, the knowledge about the employee's expertise was lost to the organization because no metaknowledge existed any longer. When the new board called for an expert in the focal employee's area of expertise, a new person was hired to fill in. If organizational knowledge was independent from individual knowledge, metaknowledge about the availability of this expertise in the organization would still have been available although all the individuals that held this knowledge in their individual memories had gone. However, because knowledge is always and exclusively bound to individual minds, metaknowledge is lost as soon as the respective individuals are gone. Transactive knowledge systems therefore represent the organization of individual knowledge within social systems.

Proposition (2)

Organizational learning is the change of individual knowledge and metaknowledge, and the change of the potential for action through the use of transactive knowledge systems

If (organizational) knowledge resides solely and exclusively within individual cognition, (organizational) learning can consequently only take place within individual cognition also. As mentioned above, besides the change in the individual knowledge base, we moreover assume that learning can result in a changed potential for action although it does not necessarily have to result in changed behaviour (see also Bandura, 1977). Learning results from taking in new information; incorporating this new information into existing knowledge structures; and evaluating this information with regard to behavioural consequences. After acquiring and processing new knowledge it might be perfectly sensible for an individual to decide that the way in which he or she acted before acquiring this knowledge was the correct behaviour, even given the new information. A stockbroker, for instance, might receive some new information about stocks she is trading. She will evaluate the information and integrate it with her existing knowledge about these stocks and the market. If the information confirms her current actions to be appropriate, she will keep buying or selling the stocks as she did before. Nevertheless, she has learned something new and added it to her existing knowledge. If the information, however, contradicts her previous knowledge structures she will most likely change her behaviour.

On the individual level, new knowledge has been learned through the change of the database. Similarly, if new knowledge is learned by one individual, the database of the organization as a transactive knowledge system will be changed. However, at least one of two conditions has to be fulfilled for that to occur. The first condition is that other members of the organization have to be aware of the knowledge acquisition of the individual. New knowledge within a transactive knowledge system will only be available if metaknowledge held by other members of the organization exists. Thus, new knowledge has to be actively incorporated into the transactive knowledge systems by 'publishing' the new acquisition. The alternative condition is that other organizational members are aware of this specific expertise of the person. If, for instance, colleagues of the stockbroker mentioned above know that she is a specialist on these stocks, she will not have to alert them of her changed knowledge base. They will routinely direct all questions regarding those stocks to her and the organization will thus utilize the changed knowledge of the stockbroker.

For organizational learning in transactive knowledge systems, this means that knowledge can change, and thereby learning occur, in three ways. First, individual knowledge can change. The stockbroker learns new information about the stocks and incorporates it into her existing knowledge base. Second, metaknowledge about the individual held by other organizational members can change. If the stockbroker's colleagues were not aware of her expertise, they would update their metaknowledge about her at the latest after a critical incident (Strauss, 1972). Critical incidents are events that prompt individuals first to question and thereafter to adjust their knowledge (Brauner, 2002). If the stockbroker, for instance, unexpectedly buys or sells stocks in large quantities, her colleagues will become aware of this behaviour and adjust their knowledge about her (that is, assume that she has gained new insights). Although this knowledge about someone else's knowledge is again stored in individual memories, it is available to the organization through its utilization by accessing someone else's knowledge. Third, and finally, organizational learning can also take place through the change of individual knowledge as well as individual metaknowledge. The stockbroker receives some special information and her colleagues get to know this. These colleagues don't have to know what exactly this new information is; they only need to know who has access to it. The stockbroker, at the same time, has to incorporate this knowledge into her knowledge base to have it available if she or someone else in the organization requires accessing it.

Thus, the organization can benefit from individual knowledge by individuals feeding their expertise into the organizational transactive knowledge system. Individuals learn and thereby change the organizational database through changing their knowledge as well as their metaknowledge about their co-workers. Through using this metaknowledge for referring to others' knowledge and using it for the pursuit of organizational goals, the organization benefits from the individuals' learning progress and expanded knowledge base.

Proposition (3)

Knowledge management is management of transactive knowledge systems (along with individual knowledge) as well as management of the change of transactive knowledge systems (along with individual knowledge)

Transactive knowledge systems delineate the social organization of individual knowledge within a social system. Individuals possess knowledge and metaknowledge about other members of the organization. Thus, knowledge available in an organization, held by individual members but scattered within or across departments and even across large geographical distances, is accessible and can be made available to other individuals and used for accomplishing their tasks. A basic requirement for this is the availability of metaknowledge held by the individual about knowledge held by the other members of the organization. Ideally, but not necessarily, metaknowledge should be mutual. This means that two or more individuals know about each other's expertise and can access each other's knowledge. Knowledge will thereby be made available to other members of the organization and, thus, to the entire organization as a social system.

However, before individuals are able to operate in transactive knowledge systems they have to acquire knowledge and metaknowledge about other members of the organization. To start, they have to decide whether they hold the knowledge required to solve a problem or to work on a task. This process is called monitoring of knowledge within the organization (cf. Brauner, 2002). Whatever knowledge is individually available to members of the organization will be monitored in a continuous process. If it is ascertained during the monitoring process that required expertise is not available, the individual will have to look for other sources and acquire necessary knowledge. Similarly as in the example of the knowledge broker mentioned above, the person will have to update his or her knowledge about others' knowledge. If it turns out that required expertise is available within reach of the individual and within the organization, it will be sufficient to store new metaknowledge and thereby new knowledge that is learned. If the monitoring process reveals that required expertise is not available, it will be essential to develop strategies to acquire new knowledge through, for instance, consultation of external experts, training and development or hiring of accordingly qualified new employees. Fundamentally important in the case of acquisition of new knowledge by any of these strategies is that all changes are incorporated into the shared metaknowledge base of the group, department or organization. This process is called control of knowledge and knowledge acquisition within the organization (cf. Brauner, 2002). Monitoring and control are the basic processes that manage the development of transactive knowledge systems and that lead to organizational learning. Thus, we define the use of transactive knowledge as well as monitoring and control of knowledge acquisition processes as knowledge management in organizations. Organizational learning is the process in which transactive knowledge systems change. Knowledge management, at the same time, is management of this change. Communication and transactive processes constitute the means by which monitoring and control is accomplished and the transactive knowledge system managed. Knowledge management is the attempt to organize processes of knowledge exchange and knowledge acquisition within transactive knowledge systems.

We have defined organizational knowledge as individual knowledge embedded in organizational transactive knowledge systems. We have furthermore conceived of organizational learning as learning that takes place when the individuals participating in the organizational transactive knowledge system learn, that is, when these individuals acquire knowledge or metaknowledge about other people's knowledge. We then delineated knowledge management as the management of transactive knowledge systems as well as the management of the change of transactive knowledge systems. The process in which transactive knowledge systems change is again understood as organizational learning. Knowledge management and organizational learning hence encompass the integration and differentiation of knowledge into transactive knowledge systems. While we use the term organizational learning to describe this process of integration and differentiation, or rather the change of knowledge and metaknowledge, the term knowledge management refers to the conscious attempt to manage and control learning and knowledge distribution in organizations.

Desiderata for the future of knowledge management

Characterizing knowledge management and organizational learning as processes that take place within and between individual members of an organization entails a number of consequences. These consequences can be classified into three categories: first, social consequences; second, institutional consequences; and third, technological consequences. We will discuss these consequences and describe desiderata for the future of knowledge management.

Social consequences

Despite the fact that we have positioned organizational knowledge within individuals, our main claim as for the future of knowledge management is that knowledge management has to become more social and more oriented towards interaction among organizational members. So far, too much emphasis has been placed on technological solutions for knowledge management (see also the third consequence, discussed below). As we have pointed out previously, metaknowledge is required to hold organizational transactive knowledge systems together. Metaknowledge is developed and learned in transactive processes. Such processes encompass social interaction and communication. Face-to-face interaction among participants in particular will enhance this process, and it is even more indispensable in more complex situations. Studies in virtual teams have shown that personalized knowledge (Pipek et al., 2003) is crucial for effective and efficient knowledge management (Hinds and Weisband, 2003; Hollingshead, 1998a, 1998b; Hollingshead et al., 2002; Maznewski and Athanassiou, 2003). All studies reflect on the major role face-to-face communication plays in knowledge-sharing. The acquisition of knowledge and metaknowledge is easier and more efficient in face-to-face interaction than in virtual, electronic media that are stripped down to the verbal aspect.

Thus, the production of metaknowledge is best achieved in small groups or smaller organizational units that will facilitate members' getting to know each other and that will allow easier communication processes. However, it is critical for the organizational transactive knowledge system that newly developed transactive knowledge within these units is also transferred to higher-level organizational units. The problems that might occur due to higher social complexity, such as more participating individuals and higher costs of co-ordination, will need further assistance and support. The larger the organization, the more acute these problems will be (Moreland, 1999). In particular, it has to be ensured that training and development aim at developing transactive knowledge and metaknowledge. As research has shown, training of interpersonal skills and development of group structure, as well as training mere communication in groups, are not as important as training of technical and task-related matters (Moreland and Myaskovsky,

2000; Salas et al., & Driskell, 1999; Thompson, 2000). Only if group members actually work together on concrete tasks can they develop an understanding of others' expertise and thereby acquire transactive knowledge (Moreland et al., 1998). These results show that transactive knowledge is in fact knowledge about other people's knowledge that is accessed and transmitted through communication and interaction.

Despite the fact that training should focus on task-related matters, factors concerning the social dynamics of groups and larger social systems affect the development of transactive knowledge systems as well. Such factors can involve trust, motivation, commitment and power. All these social dynamics develop predominantly in social interaction and communication. To decide whether an individual is, for instance, trustworthy or not, people prefer to rely on their personal judgement of the individual derived from verbal and non-verbal information gathered during personal interaction. At the same time, trust will again influence the social interaction between two or more people. Lack of trust can be critical to sharing knowledge and referring to knowledge (Eberl, 2003; Giddens, 1991; Maznewski and Athanassiou, 2003). Only if a person trusts the expertise or the willingness to co-operate of another person will he or she approach that person and engage with them in social interaction and communication. Trust in organizations can relate to either task-related issues or relationship-oriented issues. No matter whether the lack of trust concerns either one of these, a person will rather consult other sources, in some cases even accepting considerable quality loss, than co-operate with the presumably untrustworthy colleague.

Motivation and the lack of motivation can pose a further problem to knowledge management, the acquisition of new knowledge and the access to existing knowledge. According to economic theory, members of a social system tend to detain knowledge due to opportunistic reasons. So-called 'free riding' or 'social loafing' leads them to perform and co-operate less as soon as other people are present. Hollingshead et al. (2002) describe shared knowledge in an organization as a public good that cannot be withheld from anyone, no matter whether someone contributes to its production or not. Therefore, people are not really motivated to share their knowledge because free riders or social loafers could benefit from the knowledge base without contributing themselves. The identification with the organization or the team could compensate for this (Hollingshead et al., 2002). Thus, it seems crucial that organizations develop an 'info culture' that grows historically in interaction and promotes information-sharing and co-operation among organizational members. Commitment to the group or organization will be a critical factor influencing 'info culture'. Only if a person feels committed to an organization will he or she be willing to participate in knowledge management and organizational learning. Commitment will also be relevant if a member leaves the organization and is expected to help a replacement to familiarize him- or herself with the job. The higher the commitment while the person was still a full member, the more likely the transition phase will run smoothly and relevant knowledge will be passed on to the new employee.

Finally, micropolitical and power processes play an important role for the social aspects of knowledge management and organizational learning (Becker and Ortmann, 1994). Individuals, groups and even entire departments may pursue self-serving interests and consciously engage in micropolitical processes that lead to blocking off information-sharing and participation in transactive knowledge systems. In a case study described by Ortmann et al. (1990), the implementation of a production planning and controlling system was delayed for over a year because different departments pursued incompatible and conflicting goals and prevented information-sharing and co-operation. For an unencumbered and successful implementation, co-operation and knowledge-sharing among participants would have been essential. This again reflects the crucial importance of the social context for knowledge-relevant processes in organizations.

Reflecting on social processes is, in our view, crucial to successfully managing knowledge processes in organizations. Transactive knowledge systems are social systems in the first place. Communication and interaction, mandatory constituents of transactive knowledge systems and of knowledge management, are genuinely social processes. Thus, researchers should reflect more thoroughly on the social nature of knowledge management and organizational learning through the means of transactive knowledge systems.

Institutional consequences

We have defined organizational knowledge as directly dependent on the individuals that hold this knowledge. Employees, also termed human resources or human capital of an organization, consequently should play an important role in knowledge management processes. However, so far human resource management and knowledge management are not as closely related as should be wished for (Brauner and Becker, 2004). Raising awareness about transactive knowledge systems and the principles involved in transactive processes should be one major goal for the knowledge management of the future. This could be applied to all functions of human resource management, such as job analysis, recruitment, personnel development and training, as well as evaluation of employees. All these functions should be investigated with regard to knowledge management and transactive knowledge systems. Thus, if a job analysis is performed, the role of the position within the transactive knowledge system of the organization should be reflected explicitly in the job description and the specifications of required expertise. Whenever a new person is recruited and trained, his or her acquisition of transactive knowledge should be positioned in the focus of the training. Although the exact function of training is the integration of the new person into the transactive knowledge system, development of transactive knowledge is usually neglected. Furthermore, as mentioned above, training in groups usually focuses on the relationships of the individuals rather than training of task-related aspects that would enhance the development of transactive knowledge. The same applies to personnel development and training (Thompson, 2000). Evaluations of employees, finally, should include criteria that concern knowledge management and the person's embedding into the organizational transactive knowledge system. This would not only be valuable for evaluating the role and positioning of the person within the organization, but it would also benefit in case of transitions and turnover.

Thus, considerations of knowledge management should be included in all organizational functions, at least as long as personnel is involved, albeit this might rather increase the costs of training and development. According to Thompson (2000), between US$ 30 and 100 billion are spent on training and development each year in the United States. However, as knowledge management can be seen as advantageous to the competitive advantage of the organization (Becker, Duschek and Brauner, 2002; Spender, 1996), it would be sensible, in our view, to better monitor the topics of training and development. Integrating the organizational goal of knowledge management and organizational learning with the personnel function to foster the development of well-functioning transactive knowledge systems should be one main focus of human resource management.

Technological consequences

Technological solutions for the management of organizational knowledge have been developed and implemented over the past years. Most of these knowledge management tools are considerably costly, in particular pertaining to purchase and maintenance. Most of these tools differ with regard to information and data included in a database and with regard to how this information can be accessed. Examples for data included are reports, emails, websites, fax documents, documentations or even the contents of various databases. These documents can either be completely preserved or excerpts and summaries can be created. Furthermore, it is possible to create knowledge networks or knowledge maps using content analysis of documents, categorizations or analysis of language (Lehner, 2000).

However, many reports show that most of these solely technology-based approaches are either entirely failing (König, 2002; Scholl et al., 2002) or have to deal with substantial problems (Pipek et al., 2003). Several reasons account for this situation. The attempt to incorporate comprehensive expertise of employees into a knowledge management system in order to make knowledge available independently of people's willingness to share proves dangerous to the actual experts. Externalization of their expertise might make them superfluous to the organization and threaten their position as experts. Therefore, they will be less likely and less willing to actually fully incorporate their expertise.

All these systems depend on the direct maintenance by every individual who participates in the organizational knowledge management process. Because updating information by entering data into a database is more labour-intensive than talking to colleagues and thereby learning about their expertise, their knowledge and metaknowledge interactively, the maintenance of the systems is neglected. After a few months, most databases are outdated. The workload involved in the maintenance of an informative website can be paralleled to that. Updating transactive knowledge systems in social interaction is far less labour-intensive. Furthermore, mutual metaknowledge is generated without additional effort. Thus, if a person tells a co-worker about the new software that she is learning to use, the effect is twofold. First, the coworker learns about the new expertise; second, the person herself knows that the co-worker knows. Mutual transactive metaknowledge is thus created with minimal effort involved.

Social processes also kick in when information and knowledge management systems fail. Whatever cannot be accomplished by the system because the information bases are incomplete has to be compensated for by individual memories of participating individuals. These individual knowledge storages help with 'social navigation', the localization of useful knowledge. Thus, instead of referring to the information system when searching for a content, people ask other people who are expected to be knowledgeable. Thus, metaknowledge about other people's knowledge is activated in order to compensate for the deficiencies of the technological solution. Social navigation in particular turns out to be more efficient and more powerful because people relate the information sensibly to a technical and social context.

Finally, the question arises whether an individual will always be able to make his or her knowledge explicit, that is, disclose knowledge available but maybe not consciously accessible. The term tacit or implicit knowledge has been used in the literature to depict this type of knowledge (cf. Polanyi, 1966/1983; Ryle, 1962; for implicit learning see Reber, 1989, 1993). From an individual perspective, implicit knowledge is knowledge that is available to, but cannot be verbalized by, a person. From an organizational perspective this is knowledge that a person owns but does not contribute to the organization (Nonaka and Takeuchi, 1995). However, although implicit knowledge might not be explicable on a metaknowledge level, it is well activated and used if the situation requires acting accordingly. To co-workers, this implicit knowledge might become evident just through observation. An example is the development of the bread-baking machine by the Matsushita Electric Company (Nonaka, 1991). After several unsuccessful trials to construct such a machine, a software engineer became the baker's apprentice to learn the bread-baking technique through observation of his implicit knowledge about bread-kneading. Although the baker was not able to describe exactly his technique, the software engineer was able to gather the knowledge necessary for the implementation.

Thus, people's implicit knowledge will make it more difficult to feed a database completely, even though the person might be willing to share his or her expertise. Newell, Scarborough and Swan (2001) conclude in their analysis of three knowledge management projects that knowledge that is supposed to be reflected and included in these systems is often not explicable, implicit and rather scattered, which makes it difficult, if not impossible, to create a feasible database. They conclude that it is 'significant that our findings about the implications of an IT tool ultimately revolve around questions of culture, and not infrastructure or systems' (Newell et al., 2001, p. 110).

A technological support of transactive knowledge systems seems desirable despite all these problems. Organizations can become very complex social systems and single individuals or even groups of individuals will fail to keep track of the entire knowledge base. Even very well developed transactive knowledge systems are prone to errors. The studies cited above show that it is, however, not advisable to try to replace transactive knowledge systems and as an organization become independent from the human resources, namely the employees. What can be useful instead is to try to provide support to organizational members by helping them to continuously develop and update their socially based transactive knowledge system. Examples for this can be systems that don't provide the information but rather the metaknowledge that leads to the information. Thus, it would help to find the expert in that required domain. Yellow pages or knowledge brokers are examples for this technique. Essential for the implementation of specific systems is a detailed analysis of what is needed and which benefit is expected from the implementation. However, rather than relying on technology, the goal of knowledge management should always be to enhance social interaction and thereby to make knowledge management more personal, even if implementing a technological solution.

Conclusions

Our analysis of knowledge management and organizational learning intended to show that the human factor is the most crucial aspect in the future of knowledge management. We defined knowledge and learning as processes that are taking place on an individual level in individual cognition. We described the model of transactive knowledge systems that provides an idea of how individual members of an organization interact and relate to each other through transactive processes and thereby develop knowledge about each others' knowledge. This metaknowledge enables them to refer to other people and use them as an extended memory, thereby creating a knowledge network that can bridge even vast geographical distances. Important to note here is, however, that it will be neither possible nor advisable to pursue an entirely shared knowledge base. Limited information-processing capacities (Simon, 1951) will prevent this on the one hand and the necessity to preserve diversity of expertise on the other. Diversity of expertise is the justification for the existence of an organization (Crozier and Friedberg, 1980) and provides the organization with considerable resources of competitive advantage (Spender, 1996). Organizational knowledge management grants the management of this diversity through usage and development of metaknowledge through transactive processes. The principal goal of knowledge management and organizational learning should be to develop shared metaknowledge and thus provide members with direct access to knowledge (Brauner & Becker, 2001).

References

Anand, V., C. C. Manz and W. H. Glick (1998) 'An Organizational Memory Approach to Information Management', *Academy of Management Review*, 23, 796–809.
Argyris, C. and D. A. Schön (1996) *Organizational Learning II: Theory, Method, and Practice* (Reading, MA: Addison-Wesley).
Bandura, A. (1977) *Social learning theory* (Englewood Cliffs, NJ: Prentice-Hall).
Becker, A. and G. Ortmann (1994) 'Management und Mikropolitik: Ein strukturationstheoretischer Ansatz' ['Management and Micropolitics: A Structurationist Approach'], in M. Hofmann and A. Al-Ani (eds), *Neue Entwicklungen im Management* [*New Developments in Management*] (Heidelberg: Physica), pp. 201–53.
Becker, A., S. Duschek and E. Brauner (2002) 'Going Beyond the Resources Given: A Structurationist View on Knowledge and Strategic Management', paper presented at the 3rd European Conference on Organizational Knowledge, Learning, and Capabilities (OKLC), Athens Laboratory of Business Administration (ALBA), Athens, Greece, 5–6 April 2002.
Brauner, E. (2002) Transactive Knowledge Systems in Groups and Organizations habilitationsschrift, Humboldt-Universität zu Berlin.
Brauner, E. (2003) 'Informationsverarbeitung in Gruppen: Transaktive Wissenssysteme' ['Information Processing in Groups: Transactive Knowledge Systems'], in A. Thomas and S. Stumpf (eds), *Teamarbeit und Teamentwicklung* [*Team Work and Team Development*] (Göttingen: Verlag für angewandte Psychologie), pp. 57–83.
Brauner, E. and A. Becker (2001) 'Wormholes to Organizational Expertise: The Management of Metaknowledge', in M. Crossan and F. Olivera (eds), *Organizational Learning and Knowledge Management: New Directions* (London, Canada: Richard Ivey School of Business), pp. 31–48.
Brauner E. and A. Becker (2004) 'Wissensmanagement und Organisationales Lernen: Personalentwicklung und Lernen durch Transaktive Wissenssysteme' ['Knowledge Management and Organizational Learning: Personnel Development through Transactive Knowledge Systems'], in G. Hertel and U. Konradt (eds), *Human Resource Management im Inter- und Intranet* [*Human Resource Management in the Inter- and Intranet*] (Göttingen: Hogrefe), pp. 235–52.

Brown, J. S. and P. Duguid (1996) 'Organizational Learning and Communities of Practice', in M. D. Cohen and L. S. Sproull (eds), *Organizational Learning* (Thousand Oaks, CA: Sage), pp. 58–82.

Brown, J. S. and P. Duguid (2001) 'Knowledge and organization: A social-practice perspective', *Organization Science*, 12, 198–213.

Cook, S. D. N. and J. S. Brown (1999) 'Bridging Epistemologies: The Generative Dance between Organizational Knowledge and Organizational Knowing', *Organization Science*, 10, 381–400.

Crozier, M. and E. Friedberg (1980) *Actors and Systems: The Politics of Collective Action* (Chicago: University of Chicago Press).

Daft, R. L. and K. E. Weick (1984) 'Toward a Model of Organizations as Interpretation Systems', *Academy of Management Review*, 9, 284–95.

D'Aveni, R. A. (1994) *Hypercompetition: Managing the Dynamics of Strategic Maneuvering* (New York: The Free Press).

Easterby-Smith, M. and L. Araujo (1999) 'Organizational Learning: Current Debates and Opportunities', in M. Easterby-Smith, J. Burgoyne and L. Araujo (eds), *Organizational Learning and the Learning Organization: Developments in Theory and Practice* (London: Sage), pp. 1–21.

Easterby-Smith, M., M. Crossan and D. Nicolini (2000) 'Organizational Learning: Debates Past, Present and Future, *Journal of Management Studies*, 37, 783–96.

Eberl, P. (2003) *Vertrauen und Management: Studien zu einer theoretischen Fundierung des Vertrauenskonstruktes in der Managementlehre* [*Trust and Management: Studies on the Theoretical Foundation of the Construct Trust in Management Science*] (Stuttgart: Schäffer-Poeschel).

Fiol, C. M. and M. A. Lyles (1985) 'Organizational learning', *Academy of Management Review*, 10, 803–13.

Gherardi, S. (2000) 'Practice-Based Theorizing on Knowing and Learning in Organizations, *Organization*, 7, 211–23.

Giddens, A. (1991) *Modernity and Self-Identity: Self and Society in the Late Modern Age* (Stanford: Stanford University Press).

Hinds, P. and S. P. Weisband (2003) 'Knowledge Sharing and Shared Understanding in Virtual Teams', in C. B. Gibson and S. G. Cohen (eds), *Virtual Teams that Work* (Chichester: Wiley), pp. 21–36.

Hollingshead, A. B. (1998a) 'Communication, Learning, and Retrieval in Transactive Memory Systems, *Journal of Experimental Social Psychology*, 34, 423–42.

Hollingshead, A. B. (1998b) 'Retrieval Processes in Transactive Memory Systems', *Journal of Personality and Social Psychology*, 74, 659–71.

Hollingshead, A. B., J. Fulk and P. Monge (2002) 'Fostering Intranet Knowledge Sharing: An Integration of Transactive Memory and Public Goods Approaches', in P. J. Hinds and A. Kiesler (eds), *Distributed work* (Cambridge, MA: MIT Press), pp. 335–56.

Huber, G. P. (1991) 'Organizational Learning: The Contributing Process and the Literatures', *Organization Science*, 2, 88–115.

König, C. (2002) 'The future of knowledge management: Eine Delphi-Studie' ['The Future of Knowledge Management: A Delphi Study'], unveröffentl, diplomarbeit, Humboldt-Universität zu Berlin.

Lave, J. and E. Wenger (1991) *Situated Learning: Legitimate Peripheral Participation* (Cambridge: Cambridge University Press).

Lehner, F. (2000) *Organisational Memory: Konzepte und Systeme für das organisatorische Lernen und das Wissensmanagement* [*Organizational Memory: Concepts and Systems for Organizational Learning and Knowledge Management*] (München: Hanser).

Levitt, B. and J. G. March (1999) 'Organizational learning', in J. G. March (ed.), *The Pursuit of Organizational Intelligence* (Malden, MA: Blackwell), pp. 75–99.

Liang, D. W., R. L. Moreland and L. Argote (1995) 'Group versus Individual Training and Group Performance: The Mediating Role of Transactive Memory', *Personality and Social Psychology Bulletin*, 21, 384–93.

March, J. G. and J. P. Olsen (1976) 'Organizational Learning and the Ambiguity of the Past', in J. G. March and J. P. Olsen (eds), *Ambiguity and Choice in Organizations* (Bergen: Universitetsforlaget), pp. 54–68.

Maznewski, M. L. and N. A. Athanassiou (2003) 'Designing the Knowledge-Management Infrastructure for Virtual Teams: Building and Using Social Networks and Social Capital', in C. B. Gibson and S. G. Cohen (eds), *Virtual Teams that Work* (Chichester: Wiley), pp. 196–213.

Moreland, R. L. (1999) 'Transactive Memory: Learning Who Knows What in Work Groups and Organizations', in L. L. Thompson, J. M. Levine and D. M. Messick (eds), *Shared Cognition in Organizations: The Management of Knowledge* (Mahwah, NJ: Erlbaum), pp. 3–31.

Moreland, R. L. and L. Myaskovsky (2000) 'Exploring the Performance Benefits of Group Training: Transactive Memory or Improved Communication?', *Organizational Behavior and Human Decision Processes*, 82, 117–33.

Moreland, R. L., L. Argote and R. Krishnan (1998) 'Training People to Work in Groups', in R. S. Tindale, J. E. Edwards, L. Heath, E. J. Posavac, F. B. Bryant, E. Henderson-King, Y. Suarez-Balcazar and J. Myers (eds), *Social Psychological Applications to Social Issues: Applications of Theory and Research on Groups, Vol. 4* (New York: Plenum Press), pp. 37–60.

Newell, S., H. Scarborough and J. Swan (2001) 'From Global Knowledge Management to Internal Electronic Fences: Contradictory Outcomes of Intranet Development', *British Journal of Management*, 12, 97–111.

Nonaka, I. (1991) 'The Knowledge-Creating Company', *Harvard Business Review*, 69, 96–104.

Nonaka, I. and H. Takeuchi (1995) *The Knowledge-Creating Company* (New York: Oxford University Press).

Ortmann, G., A. Windeler, A. Becker and H.-J. Schulz (1990) *Computer und Macht in Organisationen: Mikropolitische Analysen* [*Computer and Power in Organizations: Micropolitical Analyses*] (Opladen: Westdeutscher Verlag).

Penrose, E. G. (1995) *The Theory of the Growth of the Firm* (Oxford: Oxford University Press).

Pipek, V., J. Hinrichs and V. Wulf (2003) 'Sharing Expertise: Challenges for Technical Support', in M. Ackerman, V. Pipek and V. Wulf (eds), *Sharing Expertise: Beyond Knowledge Management* (Cambridge, MA: MIT Press), pp. 111–136.

Polanyi, M. (1966/1983) *The Tacit Dimension* (Gloucester, MA: Peter Smith).

Reber, A. S. (1989) 'Implicit Learning and Tacit Knowledge', *Journal of Experimental Psychology: General*, 118, 219–35.

Reber, A. S. (1993) *Implicit Learning and Tacit Knowledge: An Essay on the Cognitive Unconscious* (New York: Oxford University Press).

Ryle, G. (1962) *The Concept of Mind* (New York: University Paperbacks Barnes & Noble).

Salas, E., D. Rozell, B. Mullen and J. E. Driskell (1999) 'The Effect of Team Building on Performance: An Integration', *Small Group Research*, 30, 309–29.

Scholl, W., C. König and B. Meyer (2002) 'The Delphi Study on Knowledge Management', presentation at the Conference 'The future of knowledge management', Strausberg, Humboldt-Universität zu Berlin.

Simon, H. A. (1951) *Administrative Behavior: A Study of Decision-Making Processes in Administrative Organizations* (New York: Macmillan).

Spender, J.-C. (1996) 'Making Knowledge the Basis of a Dynamic Theory of the Firm', *Strategic Management Journal* (Special Issue), 17, 45–62.

Spies, M. (2001) 'Wissensorganisation und Wissen in der Organisation – Aufgaben der Psychologie im prozessorientierten Wissensmanagement' ['Knowledge Organization and Knowledge in the Organization – The Role of Psychology in Process-Oriented Knowledge Management'], in R. Silbereisen and M. Reitzle (eds), *Bericht über den 42. Kongress der Deutschen Gesellschaft für Psychologie* (Lengerich: Pabst), pp. 712–23.

Strauss, S. (1972) 'Inducing Cognitive Development and Learning: A Review of Short-Term Training Experiments I. The Organismic Developmental Approach', *Cognition*, 1, 329–57.

Thompson, L. (2000) *Making the Team: A Guide for Managers* (Upper Saddle River, NJ: Prentice Hall).

Tsoukas, H. (1996) 'The Firm as a Distributed Knowledge System: A Constructionist Approach', *Strategic Management Journal*, 17, 11–25.

Walsh, J. P. and G. R. Ungson (1991) 'Organizational memory', *Academy of Management Review*, 16, 57–91.

Wegner, D. M. (1987) 'Transactive Memory: A Contemporary Analysis of the Group Mind', in B. Mullen and G. R. Goethals (eds), *Theories of Group Behavior* (New York, NY: Springer), pp. 185–208.

Wegner, D. M. (1995) 'A Computer Network Model of Human Transactive Memory', *Social Cognition*, 13, 319–39.

Wegner, D. M., T. Giuliano and P. T. Hertel (1985) 'Cognitive Interdependence in Close Relationships', in W. I. Ickes (ed.), *Compatible and Incompatible Relationships* (New York: Springer), pp. 253–76.

Wenger, E. (1998) *Communities of Practice* (Cambridge: Cambridge University Press).

4
Developing Organizational Narratives: A New Dimension in Knowledge Management

Georg Schreyögg and Daniel Geiger

This chapter focuses on the recent strongly advocated idea to use stories and story-telling in knowledge management. It explores the nature of narrative knowledge as compared to other forms of knowledge, in particular discursive knowledge, and discusses its merits and shortcomings. A new concept more suited to the requirements of knowledge management is proffered, which aims at discussing and validating narrative knowledge.

Introduction

Recently, organizational story-telling has come to figure prominently in studies on knowledge generation and sharing (Orr, 1996; Patriotta, 2003). Interestingly enough, some authors even claim that stories are the main source of unique organizational knowledge and therefore want narratives to take the front seat in modern knowledge management (Snowden, 2000; Reinmann-Rothmeier and Vohle, 2001). Story-telling is supposed to fulfil multiple functions in knowledge management, such as distributing effectively uncodified knowledge and tacit problem-solving competences (Pfeffer and Sutton, 1999; Swap, 2001), generating 'thick descriptions' of contexts and thereby providing actors with an adequate understanding of the complex nature of practical situations (Geertz, 1993; Orr, 1990, 1996) and setting up the basis for actionable knowing and so on. Whatever the conceptions in detail, stories are viewed as a very promising feature of knowledge management. When push comes to shove, the problem-solving power of stories and the narrative mode of thought are in many cases considered to be even more important for organizations than the power of codified knowledge and analytical mode of thought in modern organizations (Nonaka et al., 2000; Tsoukas and Hatch, 2001).

Highlighting the narrative side of organizations without any doubt provides a particularly promising template for gaining fresh and fruitful insights into organizational life and knowing processes. Quite obviously, organizations can learn a lot from the stories told in and between their departments. On the other hand, narratives are not as smooth and unproblematic as they might first appear. There is an irritating overtone in recent literature that tends to glorify organizational stories by attributing wisdom and prudence to them without any further thought. In many studies, stories or narratives simply appear as treasure and organizations are advised to search for this treasure (Gabriel, 2004). A closer look, however, reveals that narratives are much more equivocal and adverse in their effects than assumed. We should not blind ourselves to the fact that organizational narratives are as ambiguous as all other emergent artifacts and processes in organizations. In other words, narratives have dark sides as well: they can reproduce awkward stereotypes or emphatically stigmatize organizational members (witches and wizards). It is, for instance, well known that language and popular stories often carry hidden agendas that unconsciously discriminate by class, race or gender. From a more functional point of view, narratives can possibly provide grossly misleading advice, preserve ineffective solutions by narrative repetition and distribution, reconfirm outdated rules of the game and so on. We should refrain from glamorizing narratives and from treating them as sacrosanct. Taking narratives for granted is too risky. Rather, knowledge management is better advised to reflect carefully on the specific nature of narratives and the role they can and cannot play in the field of organizational knowledge and knowing.

Discussing these issues requires first of all a clear understanding of what narratives and narrative knowledge actually mean. What are the specifics of narrative knowledge as compared to other forms of knowledge? What is its epistemological architecture?

The first part of this paper seeks to provide a framework for discussing the logic of narrative knowledge. It thereby draws on the 'Lebenswelt' (lifeworld) conception. The second part addresses the question of how to reflect narratives and their relation to other more explicit forms of knowledge. The paper suggests that this can be done by providing linkages between different knowledge worlds. Finally, practical implications for a modern knowledge management are discussed.

Narratives and narrative knowledge

Stories are an integral part of organizational life and its everyday communication (Boje, 1995; Czarniawska, 1998; Gabriel, 1995); they are told and retold continually (Wilkins, 1984). By their very nature they are not construed consciously, but rather evolve from events, extraordinary situations, successes and failures and so on. In the narrative view, organizations are pervaded continuously by multiple streams of narratives told by organizational members (Boje, 1995). Some story-tellers are, however, likely to figure more prominently than others in terms of, for example frequency, intensity or credibility.

Organizational narratives cannot be conceived as well-defined entities; rather, they are basically interactive. They are evolving dynamically, being unconsciously and consciously reshaped in the telling processes. Narratives are imprinted by their tellers and listeners, their cognitions, values and emotions (Dyer, 1983; Buskirk v. and McGrath, 1992). Different versions of one story are thus likely to coexist (Gabriel, 2000, p. 42). In sum, narratives are actualized and adapted in the context of telling and listening. An analysis of organizational narratives therefore has to account for this dynamic character.

What is meant by a story and a narrative? Is there any significant difference between the notions of story and narrative? In the knowledge literature no clear distinction is drawn between them. It appears, however, that a distinction could be helpful, taking 'story' as the more pretentious and narrative as the basic and more general notion: all stories are narratives but not all narratives are stories (Gabriel, 2000, p. 5). Stories are based on a plot organized along a dramaturgical grammar with a (causal) sequence including an original state of affairs, a transforming event or a significant action and eventually the consequent state of affairs (for a more detailed discussion, see Czarniawska, 1997, 1998). Stories are told to entertain audiences. Gabriel (2000, p. 10) highlights this entertaining side to distinguish stories from other narratives, in particular from legends or myths carrying sacred meanings and tradition. Although 'story-telling' figures are prominent in the context of knowledge management, in most cases reference is actually made to incomplete forms, such as 'terses' or 'antenarratives' (Boje, 2001), not to full-blown stories. Orr (1990) suggests calling (ante)narratives that focus on challenging problems and workable solutions 'war stories'. The major emphasis is on the knowledge-sharing side of narratives (and not on the entertaining side). Knowledge management studies relate primarily to such narratives or 'war stories'.

Narratives represent more than pure facts (or, more precisely, the observation of facts, since the description of facts is, as is well known, always bound to an observation). Narratives transform singular situated experiences and events into a framework within causal linkages so that they make sense to tellers and listeners. Thus, narratives combine facts (or pseudofacts) and experiences within the context of a specific situation. 'War stories' in particular report on mastering problematic situations or failures and flops. The described context stands for the implicitly claimed validity of the narrated connections (Orr, 1990, p. 175). The context defines the situation under which a narrative is considered to be true.

From an epistemological point of view, narratives represent a specific form of knowing. They are a 'rich medium' (Lyotard, 1991, p. 68), which embraces all kind of statements and expressions: mimic, cognition, emotion, gesture and so on. All these dimensions coexist, intertwined within one narrative. The most distinguishing epistemological feature of narrative 'knowledge' is, however, its self-legitimizing character (Lyotard, 1991), brought about through implicit affirmation by telling and retelling the narrative and the story respectively. The narrated content becomes more or less automatically accepted as it is passed on. The criteria that validate narrative knowledge implicitly accompany the narration itself; they are a natural part of the story. To avoid misunderstandings it should be emphasized that narratives do not in any way explicitly raise the question of their validity – acceptance simply occurs in the flow of telling and listening. That is not to say that narrations do not have to meet any evaluation criteria such as face validity or plausibility. They do, but these criteria are not consciously reflected or even discussed. They are, rather, an implicit part of the narrative practices of a community; that is, they apply tacitly.

This unreflective mode of thought stands in sharp contrast to the scientific mode of thinking or more generally to any discursive forms of knowledge. Discursive knowledge draws on a different 'language game' or mode of thought, where the reflection of legitimation is at the heart (Lyotard, 1991). The criteria used within this language game are consciously used and explicitly accepted within a community. To put it differently, within the discursive mode of thought, assertions become accepted if and only if they meet the agreed criteria. Assertions, propositions, hypotheses and so on must be examined by means of specific criteria designed to determine whether they can be accepted ('true') or not ('false') (Kamlah and Lorenzen, 1967, p. 116; Toulmin, 1958). Assertions that have successfully passed such critical discourse are accepted as knowledge, for at least as long as a new argument emerges that can prove the contrary. Propositions which have passed such an examination distinguish themselves from propositions which have been rejected or not yet examined.

It seems important to emphasize that the discursive mode of thought does not apply exclusively to scientific communities, as is often implied in the literature (for example, Bruner, 1986). It is rather the basic mode of all reflexive operations. Aside from science, there are many other communities in a society which are accustomed to generating their knowledge in the discursive mode, for example, jurisdiction, public policy, fiscal system, IT consultants (Toulmin, 1958; Luhmann, 1984). The various subsystems bring about specific criteria focused on the evaluation of the assertions they are used to process. By implication, the various subsystems debate validity questions along their idiosyncratic criteria. For instance, in firms, the basic distinction used to qualify assertions may be 'effective' versus 'ineffective', in legal practice 'just' versus 'unjust', whereas the science system traditionally operates its selection processes on the distinction 'true' versus 'false'.

Despite all these differentiations, reflexive discourses do, however, have some basic characteristics in common, which distinguish them as being discursive:

(1) The most fundamental characteristic common to all kinds of discourse is communication. In other words, any discursive knowledge is verbalized and represents some kind of proposition, assertion, statement and so on.

(2) Since any assertion puts forward a claim, either explicitly or implicitly, proponents provide reasons (in varying forms) intended to support their claims (Toulmin, 1958, p. 11). Discourse demands reasons – a proponent is expected to explain what issues led him or her to favour one position over another.

(3) The quality of a statement depends on the justification offered. Reasons can be good or bad. Discursive knowledge settles issues by appealing to superior arguments (Fisher, 1978). A position that is advocated without the support of good reasons, without an argument, is prejudiced or biased. The idea of discursive knowledge requires examining the reasons behind a statement. Reasons are classified as good when they have successfully passed an explicit examination procedure. The criteria in use vary, as already pointed out. The examination criteria for knowledge are community-dependent and thus self-referential (Toulmin, 1958; Mittelstraß, 1974; Lyotard, 1988).

In sum, discursive knowledge is reflexive in character. In contrast, narrative knowledge, although communicative in nature, is essentially implicit and unconscious. The narratives tell something about success or failure, effective or failed solutions to problems, about good luck, justice, beauty and so on. Through listening to the narrative, the audience is (aside from being entertained) supposed to understand the clue, the claims and causality in question. As opposed to the discursive mode of thought, which requires analytical clarity, the narrative mode is, as mentioned previously, basically intertwined and ambiguous (Bruner, 1986). Narratives convey at least two different dimensions simultaneously (Lyotard, 1991): on the one hand, experiences, know-how, traditional reaction patterns (rites) and so on; on the other hand, the implicit justification of the underlying claims. In other words, narratives communicate a specific content and its evaluation at the same time. It is important to understand this distinguishing character of narration, which is at once descriptive and prescriptive. Such processes of acquiring know-how, norms, standards, assumptions and so forth and simultaneously justifying them as true and fair are also prevalent in cultural studies (Kluckhon and Strodtbeck, 1961; Schein, 1985). In a sense, culture is always affirmative and descriptive at the same time.

Organizational narratives are naturally embedded in everyday life; narrative knowledge therefore is situated by its very character. Narratives are context-bound in various ways; they are at least triply situated:[1]

Firstly, they are situated in the context of their origin (Orr, 1990, p. 175). They evolve from a specific situation (for example, a specific event, specific problem or specific time) and represent this situation in various ways. The claimed validity is thus bound to the context of origin.

Secondly, narratives stick to the context of their telling (Orr, 1990; Brown and Duguid, 2001). Narratives are told in a special language or jargon, thereby referring to implicit norms (understandable for insiders only) and to historical events of the community in question (as part of the community's history), the archetypes of the community and so on.

Thirdly, they are situated in the mode of evaluation implicitly used by the focal community (Cook and Brown, 1999). This third dimension of situated self-legitimization clearly echoes Lyotard's (1991) core criterion of narrative knowledge.

The contextual boundedness naturally constrains the sharing and applicability of narratives and narrative knowledge in and across communities (Brown and Duguid, 2001).

The situated and embedded character of the narrative mode is closely related to the phenomenological Lebenswelt conception (literally, 'life-world'), that is, the everyday context of acting and the actors' common background, the latter being taken for granted (Habermas, 1989; Schütz and Luckmann, 1989). The narrative mode of communication and of everyday knowledge-sharing represents the natural way of making and reproducing sense in the life-world and guarantees mutual understanding (Habermas, 1989; Weick, 1995). Actors refer to their life-world in a natural and naïve way. It is their ordinary way of doing things and thereby they take the narrative knowledge of their community (collective repository) for granted. Narratives assure actors of their life-world (Habermas, 1989).

This naïve sharing of the life-world is the ordinary way of getting along – at least as long as no problem (conflict, shortage and so on) emerges that cannot be solved on the basis of the standard procedures of the life-world. In all those cases, individually and institutionally, actors are not fatefully bound to luck nor wrestling for acquiring an orientation (Habermas, 2003). Rather, it is the basic proposition of modern argumentation theory that the life-world can be put into perspective; it is possible to intervene by introducing a different point of view or, as Habermas (1989) puts it, to reflexively break the symbolic reproduction of the life-world. In his view we have learned to abandon, if necessary, the narrative world and to switch to the discursive mode in all those problematic situations where conflicting claims cannot be solved on the naïve everyday level (Habermas, 1989). Pursuing this path means to introduce a second level (meta-level, if you like) that puts ordinary practices into perspective, that is, a reflexive mode. In a sense this switching can be interpreted as 'rationalization' of the life-world.[2] What does rationalization mean in this context? On a general level, it primarily refers to features such as secularization of sacred patterns of thought, dissolving of narrative dogmas through questioning their inherent claims or critical examination of prevailing norms and values. It is the basic proposition of this paper that this idea of level-switching and rationalization can make an important contribution to the recent knowledge discourse. In particular, it provides a promising avenue for discussion narratives in the context of knowledge management and for bridging the gap between the separated worlds of narrative and discursive knowledge.

Narrative knowledge and tacit knowing

As narrative knowledge is an implicit part of the life-world and organizational life respectively, it is often equated or intertwined with tacit knowing. In many cases, narratives are assumed or even supposed effectively to share tacit knowing in organizations. In our view this mingling does not get us any closer to understanding the narrative dimension of organization; indeed, it is likely to confuse the knowledge debate.

The essential differences are as follows. Drawing on Polanyi, tacit knowing refers to all those aspects of individual proficiency which are literally practical, that is, non-verbal in nature and inexplicable. Correspondingly, Polanyi (1966, p. 4) states: 'We know more than we can tell.' The individual is assumed to act on the basis of something that he or she 'knows' but cannot tell. Tacit knowing refers to the special skills of a single actor and is therefore an action-based category which cannot be separated from the knowing actor. Tacit knowing indicates a personal skill or capability, something individuals can rely on in their acting without being aware of, let alone understanding. It is a bodily skill or, as Polanyi put it, an 'embodied knowledge', that is, an inseparable part of the actor's body (Polanyi, 1958). Tacit knowing thus can only be actualized within actions and can never be removed from the actor to become something 'out there' (Cook and Brown, 1999, p. 387; Neuweg, 1999; Tsoukas, 2003; Schreyögg and Geiger, 2005).

In contrast, narrative knowledge is not embodied, but is instead verbal in nature. It can virtually exist outside of a singular action. And a second major difference is salient: narrative knowing is not an individualistic category; it is interactive and thus social in nature. Without an audience there is logically no narrative.

This distinction between narrative and tacit knowledge has far-reaching consequences at both the theoretical and the practical level. First of all, the narrative level is a separate level, with its own logic at variance from the tacit dimension. Secondly, given its embodied, non-verbal nature, tacit knowing cannot be distributed in and between organizations by narratives. There is no way to convert tacit knowing into narratives (Schreyögg and Geiger, 2005). Narratives cannot transfer or even teach bodily skills such as playing the piano or riding a bike. What narratives can do is to actualize the collective background and implicit convictions of a community. Storytellers share narrative knowledge, not tacit knowing.

Narratives in Knowledge Management

Narratives have proven to be an important feature in organizational knowledge-sharing; recent approaches to manage knowledge in organizations thus pay particular attention to them. Due to their emergent and ambiguous nature, organizational narratives cannot, however, easily be integrated into any conscious effort to manage knowledge. Narratives turn up at different places depending on specific circumstances; organizations can use them but not construe them artificially. Apart from this emergent character narratives cannot, as mentioned, be simply acquired. From a discursive point of view, narratives represent a kind of 'naïve' material, being in a natural state. As already pointed out at the beginning of this paper, using them in the context of knowledge management therefore evokes a set of intriguing issues, inclnding: whether we can actually rely on narratives; how we should evaluate narratives; how we should identify false narratives; whether the lessons to be learned from narratives are context-bound by their very nature; whether narrative lessons apply abroad (in other subsystems, other network organizations or other cultures). And in case there are contradicting or competing narratives in organizations: how we should deal with conflicting and competing narratives. Can we compare them? If so, in what way?

Whatever the approach, such issues cannot be resolved unless we can find a way to put the narrative world into perspective and to reflect on them in terms of these dimensions. And that means we have to bridge the gap to the discursive world. When seeking an answer to the questions raised above, a switching from the narrative to the reflexive level is imperative. Any such switch means partial alienation from the original ('naïve') narrative world. It implies (artificial) reconstruction and reworking: narratives have to be identified, interpreted, accepted or rejected and so on. In other words, knowledge management has to learn how to reflect narrative knowledge and how to process this reflection effectively. We suggest a three-step model to support this process. Its elements are described in the next section.

Three-step model

It has been pointed out that narratives follow an unreflective mode in a self-legitimizing world. In order to open the narrative world for knowledge management, salient narratives have to be re-worked in such a way that they can become the subject of reflection. To use narratives for management purposes, we have to introduce a second level, which basically enables our looking at narrations from an extraordinar point of view. Only by switching to this level can we find a platform for reflecting and discussing narrations in terms of the questions raised above: validity, reliability, generalization and so on. The narrative life-world level does not contain such a platform; it is a self-sustained world.

This switching from a narrative to a discursive level does not simply occur, however; it has to be deliberately brought about (Habermas, 2003). The following steps aim at explicating ways for realizing this level-switching process within the context of knowledge management. Other arenas, such as politics or jurisdiction, may require different approaches for realizing this process. In particular, they will use different criteria; the criteria agreed upon in their communities (Brown and Duguid, 1991, 1998).

Narrative knowledge has proven to be triply situated; correspondingly, three steps are suggested for elaborating on the exploration of narrative knowledge. At the core is the idea of assumption surfacing (Mason and Mitroff, 1981) or challenging strategic planning assumptions, that is, identifying the assumptions underlying narratives and reflecting on them from a discursive point of view. The three-step model set out below has been developed as a reaction to problems firms face when using narratives, in particular 'war stories', in knowledge management.

The first step

The first step aims at reflecting the original context of a narrative or a story. War stories are generated and told in specific organizational communities and they refer to specific historical situations. They are therefore closely bound to their original context (Szulanski, 2002; Brown and Duguid, 2001; Hippel v., 1994). By implication, the know-how incorporated into a narrative applies to the story's original context only. From a knowledge management point of view, such limitation is disappointing. The focal community may often face similar problems in somewhat different constellations and may possibly profit from the know-how incorporated into the war story. So the question arises whether the narrated problem solution generated in a historical situation applies to those similar situations as well. The first step, therefore, is to put the 'war story' into perspective and to examine its applicability beyond the original context to similar problems within the focal community. This exploration may be worked out in different ways, for example, trial and error or analogical reasoning.

For knowledge management it seems important to routinize such reflection on the applicability of the solutions carried along by narratives. When establishing the 'first step', two aspects are of crucial importance.

Firstly, one has to encourage and to ensure that proven successful solutions are actually narrated, that is, the organization must provide platforms or arenas that spur and support story-telling. The communities of practice (Brown and Duguid, 1991; Wenger, 1999), much quoted at the time of writing, can be used as such a measure for facilitating the story-telling process in organizations. They are organized as specialist networks for knowledge-sharing and provide common facilities. In these institutionalized exchange arenas, the applicability of a narrated problem solution beyond its original context can easily be made the subject of expert discussion.

Secondly, in case the narrated solution has actually been applied to a similar problem, the community needs feedback on the experiences and results achieved in order to find out whether such transfer worked or not. Knowledge management should therefore encourage users to explicate and share their experiences with regard to the narrated solution. Communities of practice also seem to provide a promising arena for encouraging and sharing such feedback. The more feedback on the narrated know-how generated, the broader the scope of orientation for future applications beyond the original context. The user feedback can thus be seen as a first experiential quality check of the narratives' claims.

The second step

The second step of the suggested model aims at exploring the scope of further de-contextualization and asks the question whether the narrative might apply abroad, that is, beyond the borders of the focal community. Organizations are interested in learning whether the narrated know-how that proved successful in the original context might apply also to other contexts (for example, subsystems, departments, sub-cultures). For evaluating its scope, the war story is to be made subject of a second round of exploration. The formal methods are the same: surfacing of the underlying assumptions; trial and error; analogical reasoning; six thinking hats; relational evaluation procedure (Barnes et al., 1997) and so on.

There are various organizational approaches that can support this discursive process. First of all, knowledge management can encourage interchange between different, but work-related, communities. The literature on communities of practice has begun to prove the importance of connecting or overlapping such communities. In cases where such exchange does not flow naturally, which happens more often than not, it is suggested that specialized roles be created, such as translator or moderator, that is, persons who are familiar with the context of both communities and able to act as broker between those communities (Gherardi and Nicolini, 2002, p. 434). Establishing so-called boundary objects as interfaces between communities is another approach that has proven helpful. A broad range of objects used in the communities' practices can become boundary objects: models, maps, standardized methods, charts, computer simulations and so on (Carlile, 2002, p. 451). However, boundary objects can only support the debate on the second step if both communities have some experience in working with them and use a common language when talking about them. With the help of these boundary objects, narratives can be evoked and transferred within inter-community relations (Carlile, 2004). Such object-bounded knowledge transfer, however, represents only a small part of the entire effort necessary. In addition, processes similar to those already described in step one have to ensure that the narrated problem-solution actually applies in the new context. The receiving community itself has to check whether the new problem-solution may be useful or not and share the result of its assessment. Other communities of the organization may be interested in getting involved in this assessment procedure accordingly. An open communication infrastructure again figures most prominently here in enhancing the whole process.

The third step

The third step aims at discussing the quality of the narrated 'lessons' as compared to other problem-solving approaches used or known by the organization. In other words, this step addresses the question whether the narrated practice is not only a workable solution (as steps one and two try to find out), but also a relatively good and noteworthy practice. At this stage, competing narratives told in the organization and other more codified solutions come to the fore: solutions derived from formally developed approaches; solutions shared by other narratives; solutions offered by outside consultants; and so on. Knowledge management has to bring the various solutions together and compare them in terms of efficiency or effectiveness. Discussions in step three are concerned with identifying the best solution identifying and finally deciding whether this solution should be officially dispersed across the whole organization (Schreyögg and Geiger, 2005).

How can such review processes be organized in terms of practicality? Some firms pioneered with review committees devoted to assessing the quality of emerging war stories and narrated problem-solutions respectively. Such committees are staffed with acknowledged experts in the focal field. The members are expected to discuss the surfaced and reconstructed narrative along consented criteria and eventually reach a decision on their quality. The criteria in use differ. Some examples of criteria used are given below. These stem from a case study at Shell International Exploration and Production, conducted by a Berlin research team. At Shell the experts used these criteria to evaluate new practices narrated in 'war stories' in a community of practice focusing on the field of exploring and producing hydrocarbons. The issues discussed primarily covered engineering themes on offshore deep-sea drilling techniques. At the time of the case study, the peer review committee used the following five criteria, their weighting differing from case to case:

- Health, safety and environment: At stake were health and safety risks for the staff and the impact of a solution on the environment.
- Cost estimation: What are long- and short-term costs when applying the solution; what is the proportion of fixed and variable costs as compared to other options?
- Quality/certainty: This cluster of criteria referred to the performance potential of a narrated practice. Questions of reliability, durability and transferability were given a central place here.

- Alignment with other processes: These criteria highlighted the inter-dependence with other processes. Salient questions included: Does the story's solution fit with already existing related processes or not? Is the narrated solution really new or are there already in existence processes which do a better job? Are the costs of integrating the narrated solution into already existing processes reasonable or too high? Does the narrated solution outdate an already existing solution, so that this has to be deleted?
- Urgency: How urgent is the narrated solution for improving our practices? Can we speed up the process?

As a result of such evaluation processes, some narrated practices might become recommended practice for the solution of specific problems, replacing previous less effective ones.

Obviously, different practices and performing situations require different criteria. The criteria used by the Shell peer review committee cannot be expected to apply everywhere. They are not universal. Communities have to find their own canon of criteria which are considered appropriate for evaluating narrated practices in their particular field.

The three steps together are designed to transform the narratives and render them compatible with knowledge management. In a way, doing this impoverishes the narratives in terms of magic, entertainment, fascination, complexity and so on, and questions the attraction often attributed to narratives. The suggested three-step procedure imposes analytical clarity on basically ambiguous texts. However, this does not mean that the narratives are destroyed; they will still be there. The analytical procedure works on some aspects of, rather than the whole, narrative. The three-step procedure acknowledges the fact that narratives, aside from other interesting aspects, may contain 'knowledge of regularities, or scientific principles, or general values' (Tsoukas and Cummings, 1997, p. 667). The idea is to distil discursive knowledge from the narrative and transform it into more generalized advice or, as Calori puts it, the analysis of narratives might 'reveal their lay ontology and serve to construct a higher-order theory' (2002, p. 131). By its very nature, narrative knowledge lacks a coherent structure and does not allow for any generalization without further elaboration and development. Narratives are encapsulated in their self-legitimizing nature; they cannot be analysed and discussed within the natural narrative mode. Therefore we advocate for knowledge management purposes, and only for those purposes, a 'switching' of levels, which makes the underlying assumptions of narratives subject to a discursive mode. This is a procedure which brings inherent claims to light and makes them accessible for the focal discourse community.

Embarking on this three-step procedure, narrative and discursive knowledge are not completely separated worlds, but rather can be bridged and made open to transition. It is possible to transfer previously only implicitly accepted claims (narrative mode) into the world of discursive reasoning. What has not been highlighted so far is the sequel, the re-entry of the results of discourse to the practical level. The reflected (and accepted) assertions have to be brought back to the problematic outset from which the whole process initially started. The result of the reflections may even become part of the life-world again (Habermas, 1984, p. 17). As a consequence, there is an ongoing interchange between the narrative life-world and the reflexive world of discourse: implicit validity claims can be surfaced and made the subject of a discursive assessment. The generated discursive knowledge is fed back to the life-world context where the validity claims became problematic. The new practice may replace previously narrated practices, as we know from the use of scientific results in our everyday life. Alternatively, it may actually be ignored or even rejected.

This interchange can also be interpreted as a learning process, which in some cases amounts to a special form of double-loop learning (Argyris and Schön, 1978). Through discursive assessment, implicit assumptions of narratives, once taken for granted, surface and are reflected. This reflexive practice might induce a change of these background assumptions in terms of double-loop learning as well as an actual change in everyday practices.

The crucial point here is that this reflexive process opens the door for assessing the quality of narrative knowledge and for overcoming the assumptive, sometimes even dogmatic, mentality which dominates the view of narratives in the current knowledge management debate.

This prevalent attitude of anxiously keeping narratives away from any assessment issues is all the more surprising since the broadly acclaimed resourced-based view stresses the importance of outstanding and unique organizational knowledge for corporate success (Barney, 1991, 1997). Both are characteristics which cannot be attributed unless an evaluation has taken place. Also, recently published empirical studies emphasize the practical importance of evaluating knowledge claims when generating high-quality knowledge (Lee and Cole, 2003, p. 638). For instance, Lee and Cole identified as a key driver in the Linux software development process the constant criticism of draft versions by peers: 'In the Linux development community we observe a peer review process as a structured approach to generating criticism of existing versions, evaluating those criticisms, and eliminating "error", while retaining those solutions that cannot be falsified' (2003, p. 639). In the light of our framework, the Linux knowledge-creation process can be seen as a way of transforming narrative knowledge into discursive, consented knowledge through peer-review processes set up by the Linux development team.

Implications for knowledge management

The qualifying process along the suggested three steps is designed to contribute to the improvement of knowledge management. Certainly not all organizational narratives are supposed to pass these steps. They are recommended only in cases where the inherent validity claims are called into question or challenged by competing views. Furthermore, in many cases passing step one or two may be sufficient and sometimes the discourse may proceed directly to step three. Whatever the number of cases, the basic idea of qualifying organizational narrations seems to form a new, important dimension in knowledge management, a dimension which directs attention to the content and the quality of knowledge and not only to managing the context of knowledge, as suggested in most common approaches to knowledge management. The essential precondition for integrating this new dimension is an epistemological framework that allows for a distinction between narrative and discursive knowledge.

This new dimension of qualifying narratives implies new, challenging tasks for knowledge management. Aside from currently well-known suggestions for creating a flourishing narrative context ('ba') and a story-telling supporting culture (v. Krogh, 1998), knowledge management has to institutionalize mechanisms of reflexively breaking the narrative mode of thought. Without a doubt, information and communication technology is likely to play a pivotal role here. Some companies already successfully run intranet communication platforms which automatically ask for user feedback when getting narrative advice. Later on they electronically circulate the received feedback together with the original narrative, thereby transmitting a continuously updated knowledge system (Gibbert et al., 2002). It seems to be very important to institutionalize this feedback process formally to guarantee that all war stories are reliably provided with feedback information. What is also needed is an architecture of overlapping communities. Interfaces between communities have to be established so that a constant interchange of narratives can occur.

Certainly these are only first suggestions on how such a discursive development of narratives (in particular 'war stories') can be made to work and translated into effective practices. These issues further, more detailed exploration. But all such explorations should be informed by the different epistemological natures of knowledge and narration, an issue which has too long been ignored in the debate on organizational knowledge management (Alvesson and Kärreman, 2001; Grandori and Kogut, 2002). It would appear that a 'reflexive turn' in knowledge management is due. The future of knowledge management clearly has to address questions on the quality and validity of knowledge.

Notes

1 Orr (1990) points to the doubly situated character of war stories; we add a third dimension, the context of legitimization.
2 Literally, 'Rationalisierung der Lebenswelt'. See Habermas, 1984.

References

Alvesson, M. and D. Kärreman (2001) 'Odd Couple: Making Sense of the Curious Concept of Knowledge management', *Journal of Management Studies*, 38(3), 224–231.

Argyris, C. and D. A. Schön (1978) *Organizational Learning. A Theory of Action Perspective* (Reading, Mass.: Addison-Wesley Publishing).

Barnes, D., N. Hegarty and P. M. Smeets (1997) 'Relating Equivalence Relations to Equivalence Relations: A Relational Framing Model of Complex Human Functioning', *The Analysis of Verbal Behavior*, 14 57–83.

Barney, J. B. (1991) 'Firm Resources and Sustained Competitive Advantage', *Journal of Management*, 17(1), 99–120.

Barney, J. (1997) 'Looking Inside for Competitive Advantage', in A. Campbell and L. K. Sommers (eds), *Core Competency-Based Strategy* (London: International Thomson Business Press), pp. 13–29.

Boje, D. M. (1995) 'Stories of the Storytelling Organization: A Postmodern Analysis of Disney as "Tamara-Land"', *Academy of Management Journal*, 38(4), 997–1035.

Boje, D. M. (2001) *Narrative Methods for Organizational and Communication Research* (London: SAGE).

Brown, J. S. and P. Duguid (1991) 'Organizational Learning and Communities of Practice: Toward a Unified View of Working, Learning and Innovation', *Organization Science*, 12(2), 40–57.

Brown, J. S. and P. Duguid (1998) 'Organizing Knowledge', *California Management Review*, 40(3), 90–111.

Brown, J. S. and P. Duguid (2001) 'Knowledge and Organization: A Social-Practice Perspective', *Organization Science*, 12(2), 198–213.

Bruner, J. (1986) Actual Minds, Possible Worlds (Cambridge, MA: Harvard University Press).

Buskirk V. W. and D. McGrath (1992) 'Organizational Stories as a Window on Affect in Organizations', *Journal of Organizational Change Management*, 5, 9–24.

Calori, R. (2002) 'Organizational Development and the Ontology of Creative Dialectical Evolution', *Organization*, 9(1), 127–150.

Carlile, P. R. (2002) 'A Pragmatic View of Knowledge and Boundaries: Boundary Objects in New Product Development', *Organization Science*, 13(4), 442–455.

Carlile, P. R. (2004) 'Transferring,Translating, and Transforming: An Integrative Framework for Managing Knowledge across Boundaries', *Organization Science*, 15(5), 555–568.

Cook, S. N. and J. S. Brown (1999) 'Bridging Epistemologies: The Generative Dance between Organizational Knowledge and Organizational Knowing', *Organization Science*, 10(4), 382–400.

Czarniawska, B. (1997) *Narrating the Organization: Dramas of Institutional Identity* (Chicago: University of Chicago Press).

Czarniawska, B. (1998) *A narrative approach in organization studies* (Thousand Oaks, CA: Sage).

Dyer, M. (1983) 'The Role of Affect in Narratives', *Cognitive Science*, 7, 211–42.

Fisher, W. (1978) 'Toward a Logic of Good Reason', *Quarterly Journal of Speech*, 64, 376–84.

Gabriel, Y. (1995) 'The Unmanaged Organization: Stories, Fantasies and Subjectivity', *Organization Studies*, 16(3), 477–501.

Gabriel, Y. (2000) *Storytelling in Organizations* (Oxford: Oxford University Press).

Gabriel, Y. (2004) 'The Narrative Veil: Truth and Untruths in Storytelling', in Y. Gabriel (ed.), *Myths, Stories, and Organizations: Premodern Narratives for Our Times* (Oxford: Oxford University Press), pp. 17–31.

Geertz, C. (1993) *Local Knowledge: Further Essays in Interpretive Anthropology* (London: Fontana Press).

Gherardi, S. and D. Nicolini (2002) 'Learning in a Constellation of Interconnected Practices: Canon or Dissonance?' *Journal of Management Studies*, 39(4), 419–436.

Grandori, A. and B. Kogut (2002) 'Dialogue on Organization and Knowledge', *Organization Science*, 13(3), 224–231.

Gibbert, M., S. Jenzowsky, C. Jonczvk, M. Thiel and S. Völpel (2002) 'ShareNet – the Next Generation Knowledge Management', in T. H. Davenport, and G. Probst (eds), *Knowledge Management Case Book. Siemens Best Practices*, 2 ed. (Berlin: John Wiley), pp. 42–59.

Habermas, J. (1984) *The Theory of Communicative Action, Vol. 1: Reason and the Rationalization of Society* (Boston, MA: Beacon Press).

Habermas, J. (1989) *The Theory of Communicative Action, Vol. 2: Lifeworld and System: A Critique of Functionalist Reason* (Boston, MA: Beacon Press).

Habermas, J. (2003) *Truth and Justification* (London: Polity Press).

Hippel V. E. (1994) 'Sticky Information and the Locus of Problem Solving: Implication for Innovation', *Management Science*, 40(4), 429–439.

Kamlah, W. and P. Lorenzen (1967) *Logische Propädeutik, oder Vorschule des vernünftigen Redens* (Mannheim et al.: J. B. Metzler).

Kluckhon, F. R. and F. L. Strodtbeck (1961) *Variations in value orientations* (Evanston: Row Peterson).

Krogh, G. V. (1998) 'Care in Knowledge Creation', *California Management Review*, 40(3), 133–153.

Lee, G. K. and R. E. Cole (2003) 'From a Firm-Based to a Community Based Model of Knowledge Creation: the Case of the Linux Kernel Development', *Organization Science*, 14(6), 633–649.

Luhmann, N. (1984) *The Differentiation of Society* (New York: Columbia University Press).

Lyotard, J. F. (1988) *The Differend: Phrases in Dispute* (Minnesota: University of Minnesota Press).

Lyotard, J. F. (1991) *The Postmodern Condition: A Report on Knowledge* (Minneapolis, MN: University of Minnesota Press).

Mason, R. A. and I. I. Mitroff (1981) *Challenging Strategic Planning Assumptions – Theory, Cases and Techniques* (New York: Doubleday).

Mittelstraß, J. (1974) *Die Möglichkeit von Wissenschaft* (Frankfurt a.M.: Suhrkamp).

Neuweg, H. G. (1999) *Könnerschaft und implizites Wissen. Zur lehr-lerntheoretischen Bedeutung der Erkenntnis- und Wissenstheorie Michael Polanyis* (Münster: Gabler).

Nonaka, I., G. V. Krogh and K. Ichijo (2000) *Enabling Knowledge Creation: How to Unlock the Mystery of Tacit Knowledge and Release the Power of Innovation* (Oxford: Oxford University Press).

Orr, J. E. (1990) 'Sharing Knowledge, Celebrating Identity: Community Memory in a Service Culture', in D. Middleton and D. Edwards (eds), *Collective Remembering* (London: Sage), pp. 169–89.

Orr, J. E. (1996) *Talking about Machines: An Ethnography of a Modern Job* (Ithaca: Cornell University Press).

Patriotta, G. (2003) *Organizational Knowledge in the Making: How Firms Create, Use, and Institutionalize Knowledge* (Oxford: Oxford University Press).

Pfeffer, J. and R. I. Sutton (1999) 'Knowing "What" to do is Not Enough: Turning Knowledge into Action', *California Management Review*, 42(1), 83–108.

Polanyi, M. (1958) *Personal Knowledge. Towards a Post-Critical Philosophy* (Chicago: University of Chicago Press).

Polanyi, M. (1966) *The Tacit Dimension* (London: Routledge).

Reinmann-Rothmeier, G. and F. Vohle (2001) 'Was Schiedsrichter, Manager und Rotkäppchen gemeinsam haben: Mit Geschichten Wissen managen', *zfo*, 70(5), 293–300.

Schein, E. H. (1985) *Organizational Culture and Leadership: A Dynamic View* (San Francisco et al.: Jossey-Bass).

Schreyögg, G. and D. Geiger (2005) 'Reconsidering Organizational Knowledge: Knowledge, Skills and Narrations', in G. Schreyögg and J. Koch (eds), *Narratives and Knowledge Management* (Berlin: Schmidt Verlag).

Schütz, A. and T. Luckmann (1989) *The Structures of the Life-World* (Minnesota: Northwestern University Press).

Snowden, D. (2000) 'The Social Ecology of Knowledge Management', in C. Despres and D. Chauvel (eds), *Knowledge Horizons: The Present and the Promise of Knowledge Management* (New York: Butterworth-Heinemann), pp. 237–65.

Szulanski, G. (2002) *Sticky Knowledge: Barriers to Knowing in Firms* (London: Sage).

Swap, W. (2001) 'Using Mentoring and Storytelling to Transfer Knowledge in the Workplace', *Journal of Management Information Systems*, 18, 95–114.

Toulmin, S. (1958) *The Uses of Argument* (Cambridge: Cambridge University Press).

Tsoukas, H. (2003) 'Do We Really Understand Tacit Knowledge?', in M. Easterby-Smith and M. A. Lyles (eds), *The Blackwell Handbook of Organizational Learning and Knowledge* (London: Blackwell), pp. 410–27.

Tsoukas, H. and S. Cummings (1997) 'Marginalization and Recovery: The Emergence of Aristotelian Themes in Organization Studies', *Organization Studies*, 18(4), 655–683.

Tsoukas, H. and M. J. Hatch (2001) 'Complex Thinking, Complex Practice: The Case for a Narrative Approach to Organizational Complexity', *Human Relations*, 54, 979–1013.

Wenger, E. C. (1999) *Communities of Practice: Learning, Meaning and Identity* (Cambridge: Cambridge University Press).

Weick, K. E. (1995) *Sensemaking in Organizations* (Thousand Oaks, Sage).

Wilkins, A. (1984) 'The Creation of Company Cultures: The Role of Stories and Human Resource Systems', *Human Resource Management*, 23, 41–60.

5
The Other Side of the Distinction: The Management of Ignorance

Ursula Schneider

By 2005 the area of knowledge management does not suffer from scarcity of approaches but rather from their overabundance. Although some concepts have gained visibility in the field, there is still no overarching framework.

Therefore, the future of knowledge management will probably unfold along two paths. One will seek to consolidate the multiplicity of approaches, to further differentiate contexts and to learn from empirical evidence (Mode II of knowledge generation, cf. Gibbons et al., 1994). The other will lead towards learning about the 'known' by focusing on its 'shadow' side, the 'unknown'.

This chapter will deal with the shadow side and ask the following questions:

- Following Spencer-Brown we can expect that the growth of one side of a distinction that we draw implies the growth of its other side. Does it therefore make sense in principle to manage ignorance? (cf. Spencer-Brown, 1977)
- If ignorance is not to be ignored, that is, left to contingent evolution, how can it be studied as well as (indirectly) managed?[1]
- Despite bearing a 'negative' meaning, can ignorance be useful?
- What are the effects of 'dysfunctional' types of ignorance on different performance measures of social systems?

To answer these questions, I shall first draw on complex adaptive systems theory and the law of form in order to establish ignorance as a phenomenon of necessarily growing order. In a second step, I suggest a simple typology of ignorance along the criteria of consciousness and functionality with respect to a system's purpose. Within the literature on knowledge management the distinction between knowledge exploration and knowledge exploitation (cf. March, 1991; Spender, 1992; Koza and Lewin, 1998) has proven useful to drive analysis and to discuss issues of 'right' amounts of knowledge and learning in an economic context. If they are blended with the typology of ignorance, reflections on the optimization rather than maximization of knowledge and learning will lead to the argument of positive or functional ignorance. The final paragraph will elaborate on the dysfunctional types of ignored and imposed ignorance.

The paper will close with lessons for the management of knowledge gained from the research of its mirror image, namely ignorance.

1.   Introduction: Is ignorance on the rise?

> Anything said is said by an observer.
> H. Maturana, 1970

Spencer-Brown starts his influential work on the laws of form with the order, 'Draw a distinction', and thus describes the creative act by which our minds create a (not 'the'!) universe of signifiers (cf. Spencer-Brown, 1977, p. 3). In a second step, he claims, 'there can be no distinction without motive, and there can be no motive unless contents are seen to differ in value' (ibid., p. 1). Popper has argued in a similar way when he stated in an interview: 'I believe that we actively try to impose our knowledge about nature on our environment' He declares himself a Kantian but for the assumption of an inborn understanding of time, space, cause and effect (Popper, 1991, p. 16f).

These brief references lead to two insights, provided one is ready to share their motives.

First, the insight of contingency. By drawing a distinction we establish the first simple type of form, namely the separation into a space, marked by the distinction, and an unmarked space out of the marked space's boundaries. However, the separation line could have been drawn differently through the empty space and would thus have created another marked space (cf. Spencer-Brown, 1977, p. 4). The insights gained from contingency reflect on our common distinction between description (naming) and prescription (drawing distinctions), where the former conceals that it is not possible not to apply distinctions as soon as we indicate something. In Spencer-Brown's words, 'We cannot make an indication without drawing a distinction' (ibid., p. 1). I do not intend to elaborate on epistemological questions here more than necessary for the purpose of marking the unmarked space beyond knowledge. Nevertheless, I would like to point out that such an approach seriously challenges our common concept of research, where we make indications which we transform into hypotheses, which we then submit to empirical testing. The approach also challenges the accumulative metaphor of knowledge generation confronting the law of calling (identity, repetition) with the law of crossing (marking spaces and cancelling them). While different callings follow a linear path and are a concept similar to Argyris's and Schoen's idea of single-loop learning, crossing reshuffles and redefines what has been 'accumulated' by calling. It destroys linearity. Again, I refer to Spencer-Brown's original voice: 'The "reason or the ratio" of all we have already known, is not the same that it shall be when we know more.' (ibid., p. v). Therefore the purpose of this paper is to reframe (cross), rather than to accumulate within, the still blurry but marked frame of knowledge management.

A second insight from Spencer-Brown and Popper is that distinctions are drawn on the grounds of interests and intentions (motives). This shatters our ideal of a detached and neutral researcher, who sees the world 'as it is'. The only rescue from this insight, which creates uneasiness, is to retreat to the idea of second-order observation. An observer of second order reflects in a recursive loop on the phenomenon which is observed and his or her observing it in a certain way. Researchers and managers in their corresponding systems thus become part of the 'equation'.[2] The myriad ways to define knowledge either by similar concepts such as information, capabilities, skills or experiences or by categorization along distinctions such as implicit/explicit, individual/collective, narrative/ scientific, authorized/ unauthorized and so on reflect attempts to overcome the contingent and value-driven character of indications by providing for different meanings.

A third observation needs to be added to the law of form. If knowledge is a special resource whose generation does not follow a linear path,[3] then each new distinction which is drawn will create an infinite unmarked space at its boundary. Thus ignorance grows out of proportion with the increase of what we mark as knowledge. It could be said in another metaphor that we have succeeded in the world of knowledge to create something that physics was never able to achieve: a perpetuum mobile of insatiable search for knowledge.

Applied to the concept of knowledge (management), the three insights of contingency, interest and exponential growth of unmarked space, created by the indication of any concept of knowledge, encourage curiosity to discover more about the unmarked space of ignorance. I suggest the following propositions:

1. To indicate any concept of knowledge is a first-order observation. To suppress the process of drawing the distinction between knowledge and not-knowledge (ignorance) distorts findings within the frame of first-order observation with regard to their contingent and value-driven aspects.
2. In practice, this leads to (a) accumulative concepts of knowledge management which treat knowledge as any other factor of production as if it were linear, discrete, divisible, durable and transferable, a concept well suited to data but unsuited to knowledge (cf. Schneider, 2001) and (b) blindness of knowledge management concepts to questions of power and interest which ground any activity from the very first step of its indicating knowledge. If this were better understood, failure because of resistance as evidenced in recent studies (Howaldt et al., 2004) could be handled differently.

2.   Marking the unmarked space: A typology of ignorance(s)

I will now turn to the context of business wherein systematic knowledge management became popular in the early 1990s. This context is intentional in nature. In order to mark the so far unmarked space of not-knowledge, I will introduce two new distinctions which promise to provide knowledge on ignorance. The first distinction is based on plausibility. Ignorance can be known or not known to its subject; it can be conscious, or sub- or unconscious. The interest in this distinction was expressed in the days of the ancient Greek civilization by Socrates. His famous saying, 'I know that I don't know', may be less modest than it seems at first sight. It could also be interpreted as, 'at least I know about my ignorance, whereas those absorbed by dogmatic belief don't even see what they don't see'. In a business context ignored ignorance can be expected to be detrimental to its purpose, which is commonly expressed as a certain level of profitability expected by shareholders, while accounting for restrictions resulting from expectations of influential stakeholders. A risk which is not known and thus cannot be taken into consideration in turn cannot be managed. A decision based on incorrect information should lead to a dead end. However, there are situations where ignored ignorance may enhance a purpose. This applies to its deliberate acceptance by actors who want to protect themselves from psychological destabilization and free themselves from the paralysing burden of knowledge, even though it is relevant to their purpose. As Spencer-Brown has pointed out, the act of crossing (passing from the marked to the unmarked space, re-entering the excluded) takes time. To question one's presumptions may thus mean to miss what we call windows of opportunity and consequently first-mover advantages. In such cases, incomplete and imperfect releases may be functional while a search and incorporation of additional knowledge (whose existence may be unknown to the searcher at the beginning of the search) would be dysfunctional as it may prove time-consuming. Thus dealing with the distinction of conscious or unconscious ignorance draws attention to the important question of 'how much knowledge is enough' or, more seriously, to the rules of closing the search for knowledge.

A second distinction is deduced from the binary logic of business purpose: something pays or does not pay. With regard to this logic, ignorance of a subject of reference (which could be an individual or an organisation) can be functional or dysfunctional. It can serve the purpose or undermine it.[4] Due to the contingent nature of indications (see above), we cannot expect functionality to be a constitutive and stable characteristic of knowledge or ignorance. The line of separation will change over time and depend on the situation.

Combining the two types of distinctions, explained briefly above, four types emerge:

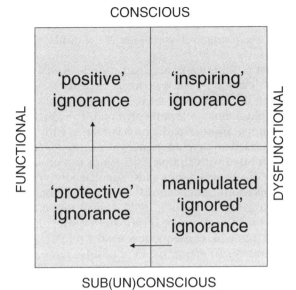

CONSCIOUS

FUNCTIONAL

'positive'
ignorance

'inspiring'
ignorance

'protective'
ignorance

manipulated
'ignored'
ignorance

DYSFUNCTIONAL

SUB(UN)CONSCIOUS

Figure 5.1   Marks in the space of ignorance

In the following paragraphs I will elaborate on those four types, starting with the contentious idea that ignorance can be functional which seems initially to contradict the basic philosophy of knowledge management.

3.   When ignorance is wise

As a first form I will illustrate and give reasons for the type of conscious (even deliberate) and functional ignorance which I have labelled 'positive'. Positive ignorance is to know what one does not need to know. This form is closely related to the knowledge management problem of overabundance of data and information[5] which is reflected in the growth rate of many indicators relating to the concept of knowledge, such as the number of publications, the number of electronic bytes added to the Internet per year, the number of living scientists and the number of different statistics provided by authorities. The annual production of structured data equals 17 times the content of the Library of Congress according to some sources (cf. 'How much information', 2003). Even if one takes into account that this includes all modes of information (data, text, pictures, movies) and all degrees of validity (from junk to thoroughly tested scientific hypotheses), it is obvious that no human mind can cope with such amounts. The documentation that is required in modern car production provides an illustration. While 202 documents were required to produce an Opel car in 1932, this number had risen to 13,850 documents by 1999. The argument is pushed to the extreme by the joke that the documentation needed to produce a Boeing 737 actually fills one. Piet Hein, a Danish poet, states the problem as follows: 'Wisdom is expiring everywhere under the dead weight of purposeless information.'

Elsewhere, I have shown that positive ignorance is an attitude as well as a skill, both of which require clear purpose and focus of (inter)action. Whereas others suggest solving the overflow problem by increasing absorptive capacities, which is without doubt a relevant concept, the distinction of positive ignorance leads along another path. In accordance with Piet Hein's words, this path is grounded on psychological evidence, as collected by Dörner and his team: confronted with complex situations test persons, responsible for the well-being of a company or a state, simulated by a computer program, make worse decisions under conditions of stress caused by information overload and ambiguity (cf. Dörner, 1998). Due to restrictions of volume, I cannot elaborate on the effects of informational stress here. I will rather conclude this section with consequences for the practice and 'future of knowledge management'. To master issues of positive ignorance at an individual as well as organizational level, technical, behavioural and cultural solutions need to be developed, from filters and smart agents to 'netiquette'[6] and means of condensation and structuring of all kinds of HRD measures to support clarity of purpose and the ability to let go of informational offers (cf. Schneider, 2005).

A second form of functional ignorance is marked by the label 'protective'. It refers to situations of risk-taking and speedy action. More generally, those are situations where 'true' decisions must be taken (cf. V. Foerster, 1993). V. Foerster points out that true decisions are decisions which cannot be made in the context of classical decision theory. This means that alternatives are uncertain and ambiguous and cannot be integrated in a calculus. Therefore, decision-makers must bear the risk that their decisions may be wrong, a state that creates uneasiness in many individuals. Organizational research has contributed the metaphor of paralysis through analysis to this picture. Uneasiness may induce decision-makers to search for more detailed information in order to gain security in marking (drawing distinctions). To mark means to take sides and to define a problem in a certain way while knowing or at least suspecting that the problem could have been stated differently. Although contradictory to the common notion of rationality (with reference to purpose), it may be wise to cut oneself off from any further search for knowledge at a certain point in the process. This seems to correspond with the concept of entrepreneurship in Schumpeter's sense (cf. Schumpeter, 1950). Instead of analysing the old, the creative destructor gets rid of it and starts building the new by daring to walk the first steps. If the leaders of great projects and the builders of all great monuments (such as space travel, the tunnel under the channel, the Eiffel Tower or Vienna's Imperial Castle) had followed risk management procedures according to the Basel II rules they would perhaps never even have started their endeavours. Protective ignorance, in the meaning suggested here, directly contradicts one basic idea of knowledge management, namely not to reinvent the wheel. As I have argued elsewhere (cf. Schneider, 2001), we need to give the notion of reinvention a closer look. If we really require from the authors of each publication, each invention and each apparently new procedure to first thoroughly study all that has been published, invented and practically accomplished over the whole world and throughout its history, we may probably find out that many basic patterns of thinking were invented a long time ago. Just think of the wisdoms of old Indian, Persian, Chinese, Japanese or classical Greek, Roman and European Renaissance and Age of Enlightenment heritage whereby this demonstration is still 'ethnocentric' as it excludes the richness of all types of indigenous knowledge. I don't believe it corresponds to the human psyche to be restricted by amounts of existing 'knowledge' which can hardly be processed in a lifetime. Humans are rather curious, with many of them, especially in the individualistic cultures of the West, tending to prefer idiosyncratic ways to mimetic learning although mimetic learning occurs as long as they live. To push the idea of not reinventing the wheel to its extreme leads us to an important and so far unsolved question in knowledge management. Instead of proclaiming the maximization of knowledge and learning, as many academics tend to (cf. Grant and Baden-Fuller, 2004; Schneider, 2003), we need to develop models which deal with stop rules. In other words, we need to develop different modes of marking and crossing between knowledge and ignorance in order to answer the simple question of how much knowledge and learning is enough. In the academic world we solve this problem by standardization (for example, of language and refereed journals) and the self-referential creation of a body of 'salient' publications. Creative destructors, though, would have to apply a stop rule to the study of those conventions if they are not to lose their creative energy under the weight of the body of commonly accepted knowledge. Thus, paradoxically it may even be rational in a psycho-'logical' sense to exclude relevant knowledge from an innovator's horizon. The innovator needs to re-enter ignorance into the marked space of knowledge.

Another type of protective or healthy ignorance is constituted by social taboos (cf. Shattuk, 2000). Humankind could not possibly survive in peace if we were to realize how rationality referring to purpose would advise us to act, that is, if full transparency were available. For instance, it seems preferable that we do not decide on each single currency unit of public spending in a collective procedure but contribute to a general pot which is then spent by a myriad of single decisions, whose result is unveiled to the public only afterwards and in broad categories. Rational theory has suggested to rid citizens of collective taxes and to leave it to their rational decision-making whether they use a public service at individual costs (cf. Mueller, 1998). I put forward the hypothesis that this would lead to a lack of public goods. In accordance with this hypothesis, ignorance or a lack of transparency serves the purpose of sustainable production of public goods better than accurate knowledge would. In social life, many so-called 'white lies' and much diplomacy are required to maintain a delicate equilibrium of cohesion. To know our mutual thoughts would shatter this equilibrium, although to approximate this knowledge is considered helpful in many training concepts or settings which allow people to share their so far unspoken ideas. No doubt, being more open in our communications can enhance our common purposes. However, being bluntly open can also escalate conflict. As the example of people whom we consider to lack social skills and delicacy illustrates, rude intervention usually rather jeopardizes than enhances a task or problem at hand.

Concluding on the functional types of ignorance I suggest the following propositions.

3. Positive ignorance, that is keeping knowledge and learning at a focused level instead of maximizing it, is functional to the purpose that a subject of reference (individual or organization) has to achieve.
4. Protective ignorance is functional to social interaction and uncertain endeavours even when and where the knowledge, which is ignored, bears relevance to the interaction or endeavour.

The argument, of course, slides on thin ice. The propositions need to be put into practice to allow for empirical testing. We cannot be precise on the lines of separation, as they too are contingent. The delicate balance between focus and serendipity in the case of positive ignorance and between functional and dysfunctional consequences of idiosyncrasy and diplomacy on the one hand and wasteful vanity and cowardice on the other depends on the situation in which it must be handled. Therefore, in a 'future of knowledge management' we will need to research situational factors that help us to be less evasive with regard to questions which are important to practitioners.

In the next section, I will complete the picture by defining dysfunctional forms of ignorance.

4.   When ignorance is unwise

The type of inspiring ignorance which is conscious and drives our search for further knowledge is a common ground of knowledge management. Therefore I will not deal with it in this paper, but turn instead to cases where ignorance is imposed on a subject of reference by a third party. This type, which is often unconscious, is labelled 'manipulated' ignorance. Here I refer to lacks of transparency and knowledge which are due to forms of strategic communication by opportunistic actors which occur as selective 'truths', as withholding of information, as disguise and fraud. Selectivity is unavoidable, but in cases of manipulated ignorance it is applied intentionally to encourage wrong conclusions in the receiver of the selective information. Fraud and counterfeiting of facts and figures are phenomena of the business world which some authors consider pervasive (cf. Stiglitz, 2002). They may be exceptions rather than the tip of an iceberg; their more harmless forms, however, are not. Those forms are all based on strategic rather than authentic communication (cf. Habermas, 1981).[7] Opportunistic withholding, fraud and selectivity can be expected to hurt the interest of the subject of reference. Again, this is not a plea for an unlimited sharing of knowledge, where co-operation is defined as the integration of complementary capabilities. While the industrial age increased efficiency by the division of labour, the post-industrial age of a 'knowledge society' will have to increase efficiency by the division, not the sharing, of knowledge.[8] On the other hand, actors need a lot of background knowledge and common ground in order to manage the interfaces of their complementary knowledge.[9] Therefore, knowledge management has already in its early years aimed at increasing transparency, for instance of business indicators, at all levels of the company. For the future, I suggest that the prevention of manipulated ignorance become a distinct task in knowledge management. As our theories tend to idealize human behaviour we have hardly included the analysis of power and interest in our knowledge management models. This needs to be done in a 'future of knowledge management' and can be done by re-entering manipulated ignorance into the marked space of knowledge.

The last form of ignorance, as marked in this paper, is constituted by the combination of the distinctions of unconsciousness and dysfunctionality. It is labelled 'ignored' ignorance, which means not to know that one does not know. Ignored ignorance can be protective in some cases (see the arrow in Figure 5.1). Mostly, it will reduce the amount of alternatives available to an actor (subject of reference) in a situation and thus restrict his or her potential to find creative solutions to a task or problem. Ignored ignorance can express itself in defensive routines, as analysed by Argyris (cf. 1997).

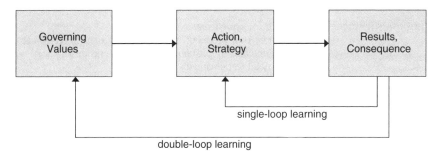

Figure 5.2   Single-loop and double-loop learning
Source: slightly modified from Argyris, 1997, p. 59)

Within the single loop individuals (and organizations) cannot detect their blind spots constituted by the programmes or frames of governing values, which are taken for granted and subconscious. Therefore, they are prevented from innovative reaction to requirements of change as in situations of strategic shift, mergers and acquisitions and reinvention in general. The high rate of failure of mergers and acquisitions as well as of change projects is an indicator that this type of ignored ignorance is detrimental to a subject's purpose of reference.

At the level of issues, ignored ignorance, such as not knowing through a process of innovation that a patent has been filed which makes the innovation obsolete, can also be detrimental. Therefore a 'knowledge management of the future' will have to re-enter ignored ignorance into knowledge management and will have to systematically create spaces where second-order observation is possible and where the search for unknown knowledge can take place on a regular basis. Table 5.1 summarizes the four types of ignorance.

Table 5.1 **Summary: Types of ignorance**

Type of ignorance	Definition	Illustrations
positive ignorance -	• to know what one does not need to know • to exclude what would distract from a focused purpose	• restrict memberships to the number of networks one can really handle • use a razor • strictly filter information
protective ignorance -	• to stop the search for knowledge where it would jeopardize action • social tabus which support social 'equilibrium'	• bold endeavours, idiosyncratic opera (e.g., PhD thesis) • white lies, diplomacy • collective 'pot' of taxes
'inspiring' ignorance	• a search for knowledge elicited by new pieces of knowledge and by problems which need to be solved in an innovative way	• science • consequences of technical and societal innovation •
'ignored' ignorance	• blind spots with regard to knowledge, which is accessible in principle • sometimes imposed by third parties, to become manipulated ignorance	• first-order observations • dogma • selective revealing, lack of transparency

5. Discussion and Conclusion

This chapter has suggested the re-entry of ignorance into the space marked by the discourse on knowledge (management). It holds that ignorance must become an important target perspective of knowledge managers in order to overcome blind spots which characterize a large portion of the over-optimistic literature on the issue (cf. Schreyögg and Geiger, 2003). Blind spots in the sense of this paper are as follows.

- The assumption that all knowledge flows in an organization are purposeful and focused at the system level. As I have tried to show, by discussing 'manipulative' ignorance, this assumption does not apply in general, but needs differentiation.
- The assumption that social capital and phenomena related to the informal organization, such as copiers and coffee corners, will enhance the purpose at the system's level by their mere existence. As I have argued, pointing to ignored, manipulated and protective ignorance, such enhancement is only one of a series of possible outcomes.
- The assumption that more is better, as in the expectation that decision-making will improve if decision-makers are provided with more information. As I tried to point out in the paragraph on positive ignorance, this assumption does not apply in an environment of fast-growing, contradictory and incommensurable knowledge.

A theory that deserves the term 'critical' has to focus on the effects and consequences of illusionary veils, that is, ignored ignorance. Such veils tend to fulfil the double function of protection and manipulation, which turns any attempt to shed light on them into an ambiguous project. Attempts to enlighten are themselves prone to falling into the trap of ignored ignorance, as they may overemphasize one-sided interpretations as in order to counterweight mainstream thinking. Therefore, the question to be asked is what benefit practitioners could take from a 'management of ignorance as a part of future knowledge management?' To supply evidence for serious economic consequences of the bad management of functional ignorance (which must be preserved) and dysfunctional ignorance (which must be fought), we will have to conduct much more research concerning the points where and conditions under which the one form turns into the other. We then have to re-enter the so far unmarked space into the marked space in theory. What that means for practice needs to be developed into a knowledge generation pattern which combines both areas.

Notes

1   Definitions and structures only serve to push ignorance to another horizon, as with each indication of one side of a distinction its other side is overshadowed.

2　It is common in management theory to introduce mathematical concepts not precisely but rather in a metaphorical manner. This may be and has been criticized (cf. among others Sokol and Bricmont, 1998). I shall keep to it never the less because of the explanatory power of metaphors, but do point out this 'mere' metaphorical meaning in accordance with the critique.

3　As I distinguish between a level of first-order observations, which follows a pattern of accumulation and a level of second-order observations, which insert recursive feedback loops so that the accumulative pattern is rearranged, linearity cannot be maintained as a condition of knowledge creation.

4　It could of course also be neutral to the purpose, that is, neither harm nor foster it. I will exclude this option because it does not influence performance.

5　At least, if information is defined as data + meaning and if the latter is considered to be determined by objective knowledge rather than subjective relevance.

6　Netiquette is defined as reflected use of e-devices: no spam, scarce use of cc and group mail functions, as well as a language that preserves a basic politeness and social glue function.

7　To draw a distinction between benevolent withholding (as parents do in order to enable the phenomenon of childhood, as Neil Postman has pointed out) and opportunistic withholding is a challenging ethical question which will not be analysed in this paper.

8　In German language, this would in both cases be translated by the same word, 'teilen', which means complementarity as well as substitution.

9　This elicits another linguistic observation. While in German and English knowledge is singular, the French language provides a plural in 'les savoirs'.

References

Argyris, C. (1997) *Wissen in Aktion: eine Fallstudie zur lernenden Organization* (Stuttgart: Klett-Cotta).

Dörner, D. (1998) *Die Logik des Misslingens. Strategisches Denken in komplexen Situationen* (Reinbek bei Hamburg: Rowohlt Verlag).

Gibbons, M., C. Limoges, H. Nowotny, S. Schwartzman, P. Scott and M. Trow (1994) The New Production of Knowledge (London: Sage Publications).

Grant, R. M. and C. H. Baden-Fuller (2004) 'A Knowledge Assessing Theory of Strategic Alliances', in *Journal of Management Studies*, 41, 1 January, pp. 61–84.

Habermas, J. (1981) *Theorie des kommunikativen Handelns, Band 2, Zur Kritik der funktionalistischen Vernunft* (Frankfurt/Main: Suhrkamp).

'How much information' (2003) http://www.sims.berkeley.edu/research/projects/how-much-info-2003/

Howaldt, J. R. Klatt and R. Kopp (2004) *Neuorientierung des Wissensmanagements – Paradoxien und Dysfunktionalitäten im Umgang mit der Ressource Wissen* (Wiesbaden).

Koza, M. P. and A. Y. Lewin (1998) 'The Co-Evolution of Strategic Alliances', *Organizational Science*, 9, pp. 255–64.

March, J. G. (1991) 'Exploration and Exploitation in Organizational Learning', in *Organization Science*, 2, 1 February, pp. 71–87.

Maturana, H. R. (1970) 'Biology of Cognition', in H. R. Maturana and F. J. Varela (1980) *Autopoiesis and Cognition: The Realisation of the Living* (Boston: Dordrecht), pp. 1–58.

Mueller, D. C. (1998) 'Redistribution and Allocative Efficiency in a Mobile World Economy', in K.-E. Schenk, D. Schmidtchen, M. Streit and V. Vanberg (eds), *Jahrbuch für Neue Politische Ökonomie*, Band 17 (Tübingen: J. C. B. Mohr), pp. 172–90.

Popper, K. R. (1991) 'Ich weiß, daß ich nichts weiß – und kaum das. Karl Popper im Gespräch über Politik, Physik und Philosophie', (Bonn: *Die Welt*, Frankfurt, A. M. Berlin: Ullstein Sachbuch).

Schneider, U. (2001) *Die 7 Todsünden im Wissensmanagement* (Frankfurt: FAZ Verlag).

Postman, Neil (1994) *The Disappearance of Childhood* (Vintage Books).

Schneider, U. (2003) 'Interorganisationales Lernen in Strategischen Netzwerken', in B. Swoboda et al. (eds), *Kooperationen, Allianzen und Netzwerke – Grundlagen, Ansätze, Perspektiven* (Wiesbaden: GWV Verlag), pp. 985–1008.

Schneider, U. (2005) *Die dunkle Seite des Wissens* (Wiesbaden: Gabler).

Schreyögg, G. and D. Geiger (2003) 'Wenn alles Wissen ist, ist Wissen am Ende nichts?! Vorschläge zur Neuorientierung des Wissensmanagements', *DBW*, 63(1), pp. 7–22.

Schumpeter, J. (1950) *Essays on Entrepreneurs, Innovations, Business Cycles, and the Evolution of Capitalism* (New Brunswick: Transaction Publishers).

Shattuk, R. (2000) *Tabu. Eine Kulturgeschichte des verbotenen Wissens* (München: Piper).

Sokol, A. and J. Bricmont (1998) *Fashionable Nonsense: Postmodern Intellectuals' Abuse of Science* (New York: Picador).

Spencer-Brown, G. (1977) *Laws of Form*, American edition with a new 'Vorwort' (New York: Julian Press) (original: London: Allen & Unwin, 1969).

Spender, J. C. (1992) 'Limits to Learning from the West', *The International Executive*, 34, September–October, pp. 389–410.

Stiglitz, J. (2002) *Die Schatten der Globalisierung* (Berlin: Siedler Verlag).

V. Foerster, H. (1993) *Kybern-Ethik* (Berlin: Merve).

Part II

Emerging Issues in Knowledge and Innovation

6
Interactive Innovation Processes and the Problems of Managing Knowledge

Sue Newell, Maxine Robertson and Jacky Swan

1. Introduction

In the early days of knowledge management both the literature and practice were relatively simplistic in orientation. Knowledge was seen as crucial in securing competitive advantage for *all* organizations and, consequently, organizations were encouraged to develop systems (often IT-based) in order to better manage their knowledge. Knowledge was typically treated as a resource, no different from any other organizational resource, such as land, labour or capital. Implicit in these approaches was the view that knowledge was a thing, or entity, located in people's heads that could, and should, be extracted, stored and circulated. Over time, however, there has been growing recognition in much of the organizational literature that this 'entitative', cognitive view of knowledge may be limited (Hosking and Morley, 1991). Recognizing these limitations, significantly more attention has been paid to conceptual developments around situated or processual views of knowledge and learning (Newell et al., 2002; Tsoukas and Vladimirou, 2001; Brown and Duguid, 2001). According to such views, knowledge is inseparable from social relationships and practice. Attention in the knowledge management literature has shifted towards addressing the organization of such relationships and practices (for example through the mobilization of social networks and 'communities of practice' – Brown and Duguid, 2001). It has also been argued that theory needs to be more sensitive to the links between knowledge management and the purposes (for example, tasks and activities) to which knowledge is being put (Hansen, 1999). For example, it has been argued that, while IT systems may support exploitation (that is, the re-use of existing knowledge and information), they are unlikely to facilitate exploration (that is, the creation of new knowledge and action – Swan et al., 2002). In this chapter we will explore, in particular, the implications for managing knowledge where the purpose is innovation.

The remainder of the chapter is structured as follows. First we outline the perspective on knowledge that we are adopting and relate this to innovation processes. Recognizing that innovation has itself been studied from a number of different perspectives, we briefly outline three different perspectives (Slappendel, 1996). In particular, we argue that innovation is best understood, not as the transfer of knowledge and physical artifacts, but as a highly *interactive process* entailing combinations and flows of knowledge among social groups and organizations seeking to develop new practices (McLoughlin, 1999; Massey et al., 1998). We then explore in more detail the nature of interactivity in innovation processes and, through empirical examples drawn from our own research over the past five years, we consider the knowledge management challenges and issues related to interactive innovation. Specifically, we focus in our analysis on the implications of different kinds of interactivity for the ways in which knowledge is created and diffused, including: interactivity between structure and agency; interactivity between different stakeholder groups and organizations; and interactivity across different episodes of the innovation process (for example, exploration and exploitation). In the light of this analysis, the final section draws some conclusions about future knowledge management theory and practice.

2.   Perspectives on knowledge

In developing our analysis we view knowledge as an integral aspect of the overall activity system of the organization (Blackler, 1995). Knowledge is not then a 'resource' that can simply be transferred (Barney, 1991); nor is it 'embedded' in organizational processes (Winter, 1987). Rather, from this perspective, knowledge is seen to emerge as people interact recurrently in the context of established (and novel) routines and procedures. Therefore, when firm members participate in organizational activities or practices, they have the potential simultaneously to create and extend the firm's knowledge (Spender, 1996; Carlile, 2002). This implies a social constructivist view of knowledge, whereby all human knowledge is developed, transmitted and maintained in social situations (Berger and Luckmann, 1966; Tsoukas and Vladimirou, 2001).

Looking more specifically at the relationship between knowledge and practice, both Nelson (1991) and Tsoukas (1996) view firms as hierarchies of routines, where most organizational knowledge is tacit and resides, not as isolated from context in the heads of individuals, but as situated in organized contexts of action. Thus, Tsoukas and Vladimirou define knowledge as 'the capability to draw distinctions, within a domain of action, based on an appreciation of context or theory, or both' (2001, p. 979). This definition highlights that knowledge is essentially related to human action (Nonaka and Takeuchi, 1995). However, in organizational settings, human action draws upon the generic rules and routines produced by the organization, hence knowledge is essentially tied to context. Moreover, each individual has only a partial view of what constitutes a particular organizational routine or practice or of the knowledge needed to design a new product or process. In other words, knowledge in organizations is distributed across social groups and communities engaged in different activities and practices (Lave and Wenger, 1991). It also needs to be acknowledged here that knowledge and learning are embedded in relationships of power and so will naturally be contested within and across communities of practice (Contu and Willmott, 2003). For these reasons, a central problem emerging during innovation is that knowledge generated in one domain does not transfer easily to another domain (Carlile, 2002).

For example, there are numerous 'breakthroughs' in scientific and technological knowledge that could drastically change medical practice. However, even where safety and effectiveness is validated (for example, through clinical trials), many such breakthroughs fail to be adopted by medical practitioners (Hilton et al., 2002). Often this is because they do not align well with existing, and highly institutionalized, professional and medical practices (Christensen et al., 2000). This means that the exploitation of scientific knowledge may require radical shifts in practices and relationships among different stakeholder groups (for example, different medical professionals, industrial scientists, academic scientists, managers, and so on). In some cases, entrenched power relationships make such shifts impossible (Hilton et al., 2002).

Innovation relies, therefore, not simply on the availability of new knowledge, but also on the ability to *integrate* knowledge across an increasingly distributed array of professional groups and organizations (Powell et al, 1996, Owen-Smith et al., 2002). As opposed to 'knowledge sharing' (that is, where groups come to appreciate and share one another's perspectives – Grant, 1996), knowledge integration emphasizes the combination and deployment of knowledge drawn from different domains in order to achieve specific innovation outcomes (for example, the development of a new product or process). This concept builds on, and extends, Okhuysen and Eisenhardt's (2002) definition of knowledge integration as a process, whereby individuals combine their information to create new knowledge. Having established our perspective on knowledge and the important role of knowledge integration in many innovations, we next consider perspectives on innovation before highlighting the challenges posed by innovation for creating and diffusing knowledge.

3. Perspectives on innovation

Innovation is used variously in the literature to describe not only both the entity or object which is new (for example, a new artifact, product or process), but also the process by which the entity is created, developed or diffused. Here we adopt the latter approach, and characterize innovation in broad processual terms as encompassing overlapping episodes of design, diffusion and implementation (Robertson et al., 1996; Alter and Hage, 1993; Clark and Staunton, 1989). Organizations appear to be more or less successful in relation to these innovation episodes, so that an organization's ability to innovate could be described as an organizational 'capability' (Zollo and Winter, 2002). At the heart of this, innovation capability is the ability to share, integrate and create knowledge within and across organizations (Spender, 1996; Grant, 1996). It follows, then, that innovation depends crucially on managing knowledge and situated learning (Lave and Wenger, 1991).

Among existing scholars that have chosen to characterize innovation in processual terms, it is also evident that very different perspectives on this process have been adopted. Slappendel's (1996) review of the innovation literature concludes that there are three major perspectives on the innovation process – the individualist, the structuralist and the interactive. These different perspectives, she argues, reflect the historical evolution of our understanding of innovation processes, with individualist perspectives being dominant in early accounts and interactive perspectives emerging more recently. Relating these to knowledge, we argue that each perspective adopts somewhat different assumptions about the nature of knowledge and knowledge management.

The individualist perspective

The individualist perspective assumes that innovation occurs through individuals making rational decisions about actions leading to specific outcomes. The focus is, therefore, on identifying characteristics of individuals that make them more likely to be innovative, for example their personality, their level of education and their cognitive style (see Rogers, 1995). This perspective places the locus of innovation at the level of the individual: the most crucial determinant of innovation is the knowledge and expertise held by the individual. Many new products, such as the bagless Dyson vacuum cleaner, associated with inventor James Dyson, are thus seen to originate from one person's genius or entrepreneurial activity and there is considerable interest in the innovation literature on the role of individual champions (Brown et al., 2004) as key determinants of successful innovation.

In relation to organizational innovation, this perspective is somewhat limited because it is apparent that within an organization there are likely to be multiple participants involved in innovation. Nevertheless, the perspective can be broadened to encompass the idea that innovation depends on the knowledge of multiple individuals who pool this knowledge to make decisions. Some of the literature also recognizes the limits to the cognitive capacities of actors (March and Simon, 1958) and so does not assume that individuals will always act rationally, that is, in their best interests.

Essentially, this amendment importantly suggests that a lack of full knowledge as possessed by an individual or group of individuals can limit or distort innovation processes.

Table 6.1 depicts the view of knowledge that underpins this individualist perspective on innovation. Thus knowledge is seen as largely embrained in the tacit understandings and cognitive processes of individual actors. The implications of such a view for managing knowledge are that these tacit understandings need to be shared and mobilized into action. This might be achieved through codification strategies (aimed at making the tacit knowledge of individuals explicit) or at personalization strategies (aimed at sharing tacit understandings through interpersonal interaction and social networks – Hansen, 1999). While there are many criticisms of this ap[...] (see Slappendel, 1996 for a review), one of its key limitations is [...]

Table 6.1   **Views of knowledge from different innovation perspectives**

	Individualist	**Structuralist**	**Interactive Process**
View of Knowledge	Embrained knowledge – in the heads of individuals	Embedded knowledge – in systems and structures	Situated knowledge sustained through and in processes of interaction among people in particular contexts
Strategy for managing knowledge	Personalization and codification	Codification	Shared practice
Mode of knowledge sharing	Through connecting individuals and/or making tacit knowledge explicit	Through organizational designs and systems, including links with other organizations	Through interactive networking, joint tasks and the formation of shared values and identities.
Knowledge stability	Knowledge stable and rationale leading to one conclusion	Knowledge stable and leading to one conclusion	Knowledge emergent from process and equivocal
Knowledge and decision-making	Individuals actively using personal knowledge to make decisions	Individuals passively responding to external influences	Individuals actively involved in the construction of the knowledge base, albeit constrained by the institutional context

privileges individual agency over structure, so ignoring (or at least de-emphasizing) the ways in which individual actors are constrained in their thoughts, behaviours and emotions by the contexts in which they exist, including group, organizational and broader institutional structures.

The structuralist perspective

This perspective on innovation has attempted to redress the limitations of the individualist perspectives by highlighting the ways in which innovation is promoted or constrained by structural characteristics of organizations, themselves embedded in wider institutional arrangements. Thus scholars have sought to establish causal relationships between structural characteristics of organizations and innovation (Damanpour, 1991), including organizational size, centralization, formalization, differentiation, professionalism and complexity (for example, the Aston Studies). However, the findings from structuralist research have been inconsistent – for example, structural complexity has been found both to increase innovation (Hage and Dewar, 1973) and to reduce innovation (Blau and McKinley, 1979). Contingency theories try to overcome these limitations by identifying the conditions in which causal relationships hold true. For example, Zaltman et al. (1973) suggest that the influence of structural variables will be contingent on whether one is focusing on the early stages of the innovation process or the later stages (initiation versus implementation). Hence, complexity may encourage initiation but it may impede implementation.

From a structural perspective, knowledge is assumed to be embedded in organizational and institutional systems and routines (see Table 6.1). The implication here is that, to manage knowledge, organizations need to be designed in such a way as to promote knowledge flows across boundaries (for example, through matrix structures or cross-functional teams). Again, rationality is stressed, since organizations are seen to adapt to their environments as appropriate to the goals of the organization. A key strength of this perspective is that it recognizes the constraining influence of social context on action. However, this is also a limitation, since it de-emphasizes the ways in which individual actors and organizations proactively shape their environment. Moreover, it fails to acknowledge that organizations and their environments are not objective realities. Rather, as Weick (1995) so eloquently points out, environments are enacted – we use our knowledge to make sense of, and construct, our environments. While there are clearly differences between individualist and structuralist perspectives, there are also some important similarities. They both adopt a 'normative-variance' approach to organizational innovation, treating innovation as a variable dependent on individual or organizational factors. Moreover, both tend to reify knowledge. Thus they assume that there are comparatively stable, codifiable bodies of knowledge (either located in the individual or in the organization) that, when pieced together, determine how, when and if innovation will happen. They also adopt a linear view of the innovation process, seeing this as dependent on the movement of knowledge from one type, or location, to another (for example, tacit to explicit – Nonaka, 1994). This linear view remains pervasive in the thinking of many managers and policy-makers, reflected in numerous initiatives aimed at the improvement of 'knowledge transfer' or the capture of 'best practice' (Massey et al., 1992; Mytelka and Smith, 2002). However, as we discuss below, there are many problems with this linear view of the innovation process.

The interactive perspective

In contrast to the linear view, an *interactive* perspective has been flagged as a more realistic way to describe innovation processes. This depicts innovation as occurring through the interactions between the practices of individuals and groups and the social contexts in which they are located. Central to this perspective is the idea that, by developing more interactive and collaborative modes of working, for example through the development of networks and joint practices, knowledge that is distributed across social and organizational boundaries can be recombined and integrated in new, often unpredictable, ways to produce new products, services and processes (Rothwell, 1994; Kline and Rosenburg, 1986). While the interactive perspective has been gaining in popularity, different authors have focused on different aspects of interactivity (for example, interaction across groups and organizations versus interaction across episodes of the innovation process). This results in conceptual confusion when considering the implications for managing knowledge. To help resolve this, we identify below three different aspects of the interactive nature of innovation processes, drawing from existing literature:

1. Interaction between structural influences and the actions of individuals

Slappendel (1996) focused on this aspect of interactivity, suggesting a duality other than the traditional dualism between structure and action (Giddens, 1984). From this perspective, innovation is influenced by, and influences, wider institutional environments. Innovation behaviour is both afforded and constrained by the organizational and institutional context. As such, any innovation is shaped by organizational and societal structures and cultures as well as by individual and group behaviour and attitudes. Similar concepts have also been advanced by students of regional economies, as for instance the theory of 'innovative milieus' (Camagni, 1995). This aspect of interactivity emphasizes that it is important to adopt a multi-level analysis when exploring any innovation process, since a focus on only one level (for example, the individual, the organizational or the institutional) will overlook reciprocal interactions between action and structure.

2.   Interaction between different phases or episodes of the innovation process

This aspect of interactivity recognizes that innovation is not a linear process from conception, through design, to implementation and diffusion but instead is typically an iterative process where recursivity is the norm and phases/episodes are conflated (Robertson et al., 1996; Clark et al., 1992; McLoughlin, 1999). Von Hippel (1988), for example, has illustrated that users can play a decisive role across all phases of the innovation process in the scientific instrument sector. Other research has shown how processes of implementation occur in parallel to, rather than following from, processes of diffusion (see, for example, Fleck's 1994 discussion of 'innofusion' in the development of manufacturing technology). This suggests the need for processual research (Pettigrew, 1985, 1990) in order to explore the dynamic and recursive nature of the production of knowledge through innovation processes over time. By contrast, the traditional linear model creates a false divide between the creation of knowledge by producers in one context and its application by users in another.

3.   Interaction between different stakeholders, within and across organizational boundaries

This aspect of interactivity stresses the involvement in the innovation process of individuals from different departments, disciplines, professional backgrounds and organizations, each with potentially a different world view (Dougherty, 1992). Empirically, authors such as Parthasarthy and Hammond (2002) show that high levels of functional integration across the whole product development process predict high levels of product innovation, hence claiming that interactivity makes a difference as a moderating factor. This suggests the need to address multiple stakeholder perspectives in understanding innovation. For example, while one group of stakeholders may assess an IT innovation project as a 'success', another group may define it as a 'failure' (Wilson and Howcroft, 2005, forthcoming).

The three dimensions of interactivity outlined above are not mutually exclusive – the interplay between the broader context and individual action, for example, will be related to the perceptions and interests of different stakeholders during the innovation process, for example. However, they are qualitatively different: the first from an appreciation of levels of analysis (individual, organizational), the second from an appreciation of temporality (innovation episodes); and the third from an appreciation of pluralism of perspectives, understandings and interests (multiple stakeholders). We can, therefore, use these different aspects of interactivity to explore the knowledge management issues and challenges that arise during innovation processes. We do this below by drawing on case examples from our own research. Given space limitations, we describe one case in detail and also provide a number of brief vignettes as illustrative examples.

4. Interactivity and knowledge management challenges – empirical examples

Case: Hospital case (Newell et al., 2003)

Midlands NHS Trust Hospital is one of a large number of Trusts in the UK that together make up the National Health System (NHS). The NHS has been under intense government pressure to improve efficiency. One of the areas targeted by the government as in need of change is the cataract diagnosis and treatment procedure. Cataract surgery, which is a 20-minute procedure, represents 96 per cent of the ophthalmology workload. In most NHS trusts, including this one, cataract diagnosis and treatment had traditionally involved the patient in a long series of visits to various specialists. Typically, patients would first go to their optometrist (the high-street optician), believing that deteriorating eyesight implied they were in need of a new prescription. However, when optometrists ascertained that the problem was actually cataracts, they would refer the patient to his or her general practitioner (GP) for a 'proper' (that is, medical) diagnosis. After a visit to the local GP who, not being an eye specialist, generally relies on the diagnosis of the optometrist, the patient would be forwarded to the hospital consultant for further examination. The patient would then go on a waiting list and would eventually be called for a brief meeting with the consultant, who would usually confirm the optometrist's original assessment. The patient would then have to make a separate appointment with a nurse for a physical examination to ensure that they were healthy enough for the surgery. Only when all of these visits were complete would the patient be placed in the queue for obtaining a date for cataract surgery. In many trusts, the lead-time for cataract surgery is over 12 months. Post-surgery, another visit to the consultant is scheduled to check on the patient and then the patient is referred back to the optometrist for a new pair of glasses. Therefore, it takes patients at least six visits and often well over a year to have a routine, 20-minute, outpatient, surgical procedure.

Given the complex and drawn-out nature of this process, a new re-engineered cataract diagnostic and treatment practice was seen as potentially beneficial by those in the Midlands NHS Trust. To facilitate that change, a designated member of the hospital's transformation team[1] was assigned to the process. This transformation team member gathered a team of eye experts from both the hospital and the community to discuss ways of reducing surgery lead times and improving patient satisfaction. Members of the cataract team included a head nurse in the eye unit, a hospital administrator, general practitioners, a set of optometrists from the local community and a surgical consultant, who was instrumental in championing the need for change and in leading the change process. Team meetings were held in the evening to facilitate attendance and were led by the transformation team member. Minutes, flow charts and other necessary documentation for the process were produced by the transformation team member and distributed to all team members after each meeting. In total, approximately five project-team meetings were held over a six-month period.

The outcome of this innovation process was that a number of changes to the existing practice were made. Visits to the patient's GP were no longer essential; the roles in the process of the consultant and the nurse were eliminated. Instead, optometrists were empowered to decide whether a patient needed cataract surgery. In doing so, they were required to fill out a detailed form that provided the consultant with specific information about the nature and severity of the cataract and to call the hospital and book a time for the patient's surgery. For their additional responsibility, the optometrists were given some extra training and received a small amount of compensation from the Trust. The preliminary pre-operation physical was replaced with a self-diagnostic questionnaire that each patient was required to fill out and return to the hospital before surgery. Nurses telephoned each patient before surgery to check the patient's details and answer any questions. Post-operation consultant appointments were also replaced with follow-up telephone calls.

The new cataract procedure resulted in a number of efficiency gains. Lead times were radically reduced from over 12 months to six to eight weeks. In addition, theatre utilization rates improved due to the addition of an administrator whose sole responsibility was scheduling theatres. Finally, and most importantly, according to follow-up phone conversations with cataract project patients, patient satisfaction improved dramatically. Moreover, busy GPS were pleased to avoid unnecessary appointments. However, attempts to diffuse this innovation to other NHS trusts were not successful.

Vignette 1:   Brachytherapy example (Swan et al., 2002)

Another good example of interactive innovation has been the development of brachytherapy treatment for prostate cancer in Europe. In contrast to traditional methods (surgery or radiation therapy), this new treatment involves irradiating the tumour from within, by accurately implanting low dosage radioactive iodine seeds directly into it. Because the treatment involves both surgical and radiological skills, multi-disciplinary teams of surgeons, radiation oncologists, general physicians and nurses need to work together in both the diagnosis and treatment of the patient. This requirement for collaborative working has been a major challenge in the development of this innovation. More specifically, in this case the major issue centred on persuading powerful groups of surgical oncologists to accept the treatment as a valid alternative to surgery and to jointly develop processes for collaborative work with, relatively less powerful, radiation oncologists.

This proved to be a challenge in part because the new treatment engendered a limited shift in the balance of professional power from the oncologists to the radiologists. Key to overcoming this challenge were the actions of the particular bioscience firm manufacturing the iodine seed implants. Instead of directly marketing their product to unwilling consumers (medical professionals) the manager in this firm went to significant effort to mobilize a new 'community of care' around the prostate cancer disease, comprising multiple professional groups and patients. Bonded by a common interest in curing the disease, this community came to share knowledge around the treatment of the disease and the practices of brachytherapy treatment.

Vignette 2:   Research team example (Newell and Swan, 2000 and Newell et al., 2001)

Exploring academic research as an innovation process provides a third example of the different aspects of interactivity involved. Newell and Swan (2000), for example, describe an academic research project, sponsored by the UK government, which involved four principal investigators and four research assistants as well as an administrator at different academic institutions in the UK. Interactivity was necessary in this project to ensure integration of knowledge, but the group failed to develop the necessary interactive practices to ensure genuine collaboration and knowledge integration. The main reason for this was that the research group was not able to overcome the knowledge boundaries created by their different disciplinary and epistemological perspectives (cf. Carlile, 2002). For example, one of the researchers came from a highly positivist tradition and another had what could be described as a weak constructivist position. These particular researchers were unable to reconcile these different positions. The outcome of the collaboration was thus relatively limited because of the research group's inability to develop a common understanding and a unifying perspective. Moreover, the difficulties which were experienced in this case were also, in part, explained by the constraints imposed on their interactive practices as a result of the institutional context (Newell et al., 2001). In particular, the funding agency required the project team to outline deliverables from the project before the research had actually been undertaken, thus restricting the degree to which knowledge could emerge out of their interaction. In addition, publications were a major basis for career advancement but the disciplinary-based educational system in the UK did not support multidisciplinary publications and so discouraged knowledge integration.

5.   Dimensions of interactivity and the production of knowledge

We can now explore the examples above in terms of the different aspects of interactivity discussed earlier.

Interactivity between structure and action

The cataract case is only explicable if we take into account the broader institutional context within which the project team was operating. Thus the NHS was striving to encourage hospital trusts to improve efficiency in key areas. This aspect of the institutional context conferred a legitimacy on the innovation that encouraged different stakeholders to become involved and to share and create the knowledge, which led to their eventually defining and introducing the new cataract diagnosis and treatment process. In this sense, then, the institutional context promoted the integration of knowledge distributed across the various stakeholders that supported the innovation process.

However, other aspects of the institutional context actually served to constrain the diffusion of this innovation. In the UK there exists a *national* health service, free to all British citizens, as well as a much smaller *private* health service for those who can pay. The interplay between the public and private services is an important structural consideration that potentially influenced the behaviour of the actors involved, constraining the diffusion of the new process. Long waiting lists for National Health Service treatment provide an incentive for some patients to opt to pay for their operation from the private service. Consultants in UK hospitals can significantly boost their incomes from their NHS work by doing private healthcare work. Reducing patient waiting lists in the NHS may not, therefore, be seen by all hospital consultants to be in their best interests, albeit from the perspective of other stakeholders this may be very beneficial. While other issues were involved in explaining the difficulties of innovation diffusion in this case (see the third subsection below), this aspect of the institutional context certainly had some influence. The institutional context thus both afforded and constrained knowledge-sharing and knowledge creation, as predicted by an interactive innovation perspective.

Similar institutional dynamics were also at play in relation to the brachytherapy case in so far as existing power structures amongst established medical professions militated against the acceptance of the new treatment. Significant efforts on the part of a medical device company marketing the equipment for the new treatment had to be made to promote the development of a new community of practice (including both oncologists and radiologists) around the disease in order to overcome the natural reluctance of the oncologists to engage with the proposed new method of treatment. In relation to the creation of knowledge by the team of academic researchers, the institutional context afforded the instigation of the research project by this particular group by providing the opportunity for a large interdisciplinary research team to be funded. At the same time however, the activities of the research team were also restricted by their institutional context. Firstly, the need to define for the funding body at the outset of the three-year project what was actually going to be produced constrained the extent to which their output could emerge from their interactions. Secondly, there were problems in relation to publishing the output from their interdisciplinary efforts because the established academic journals tend to have very strong disciplinary orientations. These constraining influences led to the research project's being divided into three separate mini-projects, each oriented to a different disciplinary perspective.

Here the theoretical lens of institutional theory (Scott, 2001) is helpful in exploring the ways in which the environment shapes (and is shaped by) knowledge integration processes that support innovation. Institutional theorists focus on understanding the ways in which innovations arise and diffuse across an organizational field (for example, DiMaggio and Powell, 1983), recognizing that the seeds of change are located both inside and outside the institutions. In particular, institutionalists examine how when regulative, normative and cultural-cognitive elements become misaligned, tensions arise that produce divergent schemas and recipes for action. Thus, institutionalists recognize the need to incorporate multiple levels of analysis, as Scott (2001) so clearly states: 'Social actions and structures exist in dualistic relation, each constraining and empowering the other. And social structures are themselves nested, groups within organizations or networks of organizations, organizations within fields, fields within broader societal and trans-societal systems. Although every study cannot attend to all levels, analysts should be aware of them and craft designs to include critical actors and structures engaged in maintaining and transforming institutions' (p. 203).

Interactivity between different stakeholders

The cataracts case indicates the importance of engaging in shared practice in generating knowledge for successful innovation. The process of re-engineering the cataract diagnostic and treatment procedure involved building meaning out of often conflicting and confusing data. This was only possible by bringing together a number of different stakeholders with different knowledge and understandings who were willing to work together in the project and share their (largely tacit) knowledge. Here a crucial aspect of the 'new' knowledge created was a holistic overview and understanding of the cataract practice, as it currently existed, which could then be re-engineered. This knowledge did not exist before the formation of the project team – each professional group had only a partial view of what constituted the particular routine or practice (Shani et al., 2000; Tsoukas, 1996) – and so had to be generated through interaction and negotiation. Bringing together individuals from different professional backgrounds was necessary in order that each group could understand and appreciate the skills and capabilities of other groups. Without this collective practice, the knowledge and understanding of the different groups would have remained unconnected and isolated, and preconceived notions of the limits of the professional competence of others would not have been challenged.

This case example echoes Boland and Tenkasi's (1995) observations about the importance of being able to understand the perspectives of 'others' (perspective-taking) in multi-disciplinary teams. More importantly they stress the need for developing a shared perspective (perspective-making) across the team for successful outcomes. In the cataracts case, the team did achieve this shared perception of the whole process and could then reconfigure which professional groups should take responsibility for different aspects of the process. Through the exchange within the project team, all of the professional groups involved in the process also started to recognize the value of, and under-utilization of, the optometrists' skills and expertise. Thus, micro-level shifts in the relative power of different professionals occurred through the practices of working together on this particular problem. Without this type of interactivity, the innovation process could not have moved forward. This accords with the conclusions of Fitzgerald et al. (2002). They also emphasize – again analysing the adoption and diffusion of innovations within health care – how knowledge is not 'objective' but tends to be continually contested and negotiated, particularly because of the presence of multiple professions. This results in adoption decisions being 'weighed', in the sense that different criteria – not just 'objective' scientific evidence – are balanced against each other and crucially shaped by networks and opinion leaders. The research team and the brachytherapy examples similarly show the influence of the contested and negotiated nature of situated knowledge on innovation processes, to the extent that in the research team example the team members were not really able to innovate because they were simply unable to develop trust in each other's ideas, coming as they did from different disciplines and epistemological positions.

Here, theoretical lenses of social constructivism (for example, Tsoukas and Vladimirou, 2001) and related frameworks on communities/networks of practice (for example, Brown and Duguid, 2001; Lave and Wenger, 1991), which emphasize the social embeddedness of knowledge, are useful. These literatures are linked by their attention to the processes of *validating* or *legitimizing* knowledge: they assume that knowledge claims ('truths') are co-constituted with political interests and institutionally embedded within network structures (Contu and Willmott, 2003). Therefore, understanding political, social and professional structures and practices surrounding the production and integration of knowledge during innovation processes is important.

A community of practice is defined as 'an activity system about which participants share understandings concerning what they are doing and what it means in their lives and their community' (Lave and Wenger, 1991,

p. 98). A critical feature of such communities is that they emerge spontan-eously through shared practice and are therefore typically made up of people from many functions, cutting across formal organization structures and hierarchies. These multi-disciplined arenas share a common identity and so provide fertile ground for the open exchange of knowledge and learning within and across organizations (Lesser and Everest, 2001). Brown and Duguid (2001) argue, therefore, that communities of practice are important arenas for local invention because they engage in constant improvisation in order to traverse the limitations of both the formal organ-ization and canonical practice. Evidence of the positive effects of communit-ies of practice and networks of practice on innovation comes from examples of local adaptations of work practices among, for example, scien-tists and technicians, in response to new problems (Orr, 1996; Brown and Duguid, 2001).

However, communities of practice can also produce barriers to innova-tion as they interpolate different identities and world views that may con-strain knowledge integration across communities (Swan et al., 2002). Thus knowledge leaks within communities of practice but sticks across them (Brown and Duguid, 2001). This can potentially have important conse-quences for interactive innovation that involves stakeholders from differ-ent communities of practice coming together (Hage and Hollingsworth, 2000). Here, then, it is likely that the constraining effects of communities of practice are likely to be more acute (Brown and Duguid, 2001; Swan et al., 2002). This aspect of interactivity therefore disrupts existing communit-ies, as was the case in the brachytherapy example (Swan et al., 2002). Thus where interactivity involves bringing together multiple professional and organizational groups, innovation relies as much upon the *dis*-embedding of existing knowledge/practice as it does upon the creation of new know-ledge (Giddens, 1984). However, as the research team vignette illustrated, the influence of these professional communities can, at times, be so strong that knowledge integration is not achieved.

The focus on knowledge legitimization emphasizes that interactive inno-vation is intimately tied up with social regimes of power. In line with our epistemological stance, power is not treated as a property of a particular individual or group, but as co-constituted with social practice and networks of social interaction (Callon, 1986). Thus, as seen in the brachytherapy case, biomedical knowledge is contested as medical professionals and scientists, with particular vested interests, seek to sustain power and control within their own knowledge domains and over their own work practices (Friedson, 1970; Abbott, 1988; Drazin, 1990). It follows that existing pow-erful networks, such as professions, are in the position to shape innovation processes that require the integration of knowledge across such networks (Brown and Duguid, 2001; Hage and Hollingsworth, 2000).

Interactivity between different episodes of the innovation process

The project described in the cataract case appeared to be successful in part because of the strong championing and leadership provided by the consultant involved. In addition, the transformation team provided resources and expertise to facilitate the knowledge generation process. Together, these factors suggest that the Midlands Hospital Trust provided a very 'receptive context' for innovation (Pettigrew et al., 1992) that was not provided in other trusts.

However, there is, we argue, a more fundamental reason why innovation diffusion did not occur. Specifically, our analysis leads us to conclude that knowledge of the new cataract diagnosis and treatment process could not readily transfer to other contexts because knowledge diffusion does not occur independently of, or in sequence to, knowledge generation. Specifically, in the Midlands Trust diffusion of the idea coincided with the development of social processes and practices needed to generate the idea. The practice of the diagnosis and treatment of cataracts was sustained by the interaction of the various collective actors and existed only through this social interaction (Gherardi and Nicolini, 2000). As Cook and Brown (1999) observe, it is groups, not individuals, that possess the 'body of knowledge'. Once developed, the new practice was captured in the form of a template for 'best practice' and made available to other NHS hospital trusts. However, when others considered the new template, they dismissed it as 'unworkable' in their context. Those in other trusts had not experienced the knowledge generation processes and, therefore, had come to appreciate neither how the whole cataracts treatment process worked nor the skills and interests of different stakeholders. As a consequence, they could not understand how the knowledge generated (the template for best practice) could apply in their own context. In Boland and Tenkasi's (1995) terms, the professionals in other trusts had not sought to develop a collective or shared perspective on the new practice (perspective-making) and so could not apply the template that had been generated at Midlands Hospital (Rowley, 2000).

This implies that, for diffusion to be successful in other trusts, it would need to have been accompanied by a knowledge generation process in the new context, which would allow those involved to understand how to apply the knowledge generated. This mirrors Szulanski's (1996) finding that absorptive capacity is the biggest impediment to the internal transfer of knowledge or innovation diffusion. Szulanski's finding highlights our contention that any given work practice is culturally mediated and, therefore, is the outcome of a web of knowledge formed through social participation, material working conditions and negotiated interpretations (Star, 1996). In this 'other' context, pre-existing ideas about normal practice limit the absorptive capacity of those involved (Cohen and Levinthal, 1990). For example, consultants that had not been through the knowledge generation process undertaken in the Midlands Trust were working from the assumption that 'opticians cannot accurately diagnose cataracts'. Acceptance of a new practice, which renders obsolete these taken-for-granted assumptions, is unlikely (Orlikowski, 2000), highlighting the need for interactivity across the different episodes of an innovation process.

Here, then, we can return to our assumptions about the nature of knowledge. In this chapter a social constructivist view of knowledge was adopted, which assumes that knowledge is essentially situated in, and inextricable from, social processes and practices (Berger and Luckmann, 1966). This situated view is often seen to be incommensurable with a view that sees knowledge as a resource, property or entity possessed by an individual, group or organization (Nonaka, 1994). Nevertheless, Cook and Brown (1999) have recently tried to bring these two views of knowledge together. They suggest that both views are useful and simply represent two different, albeit related, underpinning epistemologies: the epistemology of possession (knowledge) and the epistemology of practice (knowing). It is, they suggest, the 'generative dance' between knowledge and knowing that is important. Thus, knowledge as something possessed must be practised in a specific context to be meaningful. In this sense, knowledge is a 'tool of knowing' (Cook and Brown, 1999), making knowledgeable action, or knowing, possible.

This suggests that there are two complementary ways of looking at knowledge, each with different implications for knowledge management. Thus the epistemology of possession implies that tacit knowledge can be made explicit and transferred (for example, through the use of IT systems) independently of practice. In contrast, the epistemology of practice implies that knowledge management needs to allow the generation of new shared practice, or a shared context for knowing (Tsoukas, 1996). That said, it is important to recognize that knowledge is always a combination of tacit and explicit knowledge (Polanyi, 1966). While the knowledge as possession school tends to argue that tacit knowledge can be made explicit, Cook and Brown (1999) make it clear that tacit and explicit knowledge are inherently different and cannot simply be converted from one form to the other. Tsoukas (1996) frames this differently when he argues that tacit and explicit knowledge are mutually constituted. Thus we need both tacit and explicit knowledge to be able to engage in any given activity or practice and we need tacit knowledge to make sense of explicit knowledge. For example, in the NHS case the explicit knowledge about the new cataract practice made no sense to those who had not transformed their implicit understanding of the roles and responsibilities of different groups involved in the cataract process. The recognition that knowledge is a possession, and yet is also inherently embedded in practice, is helpful and suggests that both views of knowledge are valid. Thus, while these views suggest different approaches to managing knowledge, they are not necessarily mutually exclusive, and might even be complementary.

6.   Conclusions: Challenges for future research and practice

Our discussion of the issues and challenges of sharing and integrating knowledge to support innovation processes leads us to conclude that future research and practice on knowledge management, where the purpose is innovation, must unpack the different dimensions of interactivity explored here. Thus our analysis suggests that knowledge management research and practice needs to address different levels of analysis (interactivity between agency and structure), multiple stakeholder perspective (interactivity between different stakeholders) and the episodic nature of the innovation process (interactivity across innovation episodes).

In terms of the importance of exploring different levels of analysis, our examples have demonstrated the need to understand the creation of knowledge in innovation as a 'cultural practice' that is shaped by macro-level institutional and organizational arrangements and the actions of individuals and groups (Murray, 2001). Consequently, there is a need for a multi-level approach to knowledge management that is able to tease out the constraints and opportunities for knowledge management created by institutional and organizational contexts. For example, simply fostering links across professions (for example, through interdisciplinary fora or networks) may not result in knowledge integration where the organizational and/or institutional context reinforces separation between the practices of those professionals

In relation to multiple stakeholders, our examples have illustrated how innovation often involves stakeholders from different professions, disciplines and communities/networks of practice, each with their own particular norms, expectations and practices surrounding how knowledge is produced and legitimated (Knorr-Cetina, 1999). These differences in understanding create problems for knowledge integration, as we have seen in the example of our research team as well as in the brachytherapy case. This implies that knowledge management theory and practice needs to address the values, assumptions and invested practices that underpin the knowledge that different stakeholders hold (Carlile, 2002). For example, Robertson et al. (2003) found that lawyers are more likely than scientists to rely on codified forms of information in creating knowledge and explain this in terms of epistemic differences between these professional groups (Halliday, 1985). This has important implications for managing knowledge, since it implies that some groups (for example, legal professionals) may be more likely to respond favourably to codification strategies than others (for example, R&D professionals) because these align better with their existing work practices and values.

Finally, we have discussed the importance of addressing the episodic nature of the innovation process and the interactivity between design, diffusion and implementation. Much existing theory and practice in knowledge management is still heavily underpinned by linear assumptions regarding the production of knowledge – that is, that knowledge produced in one context can be more or less directly transferred to another (for example, Hansen, 1999). While there is much debate surrounding the appropriate vehicle for knowledge transfer in different contexts (for example, whether it should be IT systems or social networks), the assumptions of linearity still remain. In contrast, the interactivity between innovation episodes highlighted here suggests that the real challenge for knowledge management is to abandon these linear assumptions. What, for example, would a knowledge management initiative look like if the starting assumption were that knowledge transfer is impossible?

Note

1   The transformation team is a set of eight individuals who are charged with re-engineering hospital processes within this particular Midlands Trust. Other current projects include a national initiative on lead-time reduction, a project on diabetes and eyes and a project on hip replacement surgery. At any one time, numerous re-engineering projects are underway at the trust.

References

Abbott, A. (1988) *The System of Professions* (Chicago: University of Chicago Press).

Alter, C. and J. Hage (1993) *Organizations Working Together* (Newbury, PA: Sage).

Barney, J. (1991) 'Firm Resources and Sustained Competitive Advantage', *Journal of Management*, 17, 99–120.

Berger, P. L. and T. Luckmann (1966) *The Social Construction of Reality: A Treatise in the Sociology of Knowledge* (New York: Doubleday).

Blackler, F. (1995) 'Knowledge, Knowledge Work and Organisations: An Overview and Interpretation', *Organisation Studies*, 16(6), 1020–1047.

Blau, J. and W. McKinley (1979). 'Ideas, Complexity and Innovation', *Administrative Science Quarterly*, 24(2), 200–20.

Boland, R. J. and R. V. Tenkasi, (1995) 'Perspective Making and Perspective Taking in Communities of Knowing', *Organization Science*, 6(4), 350–72.

Brown, D., P. Booth and F. Giacobbe (2004) 'Technological and Organizational Influences on the Adoption of Activity-Based Costing in Australia', *Accounting and Finance*, 44(3), 329–47.

Brown, J. S. and P. Duguid (2001) 'Knowledge and Organization: A Social-Practice Perspective, *Organization Science*, 12(2) 198–213.

Callon, M. (1986) 'The Sociology of an Actor-Network: The Case of the Electric Vehicle', in J. Law and A. Rip (eds), *Mapping the Dynamics of Science and Technology* (London: Macmillan).

Camagni, R. (1995) 'The Concept of Innovative Milieu and its Relevance for Public Policies in European Lagging Regions', *Papers in Regional Science*, 74(4), 317–340.

Carlile, P. R., (2002) 'A Pragmatic View of Knowledge and Boundaries: Boundary Objects in New Product Development', *Organization Science*, 13(4), 442–55.

Christensen, C., R. Bohmer and J. Kenagy (2000) 'Will Disruptive Innovations Cure Health Care?', *Harvard Business Review*, September/October, 102–12.

Clark, P. and N. Staunton (1989) *Innovation in Technology and Organization* (London: Routledge).

Clark, P., S. ewell, P. Burcher, S. Sharifi and J. Swan (1992) 'The Decision-Episode Framework and Computer-Aided Production Management', International Studies of Management and Organization, 22, 69–80.

Cohen, W. M. and D. A. Levinthal (1990) 'Absorptive-Capacity – A New Perspective on Learning and Innovation', *Administrative Science Quarterly*, 35(1), 128–52.

Contu, A. and H. Willmott (2003) 'Re-embedding Situatedness: The Importance of Power Relations in Learning Theory', *Organization Science*, 14(3), 283–97.

Cook, S. D. and J. S. Brown (1999) 'Bridging Epistemologies: The Generative Dance between Organizational Knowledge and Organizational Knowing', *Organization Science*, 10(4), 381–400.

Damanpour, F. (1991) 'Organizational Innovation: A Meta-analysis of Effects of Determinants and Moderators', Academy of Management Journal 34, 555–90.

DiMaggio, P. and W. Powell (1983) 'The Iron Cage Revisited: Institutional Isomorphism and Collective Rationality in Organizational Fields', *American Sociological Review*, 48, 147–60.

Dougherty, D. (1992) 'Interpretive Barriers to Successful Product Innovation in Large Firms', *Organization Science,* 3, 179–202.

Drazin, R. (1990) 'Professionals and innovation: Structural-Functional versus Radical-Structural Perspectives', *Journal of Management Studies*, 27(3), 245–63.

Fitzgerald, L., E. Ferlie, M. Wood and C. Hawkins (2002) 'Interlocking Interactions: The Diffusion of Innovation in Health Care', *Human Relations*, 56(12), 1429–50.

Fleck, J. (1994) 'Learning by Trying: The Implementation of Configurational Technology', *Research Policy*, 23, 637–52.

Friedson, E. (1970) *Professional Dominance: The Social Structure of Medical Care* (New York: Atherton).

Gherardi, S. and D. Nicolini (2000) 'The Organizational Learning of Safety In Communities of Practice', *Journal of Management Inquiry*, 9(1), 7–18.

Giddens, A. (1984) *The Constitution of Society: An Outline of the Theory of Structuration* (Cambridge: Polity).

Grant, R. (1996) 'Prospering in Dynamically-Competitive Environment: Organizational Capability as Knowledge Integration', Organization Science 7, 375–87.

Hage, J. and R. Dewar (1973) 'Elite Values versus Organizational Structure in Predicting Innovation', *Administrative Science Quarterly*, 18(3), 279–91.

Hage, J. and J. Hollingsworth (2000) 'A Strategy for the Analysis of Idea Innovation Networks and Institutions', *Organization Studies*, 21, 971–1004.

Halliday, T. (1985) 'Knowledge Mandates: Collective Influence by Scientific, Normative and Syncretic Professions', *British Journal of Management*, 36(3), 421–48.

Hansen, M. T. (1999) 'The Search Transfer Problem: The Role of Weak Ties in Sharing Knowledge across Organizational Sub-Units, Administrative Science Quarterly, 44, 82–111.

Hilton, T., J. Flanzer, W. Cartwright and B. Fletcher (2002) 'Resistance to Innovation among US Drug Abuse Treatment Providers: When Organizational Knowledge Interferes with Organizational Learning', paper presented at the Organizational Knowledge, Learning and Capabilities Conference, Athens, 4–6 April.

Hosking, D. and I. Morley (1991) *The Social Psychology of Organizing* (London: Harvester Wheatsheaf).

Kline, S. and N. Rosenburg (1986) 'An Overview of Innovation', in R. Landau and N. Rosenburg (eds), *The Positive Sum Strategy* (Washington: National Academic Press), pp. 275–306.

Knorr-Cetina, K. (1999) *Epistemic Cultures: How the Sciences Make Knowledge* (Cambridge, MA: Harvard University Press).

Lave, J. and E. Wenger (1991) *Situated Learning: Legitimate Peripheral Participation* (Cambridge: Cambridge University Press).

Lesser, E. and K. Everest (2001) 'Using Communities of Practice to Manage Intellectual Capital', *Ivey Business Journal*, 65(4), 37–42.

March, J. and A. Simon (1958) *Organizations* (New York: Wiley).

Massey, D., P. Quintas and D. Wield (1992) *High Tech Fantasies: Science Parks in Society, Science and Space* (London: Routledge).

McLoughlin, I. (1999) *Creative Technological Change* (London: Routledge).

Murray, F. (2001) 'Following Distinctive Paths of Knowledge: Stretegies for Organizational Knowledge Building within Science-based Firms', in I. Nonaka and D. Teece (eds), *Managing Industrial Knowledge: Creation, Transfer and Utilization* (London: Sage) pp. 182–201.

Mytelka, L. and K. Smith (2002) 'Policy Learning and Innovation Theory: An Interactive and Coevolving Process', *Research Policy*, 31(8–9), 1467–80.

Nelson, R. (1991) 'Why Do Firms Differ, and How Does it Matter?', *Strategic Management Journal*, 12, 61–74.

Newell, S. and J. Swan (2000) 'Trust and Inter-organizational Networking', *Human Relations*, 53(10), 1287–1328.

Newell, S., J. Swan and K. Kautz (2001) 'The Role of Funding Bodies in the Creation and Diffusion of Management Fads and Fashions', *Organization*, 8(1) 97–120.

Newell, S., M. Robertson, H. Scarbrough and J. Swan (2002) *Managing Knowledge Work* (London: Palgrave).

Newell, S., L. Edelman, H. Scarbrough, J. Swan and M. Bresnen (2003) '"Best practice" Development and Transfer in the NHS: The Importance of Process as well as Product Knowledge', *Journal of Health Services Management*, 16, 1–12.

Nonaka, I. (1994) 'A Dynamic Theory of Organizational Knowledge Creation', *Organization Science*, 5, 14–37.

Nonaka, I. and H. Takeuchi (1995) '*The Knowledge-Creating Company* (Oxford: Oxford University Press).

Okhuysen, G. and K. Eisenhardt (2002) 'Integrating Knowledge in Groups: How Formal Interventions Enable Flexibility', *Organization Science*, 13, 370–86.

Orlikowski, W. (2000) 'Using Technology and Constituting Structures: A Practice Lens for Studying Technology in Organizations', *Organization Science*, 11(4), 404–28.

Orr, J. (1996). *Talking about Machines*. ILR Press, Ithaca NY.

Owen-Smith J., M., Riccaboni, F. Pammolli and W. Powell (2002) 'A Comparison of US and European University–Industry Relations in the Life Sciences', *Management Science*, 48(1), 24–43.

Parthasarthy, R. and J. Hammond (2002) 'Product Innovation Input and Outcome: Moderating Effects of the Innovation Process', *Journal of Engineering and Technology Management*, 19, 75–91.

Pettigrew, A. M. (1985) 'Contextualist Research: A Natural Way to Link Theory and Practice', in E. E. Lawler(ed.), *Doing Research that is Useful in Theory and Practice* (San Fransisco: Jossey-Bass), pp. 222–274.

Pettigrew, A. M. (1990) 'Longitudinal Field Research on Change: Theory and Practice', *Organization Science*, 1(3), 267–92.

Pettigrew, A. M. E. Ferlie and L. McKee (1992) Shaping Strategic Change (London: Sage).

Polanyi, M. (1966) *The Tacit Dimension of Knowledge* (London: Routledge and Kegan Paul).

Powell, W., W. Koput and L. Smith-Doerr (1996) 'Interorganizational Collaboration and the Locus of Innovation: Networks of Learning in Biotechnology', *Administrative Science Quarterly*, 41(1),116–30.

Robertson, M., J. Swan and S. Newell (1996) 'The Role of Networks in the Diffusion of Technological Innovation', *Journal of Management Studies*, 33(3), 333–60.

Robertson, M., H. Scarbrough and J. Swan (2003) 'Knowledge Creation in Professional Service Firms: Institutional Effects', *Organization Studies*, 24(6), 831–858.

Rogers, E. (1995) *Diffusion of Innovations*, 3rd edition (New York: Free Press).

Rothwell, R. (1994) 'Towards the Fifth Generation Innovation Process', *International Marketing Review*, 11, 7–31.

Rowley, J. (2000) 'From Learning Organization to Knowledge Entrepreneur', *Journal of Knowledge Management*, 4(1), 7–15.

Scott, W. (2001) *Institutions and Organizations,* 2nd edition (Thousand Oaks, CA: Sage).

Shani, A. B., J. A. Sena and M. W. Stebbins (2000). 'Knowledge Work Teams and Groupware Technology: Learning from Seagate's Experience', *Journal of Knowledge Management*, 4(2), 111–124.

Slappendel, C. (1996) 'Perspectives on Innovation in Organizations', *Organization Studies*, 17(1), 107–29.

Spender, J.-C. (1996) 'Organizational Knowledge, Learning and Memory: Three Concepts in Search of a Theory', *Journal of Organizational Change Management*, 9, 63–78.

Star, S. L. (1996) 'Working Together: Symbolic Interactionism, Activity Theory and Information Systems', in Y. Engestrom and D. Middleton (eds), *Cognition and communication at work* (Cambridge: Cambridge University Press), pp. 296–318.

Swan, J., H. Scarbough and M. Robertson (2002) 'The Construction of 'Communities of Practice' in the Management of Innovation', *Management Learning*, 33, 477–96.

Szulanski, G. (1996) Exploring Internal Stickiness: Impediments to the Transfer of Best Practice within the Firm', *Strategic Management Journal*, 17, 27–43.

Tsoukas, H. (1996) 'The Firm as a Distributed Knowledge System: A Constructionist Approach', *Strategic Management Journal*, 17, 11–25.

Tsoukas, H. and E. Vladimirou (2001) 'What is Organizational Knowledge?', *Journal of Management Studies*, 38(7), 973–93.

Von Hippel, E. (1988) *The Sources of Innovation* (New York: Oxford University Press).

Weick, K. (1995) *Sensemaking in Organizations* (London: Sage).

Wilson, M. and D. Howcroft (2005, forthcoming) 'Power, Politics and Persuasion in IS Evaluation: A Focus on 'Relevant Social Groups'', *Journal of Strategic Information Systems*, 14(1).

Winter, S. G. (1987) 'Knowledge and Competence as Strategic Assets', in D. J. Teece (ed.), *The Competitive Challenge: Strategy for Industrial Innovation and Renewal* (New York: Harper & Row), pp. 159–184.

Wolfe, R. (1994) 'Organizational Innovation: Review, Critique and Suggested Research Directions', *Journal of Management Studies*, 31, 405–31.

Zaltman, G., R. Duncan. and J. Holbek (1973) *Innovations and Organizations* (New York: Wiley).

Zollo, M. and S. Winter (2002) 'Deliberate Learning and Evolution of Dynamic Capabilities', *Organization Science*, 13(3), 339–352.

7
Knowledge Management and the Emerging Organizational Models of Distributed Innovation: Towards a Taxonomy

Emanuela Prandelli, Mohanbir Sawhney and Gianmario Verona

1. Introduction

One of the managerial advances that have resulted from the widespread deployment of information and communication technologies (in particular, the Internet) is the ability to greatly enhance a firm's innovation capacity by leveraging external knowledge resources. While the importance of absorbing external knowledge to support innovation has been understood for some time (for example, Cohen and Levinthal, 1990), firms have historically been limited in their ability to reach beyond their boundaries for innovative ideas for several reasons, including the absence of open standards for communication and the idiosyncrasy of knowledge (Arora and Gambardella, 1994). Consequently, the inter-organizational division of innovative labour has traditionally been limited to a few specialized industries, such as biotechnology (Shan et al., 1994; Powell et al., 1996), pharmaceuticals (Cockburn et al., 2000) and the automotive industry (Langlois and Robertson, 1992; Dyer and Nobeoka, 2000).

This situation began to change dramatically with the emergence of the Internet as an open, global and ubiquitous platform for communication. The Internet has opened new doors to firms seeking to create new organizational mechanisms to support their innovation processes. Enhanced connectivity through the Internet, for instance, allows different actors in the markets to become contributors and collaborators in the process of innovation (Iansiti and MacCormack, 1997; Prahalad and Ramaswamy, 2004). Online customer toolkits that enable leading-edge customers to provide input into innovation can greatly reduce the cost and improve the speed and quality of the innovation process (Von Hippel, 2001; Dahan and Hauser, 2002; Piller et al., 2004). Internet-enabled virtual environments offer firms new avenues to interact with suppliers (Thomke and Kuemmerle, 2002) and Internet-based communities have emerged as a powerful mechanism for enabling a highly decentralized innovation activity involving large numbers of independent contributors (Sawhney and Prandelli, 2000;

Chesbrough 2003; Von Krogh 2003). In summary, while many innovation practices and activities are still rooted in physical environments and within the four walls of the firm, the Internet is emerging as an important channel to enhance a firm's innovation capacity. Freed from the constraints of geographical proximity, the Internet greatly extends a firm's capacity to create, collect and combine knowledge by collaborating with its customers, partners and independent third parties. In so doing, it facilitates the creation of new approaches to support innovation in an open, decentralized and geographically distributed manner.

In this chapter, we investigate the emerging phenomenon of *distributed innovation*. We formally define distributed innovation as *activities in support of innovation involving a division of labour among independent and geographically dispersed actors that are enabled by information and communication technologies*. These independent actors can be firms, individual customers, communities or thirdparty organizations. While there has been a lot of recent academic and managerial interest in the areas of open innovation and distributed innovation, the literature in this domain lacks an organizing frame to map the different types of mechanisms to support distributed innovation. We address this gap by providing a detailed description of distributed innovation mechanisms, including mechanisms such as co-creation with customers, communities of creation, open source systems and virtual knowledge brokers. We also develop a framework for classifying these mechanisms based on two dimensions – the form of governance and the nature of collaborative knowledge created through the mechanism. We then provide a detailed discussion of one specific mechanism for facilitating distributed innovation: virtual knowledge brokers (VKBs). VKBs are Internet-based entities who connect, recombine and transfer knowledge among various actors to support the innovation process for firms. These independent entities collect dispersed individual and collective knowledge and distribute it to firms after organizing and elaborating it to support innovation. We discuss how VKBs are becoming important actors in facilitating distributed innovation in a wide range of industries.

The rest of this chapter is organized into three key sections. First, we review the extant literature on distributed innovation and open innovation and describe four important mechanisms for distributed innovation. Next, we focus on VKBs as a key mechanism to facilitate *mediated* distributed innovation and we present a taxonomy for classifying VKBs. We present detailed case studies for the different types of VKBs in the taxonomy. We conclude by outlining promising directions for future research in this nascent area.

2. Literature on distributed innovation: A review and a frame

The Internet has several characteristics that make it an excellent platform to support the new product development process. First, the Internet is a far more open and ubiquitous network relative to previous proprietary networks such as EDI (Afuah, 2003). It is a global medium with unprecedented reach, so independent actors can connect and collaborate without regard to constraints of time and geography (Cairncross, 1997). Second, virtual environments break the age-old trade-off between richness and reach in interactions (Evans and Wurster, 1999). In the physical world, communicating (and absorbing) rich information requires physical proximity or face-to-face communication, while sharing information with a large audience entails a compromise in the quality of the dialogue. Therefore, the number and the quality of ties that firms can develop in the physical world are limited by the trade-off between richness and reach. In virtual environments, firms can overcome this trade-off and create ties with a large number of actors without compromising on the richness of the ties. Third, positive network externalities create further incentives to extend the number of relations (Downes and Mui, 1998). On the supply side, the incremental cost to reach a new participant progressively tends to decrease, because fixed costs are far higher than variable costs in communication networks (Shapiro and Varian, 1998). As a result, firms have an incentive to attract new customers. On the demand side of the network, customers gain more value in a network as the number of users of the network increases (Gladwell, 2000), favouring the emergence of a virtuous cycle. According to the so-called Metcalfe's Law, the value of a network increases in proportion to the square of the number of people using it (see Downes and Mui, 1998). Thus the first player to achieve a critical mass of customers can potentially achieve dominance.

These properties substantially change the traditional assumptions concerning knowledge creation in support of innovation. Firms can capture distributed knowledge for innovation more directly from customers, partners or other firms. They can do so cheaply, quickly and globally. And they can tap into social knowledge that is created in communities of customers and partners (Sawhney and Prandelli, 2000).

The literature on distributed innovation has emerged at the intersection of several functional disciplines, including marketing, technology, R&D management and organization science. To organize our review of the literature, we identify two key dimensions to classify the various forms of distributed innovation mechanisms that can be crossed to create a two-by-two matrix (see Figure 7.1). The first dimension is the *form of governance* of the innovation process. Some scholars who have studied the process of distributed innovation assume a firm-centric model, where a single firm is the central actor, creating connections around itself with customers or partners. Other authors take a market-centric or community-centric perspective. In this case, the locus of the innovation process is the market itself and the innovation mechanism emerges organically as independent actors come together to collaborate. The second dimension is the *nature of collaboration* between the actors that contribute to the innovation process. Some distributed innovation mechanisms focus on a traditional form of collaboration,

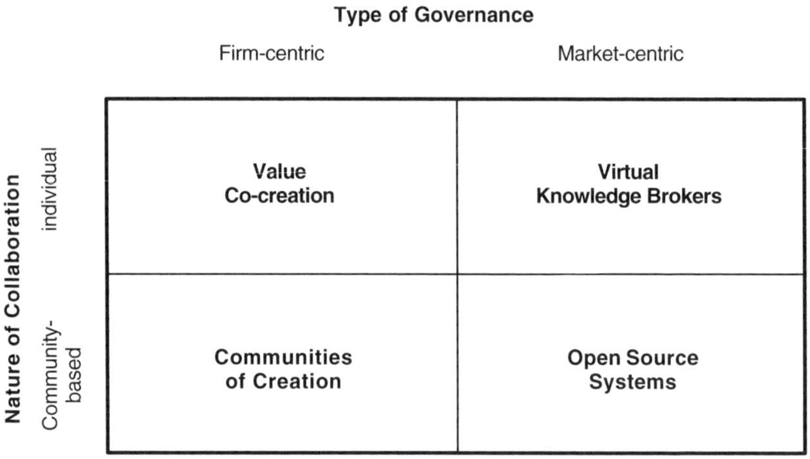

Type of Governance

Firm-centric   Market-centric

Value **Co-creation**		**Virtual** **Knowledge Brokers**
Communities **of Creation**		**Open Source** **Systems**

Nature of Collaboration — individual / Community-based

Figure 7.1   A framework for classifying models of distributed innovation

where the firm collaborates with actors in the market (customers, suppliers or partners) on an *individual basis*. Other mechanisms involve a *community approach*, where it is the web of relations among the different actors that becomes the focus of attention.

By crossing these two dimensions, we arrive at four key mechanisms for distributed innovation:

- value co-creation;
- communities of creation;
- virtual knowledge brokers;
- open source systems.

In the remainder of this section, we review the characteristics and the functioning of each mechanism and thereby derive the implications for managing distributed innovation.

2.1   Value co-creation

The model of value co-creation is based on the idea that firms can create superior products and services by collaborating with customers in the process of creating new products and services (Prahalad and Ramaswamy, 2004). Firms can benefit from the competences and insights of their customers by integrating them in co-creation of unique value (Prahalad and Ramaswamy, 2004). Instead of just working *for* customers to deliver value to customers, the co-creation model suggests that firms work *with* customers to jointly create value.

While collaboration with customers can benefit many of the firm's marketing processes, including customer relationship management, e-commerce, customer support and brand management, most scholars have focused on co-creation – collaboration with customers in the process of new product development (for example, Griffin and Hauser, 1993; Thomke and von Hippel, 2002; Dahan and Hauser, 2002). In many markets, including medical devices, computers, automobiles and mechanical equipment, leading-edge customers can contribute significantly to the creation of new ideas, new product concepts and product designs (Von Hippel, 2001). Collaborating with lead users can be very useful in markets with a segment of sophisticated customers (Stevens and Burley, 1997), in markets where the firm can learn from iterative market experimentation (Lynn et al., 1996); and in settings where customers can contribute insights through non-verbal channels (Zaltman, 1997). In advanced applications of co-creation, companies can directly involve customers in new product development using a participatory approach (Anderson and Crocca, 1993) or emphatic design (Leonard-Barton and Rayport, 1997). The application of this greater customer knowledge enhances the innovation process and allows the company to improve its external fit, since it can better anticipate market changes and satisfy market needs (Leonard-Barton and Rayport, 1997). Recent contributions to the literature show how web-based tools can simplify these activities by making it easier to manage systematic interactions with a select group of customers at a low cost (See Nambisan, 2002). These tools can include customer toolkits to support open innovation that allow customers to design and develop their own products in an Internet-enabled environment. For instance, Piller et al. (2004) describe how a customer toolkit can help customers to develop customized games for mobile phones without any advanced technical knowledge.

Firms such as Procter & Gamble have reaped significant rewards by making collaborative innovation with a wide variety of external actors an integral part of their innovation strategy. P&G calls this approach the 'Connect and Develop' strategy – where P&G looks for 'illogical', 'unpredictable' and 'unobvious' connections that link technologies in unexpected ways to create breakthrough innovations in products, processes and packages (Sakkab, 2002). The external connections that P&G pursue include connections with customers, critical supplier partnerships, universities, start-up technology firms and national laboratories. The Connect & Develop strategy has been credited with breakthroughs suchs as the Crest SpinBrush, an electric toothbrush that P&G acquired from four Cleveland-based entrepreneurs. The SpinBrush sells for $5 and has become the best-selling toothbrush in the United States, producing hundreds of millions of dollars in revenues (Chesbrough, 2003).

2.2   Communities of Creation

The community-centric model shifts the locus of innovation beyond the relationship between the individual customer and the firm, to a *community of individuals and firms* that collaborate to create joint intellectual property. This model relies on the well-known idea that knowledge is socially constructed (for example, Schmitt, 1994; Nonaka and Takeuchi, 1995; Von Krogh and Roos, 1995; Goldman, 1999), so knowledge creation can be significantly enhanced through participation in 'communities of practice' (for example, Brown and Duguid, 1991; Wenger, 1998). While communities of practice do not have to be Internet-based and the idea of communities of practice pre-dates the Internet, such communities have traditionally been considered mechanisms to catalyse situated (Lave and Wenger, 1991) and distributed (Sproull and Kiesler, 1991) learning within the individual organization, in some cases serving as an alternative to teams (Wenger and Snyder, 2000).

Virtual communities of practice focused on new knowledge creation, called *communities of creation*, allow the social creation of knowledge to extend far beyond the boundaries of the firm. The community of creation is a governance mechanism for managing innovation that lies between the hierarchy-based (closed) mechanism and the market-based (open) mechanism for innovation management (Sawhney and Prandelli, 2000). It blends the benefits of hierarchies and markets, by offering a compromise between too much structure (in a hierarchy) and complete chaos (in a free-for-all market). It overcomes the lack of co-ordination typical of markets, while emphasizing the contribution to a shared project of all contributors. Within the community, explicit knowledge as well as tacit knowledge can be shared, because participants build up a common context of experience, allowing them to socialize knowledge developed in specific contexts (Nonaka and Konno, 1998).

This mechanism seems particularly relevant at a time when knowledge is the main source of economic rents and new knowledge is being created at a furious pace. The turbulent markets at the time of writing demand speed and flexibility, variety and cohesiveness. They also demand collaborative knowledge creation with players that are outside the direct control of the firm. In such a context, the focus shifts from minimizing transaction costs for the individual firm (Williamson, 1985) to maximizing transactional value created by networks of firms, in order to increase the 'net present value of exchange relationships' (Zajac and Olsen, 1993). Thus, inter-organizational strategies – extended also to customers – that have greater joint value may be more effective in order to enhance the potential for innovation, even though they may involve the use of less efficient governance mechanisms from a transaction cost perspective. To this end, instead of designing rules that embody fixed decisions, the firm needs to act as a co-ordinator, designing rules that enable flexible decision-making, as in the 'agoric open systems' originated in the software industry for collaborative software creation (Miller and Drexler, 1988).[1]

In order to work properly, a community of creation requires a specific set of ground rules for participation. A key challenge is to create incentives for participation and co-operation within the community by recognizing the contribution of any actor who shares his knowledge assets (Kozinets, 1999). To preserve a semblance of order, a co-ordinator is also needed, as well as screening mechanisms to avoid misleading contributions. The community of creation functions like a 'gated community', where residents move about freely inside the community, but only if they satisfy some pre-specified access rules. The governance structures for a community of creation are informal, but this does not mean that they are necessarily weak (Hagel and Singer, 1999). In some cases, control can be based on restricting access to the best information assets. The community also needs a sponsor who defines the architecture and the standards around which the community is organized. The sponsor facilitates the interaction and assures that the emergent organization is both efficient and effective. Finally, a system for managing intellectual property rights is required (Thurow, 1997). To favour co-operation in knowledge creation, the property rights of *ideas*, and not only of their *expressions*, have to be recognized. New mechanisms are needed which recognize that the most innovative ideas are often the output of a joint process, within which it is difficult to discern the specific contributions of single actors. As a consequence, intellectual property rights vest in the community that creates innovation, instead of belonging to individual contributors within the community. The community-centric innovation model is more democratic than the traditional hierarchical innovation model, because it empowers peripheral players, giving them the right to contribute their own experiences and individual knowledge to the final output (Sawhney and Kotler, 2001).

2.3 Virtual knowledge brokers

VKBs are the virtual manifestation of knowledge brokers – third parties who connect, recombine and transfer knowledge to companies in order to facilitate innovation (Hargadon and Sutton, 2000). While firms can improve innovation by engaging directly in virtual environments, they need to augment *direct* virtual connectivity – namely, self-managed virtual environments – with *mediated channels* that can facilitate innovation (Verona et al., 2005). In the physical world, knowledge brokers take the form of innovation and design consulting firms (Sutton, 2002; Hargadon, 2003). In the virtual world, however, such brokers are more diverse, the scope of their activities is broader and their potential impact on the innovation process can be greater. VKBs are firms that operate in virtual environments and play a knowledge-brokering role that involves absorbing both market and technical knowledge to support innovation. Internet-based brokers like CNET.com, Homestore.com and Edmunds.com have evolved into VKBs in the technology, home ownership and automobile markets, respectively by gathering information on industry-specific products and organizing communities of interests around these indus-tries. Building upon their initial role of information intermediaries or *Infomediaries* (Hagel and Singer, 1999), they are evolving into innovation intermediaries or *Innomediaries* (Sawhney, et al., 2003). VKBs gather dis-persed individual and collective knowledge and distribute it to firms after organizing and elaborating it to support innovation. Firms are interested in this knowledge for at least two different reasons. First, they are constrained by their cognitive limits and their core competences (Leonard-Barton, 1992), and their peripheral vision often does not extend beyond their served markets. Second, their reach is physically limited by geographical and indus-trial boundaries (Sawhney et al., 2003). By working on a global and inter-industrial basis, VKBs can greatly enhance the reach and richness of connections between firms and actors who can provide knowledge to support innovation.

The activities of VKBs are characterized by four key processes: (1) network access; (2) knowledge absorption; (3) knowledge integration; and (4) know-ledge implementation. Through network access, VKBs have access to new forms of knowledge that might interest a third party for innovation pur-poses. The VKB's ability to extend the web of relations with different actors in the market improves the effectiveness of network access. The second process refers to knowledge absorption. After accessing the source of new knowledge, a VKB needs to internalize this knowledge and make the knowledge its own. This internalization requires it to possess an absorptive capacity (Cohen and Levinthal, 1990). The third process has to do with knowledge integration that allows the new absorbed knowledge to be com-bined with existing knowledge and stored in the VKB's organizational memory. Finally, knowledge implementation helps the VKB to deliver the solution to the customers that it serves. Network access is strongly empow-ered by the Internet and its ubiquitous reach. The Internet's unique proper-ties also positively influence the processes of knowledge absorption, integration, and implementation.

2.4   Open source systems

Open source systems (OSS) represent a specific evolution of virtual com-munities, completely run by and for users to mutually provide technical advice (Constant et al., 1996) and to create new products or services (Kogut and Metiu, 2001; Von Hippel, 2001; Von Hippel and Von Krogh, 2003b). They are based on the joint development of knowledge and innovation brought into being by several independent individual actors. In open source programs, individual users do not have to develop everything they need on their own, but can benefit from others' freely shared contributions.

In order to understand the OSS innovation model, it is important to briefly trace its origin. The usage of open source-based mechanisms origin-ated in the software industry, where many thousands of free and open-source software developed in time (See Fielding, 1999). Specifically, the history of OSS dates back to the early days of computer programming (Raymond, 1999). Initially, software development was carried out independently or jointly by technicians on a free basis. The knowledge needed to develop and maintain software was difficult to come by, so when individuals needed a specific bug fix or an upgrade they developed the practice of freely giving and exchanging software they had written. This became a part of the hackers' culture (Von Krogh and von Hippel, 2003b). However, it was a major event that brought the birth of an official movement: the creation of a new licence called GPL (General Public License) by Richard Stallman, a scientist at MIT's Artificial Intelligence Laboratory. Stallman found it offensive that software developed throughout this 'open' practice was then licensed to a company that commercially released it, thereby limiting the opportunity to use it as a platform for further development. Consequertly, he founded the Free Software Foundation, with the specific objective of developing a legal mechanism that would allow software developers to preserve the free status of the software by using a specific copyright that would allow a number of rights to future users (Von Krogh, 2003). These rights imply that any user may obtain a copy at no cost and then legally study its source code, modify it and distribute it to others, also for free (Lakhani and von Hippel, 2000).

Some time during 1998, the name of the movement changed 'open softwer' instead of 'free software', because this more accurately reflected its intent – open access to innovation. The OSS movement took off after this point, fuelled by the growth of the Internet as a global medium to connect actors participating in OSS projects like Linux and Apache (Kogut and Metiu, 2001). By 2003, more than 10,000 OSS projects involving more than 300,000 individuals were in progress (Von Krogh, 2003).

The OSS model is a fundamental advance in the management of distributed innovation, because it is an open model that contrasts significantly with the traditional proprietary or closed model of managing innovation (Chesbrough, 2003). The openness and inclusiveness of the OSS model make it far less susceptible to the limitations of closed innovation models, including self-referentiality, limited resources and natural limits on skills that a single firm can garner under one roof. In order to allow the OSS mechanism to work effectively, some important conditions have to be met (Von Hippel, 2001). First, at least some users should have sufficient motivation to innovate, that is, the expected benefits of innovating should exceed their costs of participation. Second, at least some users should have an incentive to voluntarily reveal their innovations and the means to do so. Finally, user-led diffusion of innovations should be able to compete with commercial production and distribution, often through for-profit firms who provide installation, maintenance and support services that complement the open source products. In fact, it was not until large commercial players like IBM, HP and Intel put their support behind open source software products such Linux that the OSS ecosystem really began to take off. These technology giants contribute technology, marketing, complementary products and software professionals to the Linux ecosystem. IBM alone has 600 programmers dedicated to Linux, and almost 90 per cent of all contributions to Linux come from programmers who work at for-profit technology companies (Hamm, 2005).

The conditions that must be satisfied to sustain OSS systems require more investigation in future research along many dimensions. First, the system of incentives to contribute to the process of innovation has not been clearly articulated. While some authors suggest that career incentives can provide an important stimulus to contribute to the process (Lerner and Tirole, 2003; Von Hippel and Von Krogh, 2003b) and enhancement to one's own reputation and expectations of reciprocity, together with commitment to the group and the awareness of affecting the environment, can represent powerful incentives (Kollock, 1997), still much of the reputation-based incentives have to be disclosed. Second, the evolution pathways for the governance of OSS projects are still unclear. For instance, the Linux ecosystem, while very decentralized, had until recently been very tightly and dictatorially controlled by Linus Torvalds, the author of Linux. More recently, the governance has been delegated to a community called Open Software Development Labs (OSDL) and a team of experts overseen by Torvalds. This change in governance suggests that as OSS projects become more global, more complex and more commercially important, some elements of hierarchy may need to be introduced into the community-based governance model to prevent the fragmentation of the community. Third, even if OSS mechanisms have been extended beyond the software industry to other industries involving the development of physical products, such as in the sportswear industry (Von Hippel, 2001), the OSS model is still largely confined to the software industry. The OSS model seems to be less viable for contexts where components of a new product cannot be created, delivered and assembled over the Internet. This may represent an important limitation that needs to be overcome for the adoption of the OSS model in different industries.

2.5 Towards etherarchical approaches

In Table 7.1, we summarize the four different mechanisms for distributed innovation and provide a summary of the key properties of these mechanisms. The main differences among the mechanisms go beyond the two dimensions that define their identity, namely the type of governance and the type of collaboration. For instance, the type of knowledge they help generate may range from unstructured information and ideas for innovation to completely developed solutions. The interaction needed to support the creation of such knowledge can be spot or continuous, depending upon the firms' needs and the customers' competences. Further, the incentives offered to contributors may also be different across the mechanisms. Opinion leadership and reputation may be adequate pay-off to stimulate participation in OSS and in communities of creation, where the sense of belonging is a significant motivator. More concrete incentives may be required to stimulate involvement in value co-creation and virtual knowledge brokerage activities, wherein participants may want something of tangible value in return for their participation.

Table 7.1 **Models of distributed innovation**

	Value Co-creation	**Communities of Creation**	**Open Source Systems**	**Virtual Knowledge Brokers**
Governance	Firm-centric	Firm-centric	Market-centric	Market-centric
Collaboration	1-to-1	Community-based	Community-based	1-to-1
Incentives of collaboration	Early access to new products, influence over innovation, economic incentives	Reputation and passion	Career; reputation	Specific fees
Type of outcome	Data and competences through self-designed products	Insights or specific knowledge for innovation	Chats ('free talk') or products ('free beer')	Specific codified knowledge for innovation (e.g. patents, licenses, products)
Type of Interaction	Spot. Based on the firm's contingent needs	Continuous. Based on ground rules for participation	Spot or continuous on the basis of individual available competences	Spot or continuous on the basis of the network of firms' contingent needs
Examples	Siemens, P&G	Ducati, Sun Microsystems	Linux, IBM Alphaworks	Innocentive; Yet2; TechEx
Limitations	Knowledge from individual customers	Bias of the firm as community coordinator	Public knowledge, industry-specificity	Knowledge delivery

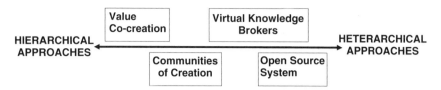

Figure 7.2   The governance continuum for models of distributed innovation

An important implication of these considerations is that each mechanism supports different types of innovation and in different ways. Therefore, the different mechanisms complement each other. Hence, a firm that wants to pursue competitive advantage through innovation on an ongoing basis should employ a portfolio of such mechanisms to overcome limitations of specific mechanisms.

The four modes also present different elements of governance and are characterized by different degrees of involvement of external actors. Based on this distinction, we can arrange them along a continuum from hierarchical approaches to etherarchical approaches (See Figure 7.2). Models of co-creation are characterized by a strong degree of autonomy and hence can be considered analogous to hierarchical models typical of the classic approach of innovation management. The more we move to community-based models, from communities of creation to VKBs and OSS, the more the mechanism looks like an etherarchical approach, characterized by emergent and unplanned behaviour.

3.   VKBs: Towards a taxonomy

While there is a rich academic literature on value co-creation, OSS and communities of Creation, the mechanism of VKBs has just started to be discussed. Therefore, it is important to analyse this mechanism in more detail. In contrast with other distributed innovation mechanisms, the VKB model is characterized by the presence of a dedicated individual operator (the firm that brokers the knowledge for innovation) that relies on a one-to-one relation with the firm that wants to innovate. Based on primary research across a range of industries, research based on secondary data and document analysis,[2] we have identified four types of VKBs:

- innovation marketplace;
- customer network operator;
- technology marketplace;
- community network operator.

Degree of Specialization

	Back-end	Front-end

transaction	**Technology Market place** Tech-ex Yet2 Pharmalicensing	**Customer Network Operator** ComScore Networks Nielsen Netratings
solution	**Innovation Market place** e.g. Innocent NineSigma	**Customer Community Operator** e.g. Edmunds Gizmodo

Type of Relationship

Figure 7.3   A taxonomy of virtual knowledge brokers

As Figure 7.3 shows, some of these VKBs help at the front-end of the innovation lifecycle, providing insights into the market and customers, while other VKBs are more useful at the back-end of the process. Another key difference among various types of VKBs is that some of them provide pre-packed knowledge that is not customized to the specific needs of a specific firm, while others work on a customized basis on the specific solutions requested by a client firm. Next, we discuss each of the four types of VKBs in more detail.

3.1   Technology marketplace

The technology marketplace operator employs a 'many-to-many' mechanism whose purpose is to connect sellers of technology with potential buyers. The type of knowledge available for sale is the specialized expertise of professionals which has already been pre-codified, typically through patents or licences that are made public on a dedicated website. The key characteristics of these VKBs is the ability to connect demand and supply on existing relevant problems related to innovation for which possible solutions are already available in the broad inter-industrial technology market. These operators make money based on a transaction fee for buying a selected technology or intellectual property. Many of these operators also collect fees related to the opportunity to transact. Technology suppliers may be asked for a fee to post their technology on the website; buyers may be asked for a membership fee to get access to a database of technology solutions available for sale. While most technology marketplaces are inter-industrial, these VKBs tend to focus on industries that rely heavily on patents (for example, chemical, biotech and pharmaceuticals). To study this type of VKB in more detail, we focus on two such entities – Yet2.com and TechEx.

Yet2.com was founded in 1999 in Cambridge, Massachusetts and in a short period of time it became the biggest worldwide market for patents. Specifically, it has extensive experience in matching demand and supply for intellectual property assets: from patents to complete packages of technology and know-how. The purpose is to allow all parties to maximize the return on their investments. Whether the users are working with a team of their licensing experts or they are using the virtual technology marketplace, Yet2.com offers companies and individuals the tools and expertise to acquire, sell, license and leverage valuable intellectual assets. In 2002 Yet2.com was bought by Schiper Plc, a British company leading in patent- and product-licensing across Europe. With over 80,000 users, in December 2004 Yet2.com represented more than 30 categories, from chemicals to new materials, from electronics to consumer goods. As a technology marketplace, the company is a traditional many-to-many operator, where seekers of specific technologies may find sellers of patents. Sellers can remain anonymous until they have qualified a buyer and they can set restrictions, exercise listings at any time and accept only the introductions they consider adequate. Potential buyers can be supported in their search for a specific technology by services such as the 'Free patent search', which allow users to save, manage and organize their patent search, and the 'Consult with an expert', which provides professional consulting and expert witness services from over 10,000 industry experts covering 30,000 areas of science, engineering, regulation and business. Seekers of specific technologies can remain anonymous, but they have to provide some information such as company type, annual revenue, years in business and geographic area of their activity. The TechNeed Challenge periodically highlights TechNeeds that individuals and their organization may be able to meet. A description of the required technology is provided, together with a desired timeframe, the field of use and intended application and the desired outcome. Among the customers that sponsor and use the website are large companies like 3M, AlliedSignal, The Boeing Company, The Dow Chemical Company, DuPont, P&G and other international companies such as Toyota Motors and Bayer.

TechEx has built a network of research and licensing professionals in the biomedical industry, providing a virtual marketplace for buying and selling biomedical technologies in five main areas: agriculture, chemicals, diagnostics, genomics and medical equipment. Founded at Yale University at the end of the 1990s and acquired by UTEK Corporation in May 2002, TechEx is used by thousands of technology transfer and research professionals to efficiently exchange licensing opportunities and innovations available for partnering. It is considered a premier source for emerging technologies in the biomedical field. New discoveries from corporate, government and academic laboratories are listed at Techex.com every day. These technologies are immediately compared against the interests of the world's leading biotechnology development organizations to ensure the fastest communication of biomedical breakthroughs. TechEx is a members-only system and is restricted to approved users. There are three types of participants: licensing professionals from research institutions; corporate licensing professionals capable of bringing early-stage inventions to market or otherwise providing significant value-added development; and venture capitalists capable of providing financial assistance to commercialization efforts. At the buyer end, corporate licensing professionals and venture capitalists establish a confidential and secure interest profile describing licensing opportunities of interest to them. They can specify the applications or pathologies they are particularly interested in, define the development stage (from discovery to Phase II), set geographical limitations and define technological sources (for example, research centres or corporations only). At the seller end, research institutions and corporations with technologies to license provide non-confidential descriptions of their technologies. They have to specify the industry where these technologies are applicable, the licensing conditions and the type of partnership they are interested in. TechEx matches opportunities with interests and sends complete information to all parties. The total number of inventions made available on TechEx is close to 7800; over 600 corporations and 340 research institutions participate in the marketplace. A division of UTEK – Pax Technology Transfer Ltd. – operates in Europe to assist local clients. Another *ad hoc* organizational unit has been created to serve the Asian market. TechEx has two main revenue sources: an annual fee ($2500) and a fee per listing ($250). As an option, users can also pay a pre-defined amount of money to gain unlimited access to the TechEx website and its services. There are no commissions on completed transactions and non-profit institutions do not have to pay a fee per listing. Universities can also create 'Gateway' websites for free to sell their own technologies and buy new ones. For instance, Harvard University has set up the Harvard Biomedical Community Technology Gateway to aggregate and provide visibility to all the research activities run by Harvard in the biomedical field.

3.2   Innovation marketplace

An innovation marketplace is also a 'many-to-many' operator. In this case, the innovations are typically intellectual property – a discovery, patent, or kind of know-how. The main difference between these VKBs and the technology marketplace is that the innovation marketplace works on a customized basis to provide *ad hoc* transactions for specific customers. In so doing, it goes beyond offering a pre-packed technology or patent, by providing solutions on request and consulting services related to innovation. To understand how innovation marketplace operators function, consider an example from the pharmaceutical industry. Businesses in this industry are constantly searching for ways to improve the speed and lower the cost of their innovation process. In June 2001, Eli Lilly created an Internet-based platform called InnoCentive that would support innovation by facilitating direct dialogue between the company on one side and lead users and communities of experts on the other. InnoCentive quickly evolved into an innovation marketplace by acting as an independent third party to connect a broad range of 'solution-seeker' companies with a vast base of potential problem-solvers. InnoCentive operates as a subsidiary of Eli Lilly. It is managed by an autonomous team and it is located in Andover, Massachusetts, far from its Indianapolis-based parent. Although InnoCentive started with small-molecule synthetic chemistry problems, within a year of its formation it had expanded its innovation services to the pharmaceutical, chemicals, biotechnology, agribusiness and consumer product sectors.

InnoCentive's approach is very different from the way contract research is typically outsourced. Its process comprises four steps. First, scientists review the problems posted by companies in need of solutions. The details of each problem include a molecular structure, problem specifications, the cash incentive and the deadline for submission of proposed solutions. Next, if scientists wish to participate in the competition, they register on site as potential problem-solvers. In the third step, they choose a specific problem to work on, sign the agreement that transfers ownership of the resulting intellectual property to the company and get a project room where they can deploy their work, either as individuals or as members of a team. The project room is a virtual space on the site that allows scientists to post submissions, store documents and conduct conversations with the seeker company in order to get clarifications or further details about the challenge. Eventually, they can upload a proposed solution in their project room. In the final step, InnoCentive reviews all the proposed solutions, determines the best one that can be reproduced in a laboratory and awards a cash prize to the scientist or team that came up with the winning solution.

For seeker companies, InnoCentive is a cost-effective, convenient and speedy mechanism for tapping into scientific knowledge distributed across the globe. It allows them to expand their research and development capacity flexibly, without adding to employee costs. And since all payments are contingent upon satisfactory solutions, companies incur no additional expenses as more and more solvers take on a specific problem. Further, because scientists from diverse disciplines and locations can address the innovation challenges, problems that were deemed unsolvable have been conquered by scientists from very different disciplines who have taken unconventional approaches to solving problems from outside their fields. For potential problem-solvers, InnoCentive provides an easy and quick way to find challenging problems that match their experience and expertise and offer the promise of a financial reward. By June 2003, more than 10,000 scientists from 105 countries had registered on InnoCentive's website, with more than half of that number from outside the United States. Over 3000 project rooms had been opened and 14 awards had been announced, ranging from $2000 to $75,000; several dozen more awards were in the pipeline. Scientists who participate include retired researchers, university professors, researchers working for independent clinical research organizations and even scientists working for non-competing pharmaceutical firms. Although the cash payments are modest by US standards, they are significant for scientists from developing countries. The satisfaction of solving a difficult problem also seems to motivate many scientists to participate in InnoCentive challenges. Innovation marketplace operators like InnoCentive blend the benefits of the distributed mechanism that are central to the success of the open-source approach to innovation with those that come from having a sponsor organization that co-ordinates the marketplace, sets the ground rules, gains trust and creates incentives for participation. The innovation marketplace operator maintains the balance between structure and chaos that is so important in managing distributed innovation.

3.3 Customer network operators

While the Technology marketplace and the innovation marketplace work on the back-end of the innovation process, the other two VKBs work at its front-end with the specific objective of importing the voice of the customer to facilitate the early stages of the innovation process. Customer network operators are like online versions of market research vendors that operate customer panels. They support innovation by recruiting and maintaining networks of customers and providing companies with access to specific customer segments for the purpose of soliciting feedback. Customer network operators are most useful in the stages of concept testing or test marketing, when firms want to know how customers will react to new product concepts or new products. Firms interact with customers through surveys or by monitoring purchase behaviour, so the knowledge they obtain is explicit rather than tacit. In other words, they can use the VKB to find out what customers 'know they know' and what they actually purchase, but not what they know but can't express directly or what they do without being fully aware of their behaviour.

An example of a customer network operator is the online market research company ComScore Networks. ComScore has recruited a global sample of more than 1.5 million panelists who have agreed to have their Internet behaviour confidentially and anonymously monitored. The company uses this large panel to provide information to companies about their customers their competitors' customers or prospective customers; it tracks what people buy, how often, from which sites and how they respond to online advertising and marketing offers. ComScore aggregates the panelists' online buying information and combines it with data about their offline buying behaviour (gleaned from such sources as retail-store scanners and credit card databases) to create a 'customer knowledge platform' – a 360-degree view of the surfing and buying behaviour of customers over the entire Internet. In addition to general customer buying behavior, comScore offers a 'private network service' to companies that want to understand and interact with specific customer segments. To set up a private network, comScore recruits a panel of customers in accordance with the client's needs and then monitors their Internet activities. Companies can use private networks to test alternative new product concepts, marketing offers and marketing communications with a select group of customers located within a 'walled garden'. The company also allows its private network clients to conduct surveys so that they can collect preference and perceptual data in addition to behavioural data.

3.4   The customer community operator

While customer network operators help companies to import knowledge from individual customers, they cannot help with knowledge that is generated through interactions *among* customers. The customer community operator is a VKB that specializes in connecting firms with customers who form a community based on common interests. Community Operators commonly begin life as infomediaries, creating communities in order to facilitate transactions. They then evolve into a VKB role. They are particularly useful at the ideation stage in the innovation process, when companies are trying to understand customer lifestyles, motivations and unmet needs. They are also valuable at the product design stage, when product designers and managers need to communicate and collaborate with customers to optimize their designs. Community operators can also help companies to identify and profile influencers and opinion leaders within a customer population, to shape the opinions of early adopters and to accelerate the diffusion of new products through word of mouth or 'word of mouse'.

An example of a community operator is Edmunds (www.edmunds.com), an infomediary that empowers automotive customers to make better buying and ownership decisions by providing detailed and unbiased information for automobile buyers. Edmunds focuses on editorial content and community management, and generates revenues by referring qualified leads to marketing partners that include auto dealers, manufacturers and finance and insurance companies. More recently, Edmunds has begun to play the role of a VKB. It realized that its community-named Town Hall could actually be a valuable resource for its automobile OEM partners. It now allows automobile OEM executives to host discussions as guests or to answer questions posed by customers. OEM product managers can even create their own sub-communities about, for example, a new model that they may be bringing to market in the future. Some automotive companies have gone further, creating private communities for which they pay Edmunds a monthly fee to host and run their part of the site. For instance, Edmunds' partners like Subaru have begun to make use of its million-strong customer community to obtain specific feedback from a diverse group of customers regarding their products. This feedback is analysed and repackaged by Edmunds to suit Subaru's specific knowledge needs and to support its new product development activities. By partnering with Edmunds, Subaru can maximize the quality of customer contributions and filter out less insightful conversations. When Edmunds hosts live chat events, it is able to engage more than 200 participants per session, who act as a clinical group, providing comments and advice about products and product experiences to product managers, who can intervene to appropriately stimulate their knowledge-sharing. Beyond operating *ad hoc* virtual communities, Edmunds also offers Edmunds Information Solutions to automotive manufacturers, which provides competitive intelligence, consideration sets, customer preferences and buying behaviour to support the new product development and product-marketing processes for automotive OEMs. In this way, Edmunds helps OEMs to connect with customers who are more committed, active and informed than those who visit websites run by individual manufacturers.

In a similar way, but in a different industry, the community operator Liquid Generation (www.liquidgeneration.com) provides information useful to firms interested in better understanding teenagers who belong to the so-called 'Generation Y', a segment whose economic importance is growing. When the company was founded in August 2000, it planned to create a portal and generate revenue through advertising and selling merchandise. However, soon the firm realized that the real opportunity laid in addressing problems faced by every firm that seeks to market to teenagers: understanding the fickle needs of this population and motivating hard-to-reach teenagers to provide information about their needs and preferences. The website functions as an entertainment site that hires young people who understand the culture and can interact effectively with the target demographic that the company wants to involve in deep conversations. This content is analysed and interpreted by Liquid Generation to answer its clients' needs of specific feedback and ideas related to individual products. For instance, one of the firm's clients – a company that makes stuffed shirts – wanted to survey the age group about a new product and its most appropriate attributes. Liquid Generation incorporated the survey questions into a funny online presentation, leveraged its relationships with 3.5 million unique visitors a month and in about 36 hours was able to provide relevant customer input to its client.

4.   Conclusion

In this paper we have tried to explore alternative organizational modes for innovation. Our argument is rooted in the emerging trend of dividing the innovative labour beyond the boundaries of the firm. The complexity of products in several industries and the difficulties related to the management of the organizational competences for innovation has spurred firms to explore new avenues for supporting innovation. Thanks to the Internet, firms can today leverage new solutions that extend their innovation capacity and provide creative alternatives to the traditional hierarchical model with which innovation has been conceived since the seminal description of the so-called Schumpeterian entrepreneur (Schumpeter, 1917). The management of knowledge to support innovation in today's environment requires a geographically distributed and diverse set of actors that use the Internet to collaboratively create knowledge.

We have identified four different organizational modes (namely, value co-creation, communities of creation, VKBs and OSS) for distributed innovation. We have also explored VKBs as an important new mechanism for facilitating mediated distributed innovation. Through detailed case studies, we have highlighted how VKBs extend a firm's reach and the richness of interaction that it can have with technological as well as market sources of knowledge.

We hope that future research will explore these different models for distributed innovation and provide further insights into how the different mechanisms complement each other and their relevance to different industry and market contexts. In today's fast-paced competitive business environment, firms must produce a constant stream of innovations. By harnessing the power of distributed innovation enabled by the Internet, firms can rise to the innovation challenge and outpace competitors in the never-ending race for competitive advantage.

Notes

1   An agoric system is a software system using market mechanisms, allowing for software to be distributed across and to serve different owners pursuing different goals. The proponents of agoric systems argue that decentralized planning is potentially more rational, since it involves more minds taking into account more information. However, the agoric system is more complex than classic decentralization, because decentralization has to be combined with a central direction of resource allocation. Therefore, a hierarchical structure remains the basic governance mechanism for co-ordinating knowledge socialization processes, but these processes are fed and catalysed with the contribution of the market for transaction types that are not effectively supported within hierarchical organizations (Miller and Drexler, 1988).

2 There is little academic literature on the organizational experience of firms that play as VKBs. Hence, we adopt an exploratory approach by which to derive patterns and implications. We have followed the logic of grounded theory (Glaser and Strauss, 1967), by employing a multiple-case study methodology (Eisenhardt, 1989; Miles and Huberman, 1994). In the tradition of other qualitative approaches used in business research, we rely on a small number of highly visible examples of the object of our inquiry to develop our insights (Pettigrew, 1990). The companies we selected are intensively leveraging the Internet to engage actors for third parties' innovation purposes. Our case studies were based upon a series of in-depth interviews with senior managers. The interviewees within each firm were chosen on the basis of their specialized knowledge and experience, following a key informant approach (Philipps, 1981; Kumar, et al., 1993). In-depth interviews were conducted during 2003 and early 2004. The approach was non-directive, based on individual semi-structured interviews (McCracken, 1990) that are flexible, but also controlled (Burgess, 1982). An open-questions frame helped us in categorizing the key themes. The analysis also included a detailed archival and Internet data collection based on financial statements, internal documents and industry publications.

References

Afuah, A. (2003) 'Redefining Firm Boundaries in the Face of the Internet: Are Firms Really Shrinking?', *Academy of Management Review*, 28(1), 34–53.

Anderson W. L. and W. T. Crocca (1993) 'Engineering Practice and Co-development of Product Prototypes', *Communications of the ACM*, 36(4), 49–56.

Arora, A. and A. Gambardella (1994) 'The Changing Technology of Technological Change: General and Abstract Knowledge and the Division of Innovative Labor', *Research Policy*, 23, 523–532.

Brown J. S. and P. Duguid (1991) 'Organizational Learning and Communities-of-Practice: Toward a Unified View of Working, Learning and Innovation', *Organization Science*, 2(1), 40–57.

Burgess, R. (1982) 'The Unstructured Interview as a Conversation', In R. Burgess (ed.), *Field Research: A Sourcebook and Field Manual* (London: George Allen and Unwin) pp. 107–110

Cairncross, F. (1997) *The Death of Distance: How the Communication Revolution will Change our Lives.* (Boston: Harvard Business School Press).

Chesbrough, H. W. (2003) 'The Era of Open Innovation', *MIT Sloan Management Review*, Spring, 35–41.

Cockburn, 1., R. Henderson, and S. Stern, (2000) 'Untangling the Origin of Competitive Advantage?', *Strategic Management Journal*, 21, Winter Special Issue, 1123–1145.

Cohen W. M. and D. A. Levinthal (1990) 'Absorptive Capacity: A New Perspective on Learning and Innovation', *Administrative Science Quarterly*, 35, 128–52.

Constant D., L. Sproull and S. Kiesler (1996) 'The Kindness of Strangers: The Usefulness of Electronic Weak Ties for Technical Advice' *Organization Science* 7(2) 119–35.

Dahan E. and J. R. Hauser (2002) 'The Virtual Customer', *Journal of Product Innovation Management,* 19, 332–53.

Downes, L. and C. Mui, (1998) *Unleashing the Killer App: Digital Strategies for Market Dominance* (Boston: Harvard Business School Press).

Dyer, J. H. and K. Nobeoka (2000), 'Creating and Managing a High-Performance Knowledge-Sharing Network: The Toyota Case', *Strategic Management Journal*, 21, 345–367

Eisenhardt, K. M. (1989) 'Building Theories from Case Study Research', *Academy of Management Review*, 14(4), 532–50.

Evans P. and T. Wurster, (1999). *Blown to Bits: How the New Economics of Information Transforms Strategy*, (Boston: Harvard Business School Press).

Fielding, R (1999) 'Leadership in the Apache Project', *Communications of the ACM*, 42(4), 42–43

Gladwell, M. (2000) *The Tipping Point: How Little Things can make a Big Difference* (Boston: Little, Brown & Co).

Glaser, B. and A. Strauss (1967) *The Discovery of Grounded Theory* Chicago: Aldine.

Goldman A. I. (1999) *Knowledge in a Social World* (Oxford: Oxford University Press).

Griffin, A. and J. Hauser (1993) 'The Voice of the Customer', *Marketing Science*, 12(1), 1–27.

Hagel, J, III and M. Singer (1999) *Net Worth: Shaping Markets when Customers Make the Rules* (Boston: Harvard Business School Press)

Hamm, S. (2005) 'Linux, Inc.', *Business Week*, 31. January

Hargadon, A. (2003) *How Breakthroughs Happen: The Surprising Truth about How Companies Innovate* (Boston: Harvard Business School Press).

Hargadon, A. and R. Sutton (2000) 'Building an Innovation Factory', *Harvard Business Review*, May/June 157–66.

Iansiti M. and A. MacCormack (1997) 'Developing Products on Internet Time', *Harvard Business Review*, September–October: 108–17.

Kogut, B. and A. Metiu (2001) 'Open-Source Software Development and Distributed Innovation', *Oxford Review of Economic Policy*, 17(2), 248–64.

Kollock P. (1999) 'The Economics of Online Cooperation: Gift and Public Good in Computer Communities, in *Communities in Cyberspace*, M.Smith and P. Kollock (eds) (London: Routledge), pp. 3–25

Kozinets, R. (1999) 'E-Tribalized Marketing? The Strategic Implications of Virtual Communities of Consumption', *European Management Journal*, 17(3), 252–64.

Kumar, N., L. Stern, and J. Anderson (1993) 'Conducting Interoganizational Research Using Key Informants', *Academy of Management Journal*, 36(6), 1633–51.

Lakhani K. and E. von Hippel (2000) 'How Open Source Software Works: "Free" User-to-User Assistance, Working paper MIT Sloan School of Management, 4117, 1–39.

Langlois, R. N. and P. L. Robertson, (1992) 'Networks and Innovation in a Modular System: Lesson from the Microcomputer and Stereo Components Industries', *Research Policy*, 21, 297–313

Lave, J. and E. Wenger (1991), *Situated Learning* (Cambridge, MA: Cambridge University Press).

Leonard-Barton, D. (1992) 'Core Capabilities and Core Rigidities: A Paradox in Managing New Product Development', *Strategic Management Journal*, 13, 111–25.

Leonard-Barton, D. and J. F. Rayport (1997). 'Spark Innovation through Empathic Design', *Harvard Business Review*, November/December, 102–13.

Lerner J. and J. Tirole (2003) 'The Scope of Open Source Licensing, NBER Working Paper No. 9363.

Lynn, G., J. Morone and A. Paulson (1996) 'Marketing and Discount Innovation: The Probe and Learn Process', *California Management Review*, 38(3): 8–37.

McCracken, G. (1990) 'Culture and Consumer Behavior: An Anthropological Perspective', *Journal of the Market Research Society*, 32(1), 3–11.

Miles, M. B. and A. M. Huberman, (1994). *Qualitative Data Analysis. An Expanded Sourcebook* (Thousand Oaks, CA: Sage Publications.

Miller, M. S. and K. E. Drexler (1988) 'Markets and Computation: Agoric Open Systems', in B. Huberma (ed.), *The Ecology of Computation* (Amsterdam: Elsevier Science Publisher), pp. 58–69.

Nambisan, S. (2002) 'Designing Virtual Customer Environments for New Product Development: Toward a Theory', *Academy of Management Review*, 27(3), 392–413.

Nonaka, I. and N. Konno (1998) "The concept of "Ba": Building a Foundation for Knowledge Creation', *California Management Review*, 3, 40–54.

Nonaka, I. and H. Takeuchi (1995) *The Knowledge-Creating Company* (New York: Oxford University Press).

Pettigrew, A. (1990) 'Longitudinal Field Research on Change: Theory and Practice', *Organization Science*, 3, 267–92.

Piller, F., I. Chrsoph, J. Fuller and C. Stotko (2004) 'Toolkits for Open Innovation – The Case of Mobile Phone Games', Proceedings of the 37th Hawaii International Conference on System Sciences.

Philipps, L. W. (1981) 'Assessing Measurement Error in Key Informant Reports: A Methodological Note on Organizational Analysis in Marketing', *Journal of Marketing Research*, 18(November), 395–415.

Powell, W. W., K. W. Koput, and L. S. Doerr, (1996) 'Interorganizational Collaboration and the locus of Innovation: Networks of Learning in Biotechnology', *Administrative Science Quarterly*, 41, 116–45.

Prahalad, C. K. and V. Ramaswamy (2004) 'Co-creation Experiences: The New Practice in Value Creation', *Journal of Interactive Marketing*, 18(3), 5–14.

Raymond E. S. (1999) 'A Brief History of Hackerdom', in C. DiBona, S. Ockman, M. Stone (eds) *Open Source: Voices from the open Source Revolution* (O'really and Associates).

Sakkab, N. Y. (2002) 'Connect & Develop Complements Research & Develop at P&G', *Research Technology Management*, March/April.

Sawhney M. and P. Kotler (2001) 'Marketing in the Age of Information Democracy', in D. Iacobucci (ed.), *Kellogg on Marketing* (Chicago, IL: John Wiley and Son)., pp. 386–408

Sawhney M. and E. Prandelli (2000). 'Communities of Creation: Managing Distributed Innovation in Turbulent Market', *California Management Review*, 42(4) 24–54.

Sawhney, M., E. Prandelli and G. Verona (2003) 'The Power of Innomediation', *MIT Sloan Management Review*, 44(2), 77–82.

Schmitt, F. F. (1994) *Socializing Epistemology – The Social Dimensions of Knowledge* (Boston: Rowman & Littlefield).

Schumpeter, J. (1934) *The Theory of Economic Development*, Boston: Harvard University Press', first edition in German 1917

Shan, W., G. Walker and B. Kogut (1994) 'Interfirm Cooperation and Startup Innovation in the Biotechnology Industry' *Strategic Management* Journal, 15, 387–394.

Shapiro, C. and H. R. Varian (1998) *Information Rules: A Strategic Guide to the Network Economy* (Boston: Harvard Business School Press).

Sproull L. and S. Kiesler (1991) *Connections: New ways of Working in the Networked Organization* (Cambridge, MA: MIT Press).

Steven, G. and J. Burley (1997) '3,000 Raw Ideas = 1 Commercial Success!', *Research and Technology Management*, May/June, 16–27.

Sutton, R. (2002) 'Weird Ideas that Spark Innovation', *MIT Sloan Management Review*, 43(2), 83–7.

Thomke S. and W. Kuemmerle (2002) 'Asset Accumulation, Interdependence and Technological Change: Evidence from Pharmaceutical Drug Discovery' *Strategic Management Journal*, 23(7), 619–635.

Thomke, S. H. and von E. Hippel (2002) 'Customers as Innovators: A New Way to Create Value', *Harvard Business Review*, 80(4), 74–81.

Thurow, L. C. (1997) 'Needed: A new System of Intellectual Property Rights', *Harvard Business Review*, September/October, 95–103.

Verona, G., E. Prandelli and M. Sawhney (2005) 'Innovation and Virtual Environments: Towards Virtual Knowledge Brokers', *Organization Studies*, forthcoming.

Von Hippel, E. (2001) 'Perspective: User Toolkits for Innovation', *Journal of Product Innovation Management*, 18, 247–257.

Von Hippel, E. and G. Von Krogh (2003a) 'Editorial', *Research Policy*, Special issue on open source software development, 1149–57.

Von Hippel, E. and G. Von Krogh (2003b) 'Open Source Software and the "Private–Collective" Innovation Model: Issues for Organization Science', *Organization Science*, 14(2), 209–223.

Von Krogh, G. (2003) 'Open-Source Software Development', *MIT Sloan Management Review*, Spring, 14–18

Von Krogh, G. and J. Roos (1995) *Organizational Epistemology* (New York: St. Martin's Press.

Wenger, E. (1998) *Communities of Practice: Learning, Meaning, and Identity* (Cambridge: Cambridge University Press).

Wenger, E. and W. M. Snyder (2000) 'Communities of Practice: The Organizational Frontier', *Harvard Business Review*, January/February, 139–145.

Williamson, O. E. (1985) *The Economic Institutions of Capitalism*, New York: The Free Press.

Zajac, E. and C. Olsen (1993) 'From Transaction Costs to Transactional Value Analysis: Implications for the Study of Interorganizational Strategies', *Journal of Management Studies*, 30, 131–45.

Zaltman G. (1997). 'Rethinking Market Research: Putting People Back', *Journal of Marketing Research*, 34, 424–37.

8
Equipment-Related Knowledge Creation in Innovative Online Basketball Communities

Johann Füller, Gregor Jawecki and Hans Mühlbacher

This chapter investigates how knowledge related to basketball equipment emerges and spreads within online basketball communities. Our netnographic research shows that within online basketball communities commonly shared knowledge arises through shoptalk of members' product usage experiences, basketball-related know-how and opinions. Knowledge-sharing is not only supported by vivid stories but also by uploaded pictures and drawings to which community members are referring. Valuable discussions are archived and can be easily found and accessed by every community member. New knowledge emerges within online basketball communities by members' jointly working on problems or tasks self-stated by individual, well-respected community members in the form of 'friendly' competitions. While many community members provide their product judgement and engage in discussions on how to improve the user-generated designs, only a small number of community members possess sufficient creativity, domain-specific skills and motivation to develop new basketball shoes. The high quality and variety of community members' knowledge seems to be a promising source of innovation. In addition, various examples indicate community members' positive predisposition to share their know-how and ideas with producers. This leads to discussing how creative communities can be virtually integrated into a company's innovation process.

1. Introduction

Nowadays, 'technology has become so sophisticated, broad, and expensive that even the largest companies can't afford to do it all themselves' (Leonard-Barton, 1996, p. 135). Absorbing external knowledge is becoming indispensable for the creation of successful innovations (Cohen and Levinthal, 1990; Sawhney and Prandelli, 2000). In general, knowledge can be understood as information combined with experience, context, interpretation and reflection (Davenport and Prusak, 1998). To sustain the pace of innovation resulting from fast-changing technologies and customer needs,

Leonard-Barton (1996), Teece et al. (1997) and Lengnick-Hall (1996) suggested integrating customers into value creation and absorbing customers' knowledge to strengthen the company's capabilities (Cohen and Levinthal, 1990). In a new era of 'open innovation', researchers as well as consultants proclaim to create unique value in co-operation with customers and to engage them into new product development in a much more active way than traditional market research allows (Chesbrough, 2003; Kambil et al., 1999; Prahalad and Ramaswamy, 2004; Sawhney and Prandelli, 2000; Vandenbosch and Dawar, 2002; Von Hippel, 2002).

Due to the existence of the Internet as an interactive and multimedia-rich technology that has lowered the costs of communication (Dahan and Hauser, 2002a, 2002b; Dahan and Srinivasan, 2000; Urban and Hauser, 2004), new, simplified modes of large-scale interaction between producers and consumers have emerged. With its current one billion users (Almanac, 2004), the Internet offers an enormous pool of knowledge. The Internet serves as a virtual meeting place for consumers sharing interests (Hemetsberger and Pieters, 2001; Kozinets, 1999, 2002; McAlexander et al., 2002; Muniz and O'Guinn, 2001). In online communities, like-minded people with similar interests virtually get together, for example to exchange experiences, to discuss certain points of view and to create shared visions and ideas. Experiences with specific products are exchanged, problems shared and solutions created in order to modify existing products or even develop new ones. Among others, Bagozzi and Dholakia (2002, p. 5) point out that online communities present an aggregation of collective expertise that is difficult to match elsewhere. Researchers like consultants agree upon the enormous, so far by and large unexploited, potential of online communities for marketing and product development (Armstrong and Hagel, 1996; Hagel III and Armstrong, 1997; Kozinets, 2002; Prahalad and Ramaswamy, 2000, 2004; Sawhney and Prandelli, 2000; Sawhney et al., 2003). Except for some examples of knowledgeable online consumer groups such as the 'Harley-Owners-Group' (http://www.hog.com) (McWilliam, 2000) or the 'alt.coffee' community (Kozinets, 1999), little is known about how new knowledge is created and transferred within online communities. As knowledge creation strongly depends on context (Tyre and von Hippel, 1997), it is worth investigating knowledge creation processes within online consumer groups in more detail. While there is agreement on the fact that the Internet is capable of transferring information and explicit knowledge (Barrett et al., 2004; Carayannis, 1998; Descantis et al., 2004; Sawhney and Prandelli, 2000), the Internet has been considered inadequate for user collaboration on highly complex tasks, such as product innovation, which require high levels of creativity and flexibility (Nemiro, 2002; Nonaka et al., 2000). The research described in this paper sheds some light on: (1) how product-related knowledge is generated and transferred within online basketball communities; (2) whether communities use their knowledge to innovate new products; and (3) how innovation-related knowledge could be accessed and used for a company's innovation process. Finally, the potential of virtually integrating communities to reinforce a company's innovation process is discussed.

2. Knowledge creation in online communities

Depending on the school of thought, different definitions and explanations of knowledge can be found conceptualizing knowledge as information combined with experience, context, interpretation and reflection (Brown and Duguid, 2001). Two kinds of knowledge can be distinguished: explicit and tacit. The former is sometimes described as declarative, the latter as performative (Garud, 1997). How explicit knowledge can be created and shared in online communities may be explained by the concept of 'ba' (Nonaka and Konno, 1998).

The concept of 'ba'

Nonaka and Konno's (1998) concept of 'ba' offers a way to understand how knowledge can be created and shared within online communities. 'Ba', which roughly means 'place', is defined as a common space – either physical, virtual or mental – in which knowledge is shared, created and utilized (Nonaka et al., 2000). In 'ba', new knowledge is created in a spiralling process of interactions among individuals with different types and contents of knowledge. Nonaka and Konno (1998) introduce the SECI model, a four-step process consisting of socialization, externalization, combination and internalization to describe the continuous conversions of tacit to explicit and individual to social knowledge that lead to the creation of new knowledge. Within several loops of interaction where community members share their experiences, ideals and ideas with others, new knowledge – individual as well as collective – emerges. In the process of knowledge creation, individuals self-transcend their own limited perspectives and boundaries and, as a result, change themselves, others and the place itself (Nonaka et al., 2000). Knowledge embedded in the shared spaces of 'ba' can be acquired through one's own experience or reflections on the experiences of others. Knowledge creation processes have been studied both in communities of practice and in user innovation communities.

Communities of practice

Communities of practice are 'groups of people informally bound together by shared expertise and passion for a joint enterprise – engineers engaged in deep-water drilling, for example, consultants who specialize in strategic marketing [...] Some communities of practice meet regularly – for lunch on Thursdays, say. Others are connected primarily by email networks' (Wenger, 2000, p. 139). Members of communities of practice continuously interact and communicate: they talk about their work; pose questions; raise problems; offer solutions; construct answers; laugh at mistakes; or discuss changes in their work (Brown and Duguid, 1991; Wenger, 2004). In all their activities they keep each other up to date about what they know, what they have learned and what they are doing (Brown and Duguid, 2000). They develop a pool of collective knowledge which transcends any individual member's knowledge and which is openly accessible for all members. If community members are confronted with an unfamiliar situation which cannot be solved with their current know-how, they conduct a series of alternating experimentation and improvisation stages, accompanied by the sharing of and reflecting on stories of similar situations which at the end lead to a solution to the problem. This process of improvisation resembles what Levi-Strauss (1966) termed 'bricolage': the ability to perform tasks and find solutions with whatever materials and tools are at hand, from 'odds and ends' (Brown and Duguid, 1991).

User innovation communities

In user innovation communities, members actively discuss provided ideas, offer possible solutions, further elaborate them, test them or just give their opinion. User innovators get in contact with their friends, peer group members, relatives and acquaintances because they look for complimentary knowledge and skills, needed to realize their new product ideas (Von Hippel, 2005; Von Hippel, 2002). Being confronted with an innovator's new product, discussing it and providing feedback on it creates a common understanding about the innovation; new common knowledge emerges (Hienerth, 2004; Sawhney and Prandelli, 2000). Through the ongoing dialogue the innovator is constantly challenged. She may rethink her innovation with respect to the suggestions made by the community members and may be able to overcome so far unsolved problems. The innovator learns from the community and complements her knowledge. In addition, the disseminated knowledge will inspire other community members to build on this idea. Through intense interactions, finally a new product may result that is superior than if it had been innovated by a single user and that is 'superior to the sum of the individual outputs, because new knowledge is created through the emerging relationships' (Sawhney and Prandelli, 2000, p. 26).

While explicit knowledge can be codified and expressed in words and numbers and shared in the form of data, formulae and manuals, tacit knowledge is highly personal, subject to automatic processing and, therefore, difficult to formalize, to communicate or to share with others (Nonaka and Konno, 1998, p. 42). Tacit knowledge is often classified as 'sticky' (Andersen, 1999; Ogawa, 1998; Szulanski, 1996; Von Hippel, 1998; Von Hippel, 1994).

Hemetsberger and Reinhardt (2004) have shown that virtual communities can overcome the problems related to the transfer of sticky information and tacit knowledge through technological tools, task-related features, collective reflection, stories and usage scenarios. Thus, even more complex tasks such as joint innovation may be realized on the Internet. The open-source network constitutes a real-life best-practice example for collective knowledge creation within online communities (Hemetsberger and Reinhardt, 2004). In order to deal with the huge amount of knowledge, an online community builds a collective group memory and organizes content. Hence, participants do not necessarily have to possess all knowledge at all times. They rather know where to find information or which members to ask for help with a specific problem. Innovating members comment on their actions, thus allowing other participants to re-experience their line of thought and to accumulate their specific knowledge. Typically, new members are introduced slowly and often rigidly guided by experienced participants, to enable their understanding of the cultural norms of the community and familiarity with the collective knowledge pool (Descantis et al., 2004). Processes of conceptualizing problems and jointly reflecting on possible solutions are applied to stimulate the creativity of the entire community. In order to create a common understanding of their future action, the members of an online community create a 'virtual' world, that is, a constructed representation of the future realization of their ideas. Just as social and physical settings play an important role for knowledge creation in offline contexts (Tyre and von Hippel, 1997), they are essential for knowledge creation in virtual environments. Along with the social context (for example, shared language, rules, values and understanding), the technical infrastructure (for example, stability, speed, effective tools) as well as the virtual design (for example, navigation, look and feel, media richness, interactivity and user-friendliness) highly influence learning and knowledge creation on the Internet (Barrett et al., 2004; Descantis et al., 2004, Butler et al., 2002; Kettanurak et al., 2001).

Although knowledge creation has been extensively researched in organizational contexts, little is known about the creation and transfer of knowledge within online communities centring around consumer products. Further, no empirical study addresses how the knowledge of online consumer groups could be systematically used for a company's innovation process. Our research sheds light on the creation and transfer of equipment-related knowledge within online consumer groups by its investigation of online basketball communities.

3. Research field

Online communities dedicated to basketball shoes were selected as our research object based on three considerations. First, basketball is played and watched by a great number of people all over the world. Thus, a high number of online communities could be expected. Second, as basketball is typically played in teams, players probably would have tight relations, keen to share their experiences. Third, one of the authors enthusiastically played basketball for more than ten years and possesses profound knowledge about basketball footwear, which was considered indispensable to understand the conversation among community members.

The basketball shoe sector is a highly competitive market with few established brands and a variety of new models introduced every year. New products are mainly limited to modifications mostly in the appearance of shoes. Radical innovations are rare and often require a very long development time. For instance, Nike spent 16 years from conception to creation of its new cushioning technology (Von Wartburg, 2002).

4. Methodology

For this research, a methodology based on netnography (Kozinets, 1999, 2002) was selected. Netnography has its origin in ethnography (Arnould and Wallendorf, 1994) and is adapted to the Internet. It uses information publicly available on the Internet to study the nature and behaviour of online consumer groups. The netnographic approach describes how to identify and get in contact with online communities and how to analyse and check trustworthiness of community insights. Further, netnography covers ethical behaviour in conducting marketing research in an online environment. It is mainly used to gain 'grounded knowledge' (Glaser and Strauss, 1967) concerning a certain research question.

Table 8.1   **Message board of each basketball community in the research sample**

Community	Members	Description
Niketalk (US)	30,000	• Best community based on content and number of members • No official affiliation with Nike, Inc.
Basketballboards (US)	11,000	• Members are of younger age • One forum specifically for apparel
Instyleshoes (US)	6,200	• Often mentioned as second best online community • All brands are frequently discussed
Kickz101 (AUS)	3,300	• Message board of a basketball apparel store based in Australia • Interesting because of international perspective
Kicksology (US)	n.a.	• Private site with reviews of more than 150 basketball shoes • Reviews have a strong influences on purchase decision of many users

The study was conducted by following a four step approach: (1) determination of user characteristics; (2) community identification and selection; (3) observation and data-gathering; and (4) data analysis and interpretation of findings. Overall, more than 500 online communities dedicated to basketball-related topics were identified. After extensive screening related to quality of content, posting frequency and professionalism, five message boards were identified as most promising for this research: Niketalk, Basketballboards, Instyleshoes, Kickz101 and Kicksology. Table 8.1 provides a brief description of the selected basketball communities. All five communities were observed over a period of six months, from October 2003 to March 2004. During this time all equipment-related content was monitored. More than 240,000 posts in more than 18,000 discussions were screened and the most relevant ones filed electronically. Finally, 460 discussions – current and past discussions as far as archived – including 11,000 posts were analysed and interpreted by the use of QSR NVivo software.

5. Findings

Communities and their members

The members of online basketball communities are typically very interested to find out what personalities are hidden behind the user names of other members. Thus, they start threads from time to time in which they introduce themselves to the community. The participation in such topics is usually very high and members not only give information about their age, their location and their profession, but also often attach photos of themselves and their basketball shoe collections. Because of these threads, a good picture of the members of online basketball communities can be acquired.

Typically, members are between 15 and 25 years old and go to school or university. Nevertheless, some older members can be met as well:

> ... just wanted to let all those 30+ guys out there know: You are not alone, but I still think we're outnumbered like 20:1 by the teenagers.

Interestingly, numerous employees of sporting goods stores also participate, not with the intention of advertising their stores but because they too want to satisfy their passion for basketball footwear. In terms of the location of members, it can be observed that a clear majority is from the United States. However, members from other countries spread throughout the world participate as well. The most enthusiastic members of each community are highly involved in the field of basketball shoes, as shown by their amazing shoe collections. Such collections often include between fifty and one hundred, and in some cases even up to several hundred, different pairs of high-end basketball shoes of the major brands. Collectors spend a significant amount of money on their main interest:

I got 49 pairs, soon to be 50 because my birthday is in 2 weeks. I wear all my shoes and get the majority of them for birthday and Christmas and whenever I get a paycheck. I'm sure I have spent $1000+ on them, but its all worth it to me.

On account of their frequent use of basketball shoes while playing (and even wearing off-court) as well as the significant time they spend with other activities related to their hobby (for example, reading basketball magazines), the most enthusiastic members have a very extensive knowledge about basketball shoes. For instance, they know the exact name of a model when they see only a picture of it, are aware of each shoe's pros and cons and have detailed knowledge about upcoming models: 'the heads on this board are some of the most knowledgeable people about shoes in the world'.

For these most enthusiastic members, the online community is like a virtual family ('Niketalk really has grown into a family, nationwide!'), which gives a sense of belonging: 'It does feel like a community, even way out here in Tokyo'.

Hence, members spend numerous hours each day within the community:

I have to admit that I'm excited about this because it has been a looooong while since we've all stayed up until the wee hours of the morning hitting 'refresh' on our browsers, waiting for that special something to appear.

Social ties among the most active participants are so strong that they even organize so-called 'summits' where they meet and get to know each other offline: 'Brandon, I cant wait to meet you! I'm so excited!'.

The communication among members is typically marked by mutual respect:

I think there were just a few miscommunications here and there, but it's good to see that the Niketalk community is all about respect and love.

While each of the selected communities has several thousand members, the majority of all postings are made by a much smaller group of users. At Instyleshoes for example, 58 per cent of all members can be considered lurkers (Nonnecke et al., 2004), while 80 per cent of all postings are made by only 3 per cent of all members (see Table 8.2). In each community a group of highly active, well-known and knowledgeable insiders can be found. What these 'opinion leaders' express is immediately adopted by most other members of the community:

What I noticed is that whenever ekin or airmax puts up a post everyone magically does not ever affront him, says the shoes suck, ... like he or she is a god or something.

Table 8.2   **Categorization of members of Instyleshoes community based on their posting frequency**

Instyleshoes 6,216 members	Absolute number	Percentage of total members	Behaviour and role in community
Lurkers	3,605	58	• Registered members who rarely contribute • Passively observe communication to gather information and to read interesting discussions • Do not hold social ties to other members • Numerous unregistered lurkers can be expected
Posters	2,399	39	• Contribute regularly to topics of interest • Share shoe reviews with other members • Are interested in social interactions besides footwear-related discussions
Frequent posters	212	3	• Contribute frequently or even daily • Hold strong social ties to other frequent posters • Possess extensive product-related know-how • Most respected members of their communities • Some take the role of opinion leaders

Knowledge-sharing

The members of online communities typically do not keep their knowledge about basketball shoes secret but share it with others free of cost. The motivations to do so include the desire to give back to the community; striving for recognition from other members; awareness of community norms; and the satisfaction when interacting with others who share the same enthusiasm for basketball footwear. However, one of the strongest motivations is the desire to help others, as shown by detailed shoe reviews in which members share their personal experiences and opinions on a specific model. Such reviews not only concern the shoe as a whole but often include detailed judgements of specific components (for example, cushioning and comfort) by the help of a commonly acknowledged categorization scheme (one to ten points). Reviews help other members in their purchase decisions:

> Thanks for the review, I've been thinking about getting a pair but since I've been hearing so many good reviews about them I might pick a pair up.

At the same time, reviews are often the starting point for innovative ideas

> Eric, why do you say the cushioning feel would be bad? To me it seems very simple: if the sockliner and a unit at the heel lead to very responsive cushioning, wouldn't an extra full-length unit make it even more responsive?

In total, our analysis identified more than 20 components and attributes of a basketball shoe which are frequently discussed.

An example which illustrates that individual knowledge is freely shared even when it is of high value for its owner is insider information on upcoming models. From time to time the major companies launch a limited number of a certain basketball shoe model, which is distributed in selected stores only. Such so-called 'limited releases' then become sought-after collectors' items and are not uncommonly sold for several hundred dollars among collectors. However, it can be observed that even information regarding when and where someone can purchase such upcoming limited models (for example, sales place and release date) is also shared freely with others, even though it reduces the chance of the knowledge-holder to buy one of the few pairs when thousands of enthusiastic basketball players read about it in the community.

Through the process of knowledge-sharing, common knowledge is created in the community. In all analysed basketball communities it can be observed that as soon as so far unsolved problems or questions arise, members combine their individual knowledge to find the best answer to the problem at hand. Thus a pool of shared community knowledge evolves, from which all members can draw at any time. An example for this process is shoe-painting guidelines. In order to stand out from the crowd, many basketball shoe enthusiasts customize their footwear by applying paint, glitter and even denim (see Figures 8.1 and 8.2). However, to do so they have to overcome some difficulties, such as how to make the paint flexible and thin in order to avoid creases:

> I would also like to note that this paint mixture doesn't really chip but it may tear due to lot of creasing and stress depending on the number of coats.

Typically, members who modify their shoes share their experiences and give detailed advice on how to achieve the best results, such as which acetone to use, the best ratio to mix acetone and paint and how many coats of paint to apply:

> I stripped the first layer of the paint that was on there with Acetone [...] then I painted the paint normally for about 5 or 6 coats [...] then i put 2 layers of sealer on [...] so far, they holding up [...].

Figure 8.1 Customized basketball shoe by *KBCustomz* (Modification: originally all-white)

Source: Instyleshoes, Dec 2003

Figure 8.2 Customized basketball shoe by *kbtoyz0902 (*Modification: denim attached)

Source: Niketalk, Dec 2003

Over time, a step-by-step set of guidelines evolves which provides answers to all painting-related questions: 'That essay was very insightful. I didnt even think of putting multiple coats of acetone prior to painting.' In the Niketalk community, useful guidelines are moved to the so-called Archives, which is a separate section with permanently saved messages. Thus, whenever members have a question related to shoe-painting, they do not have to look for an individual member who possesses the information which is required for the specific interest, but can go to the Archives and look for the answer themselves: 'This post should be archived or sticky because it is helpful with a lot of people trying to paint their kicks.'

Another example illustrating how members integrate their knowledge into a commonly shared knowledge base is the topic of so-called 'fakes', which are illegal, low-quality imitations of branded basketball shoes. As they look very similar to original basketball shoes, the problem arises how to recognize them when buying basketball shoes from private sellers on the Internet:

> I have to agree with you guys that fakes are getting better [...] a clueless buyer wouldn't be able to distinguish which is the real deal.

Expert community members contribute their knowledge, thereby helping less experienced members to avoid buying fakes:

> Thanks Kookies, your last post on the fakes and their boxes has already helped me out, now I just gotta keep my eye open for some real ones.

In some cases these instructions are so in-depth that even the smallest details, such as the shape of the stitching, are used as distinguishing criteria between fakes and branded basketball shoes:

> the stitching behind the triangle has more of a 'rounded' appearance vs. the fake pair that comes to more of an angle.

At the same time, often pictures are used to visualize the differences between imitations and originals (see Figure 8.3).

The consequence of thousands of members sharing their knowledge is, besides the enjoyment members perceive when meeting like-minded others, that the role of the community as an almost unlimited source of footwear-related knowledge and information is an important reason for many members to participate: 'I come here for the information and stick for the comedy.'

The members of the online basketball communities in the sample can not only draw from an extensive amount of knowledge. They often receive information earlier than non-members and even firms in the basketball

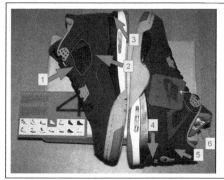

1 The rubber covering the mesh should be lined up with the top of the panel, not the bottom. 2 Stitching looks bad, common on most fakes. Lines all over the shoe are not straight, again, common on fakes. 3 Foam sticks out way too far. 4 'Butt' of the shoe is too flat. Should have more contour there. 5 Shape angle on that corner. This is the easiest way to spot fakes. All of the fakes on ebay show this. 6 Tag is positioned too high on inside of tongue.

Figure 8.3   Instructions on how to distinguish a branded basketball shoe from a fake version

Source: Niketalk, April 2004

shoe industry. Typically, the major companies consciously determine when to reveal first information and pictures of their upcoming top-of-the-line models in order to avoid competitors gaining a competitive advantage. However, within online basketball communities first information about a new model often emerges several months before the model is officially launched in the market, at a point when the company is of the opinion that all information is still strictly confidential:

> This whole post shows how fast an idea laid out on desk can hit the streets and the public eye in one second.

When the authors showed pictures of upcoming models to the basketball innovation managers of a leading sporting goods company, they acknowledged that some of their products, which they thought were strictly secret at that time, were already being discussed in online basketball communities. The origin of such proprietary knowledge and pictures is typically unknown. In most cases one member shares them with the community but does not want to disclose the sources:

> A little something for my friends at Niketalk – Air Zoom Lebron II – from an old pal.

Interestingly, it can be observed that once the first pictures of a new basketball shoe emerge in an online community, often members do not like it at all. But as the launch date comes closer, they change their opinion and most of them end up buying the basketball shoe they did not like in the beginning:

> We all know how much everyone hated the XIX when they first saw pics, but how 3 days before the Release Date everyone was all over them [...] I'd say 85% of the people who reply dislike them [...] those numbers will change dramatically before the Release Date.

Possible explanations for this phenomenon may be that the community members get used to the design; that they are positively influenced by some launch campaigns; or that they are fond of the brand and just want to have the latest equipment.

Creating innovation-related knowledge

The members of the five online basketball communities not only share their opinions on existing and future basketball shoes of the major companies but also generate innovative ideas for entirely new technologies and basketball shoes from scratch. Approximately 4000 members of the five online basketball communities engage in innovation activities in one way or another. Innovative ideas, often visualized in the form of drawings or even computer renderings of numerous shoe components, for example, design, cushioning, lacing and ventilation, could be found. Similar to knowledge on existing models, innovation-related knowledge is shared freely within the community: 'Continue producing your masterpieces and thank you for always sharing with the community.'

While some of the innovations are triggered by the perception of a so far unsatisfied need:

> I think basketball is a leading cause of injuries [...] I've hurt my wrist, both my ankles, knees, and shoulders. I think it's because there's no protective equipment for the sport.

obviously the main motivations are the fun of the activity itself – 'Hey, these renderings should be interesting, I can't wait!' – and members' desire to improve their skills through feedback from a knowledgeable audience – 'Thank you very much for your kind feedback. It's nice to get critics and try to top my own limits'.

Many more innovations are triggered by the enjoyment, the fun and pleasure some members experience when engaging in innovation activities than by a specific requirement. Approximately 80 per cent of all innovations are generated by community members who derive enjoyment from the creative activity; only about 20 per cent are the result of a so far unmet need.

The small number of most enthusiastic enjoyment-driven innovators who repeatedly engage in creative activities are commonly known as 'designers' in their community. For instance, approximately 20 members of the total 34,000 members in the Niketalk community belong to the group of 'designers'. They contribute by far the highest number and quality of innovative ideas. In contrast to innovators driven by need who mostly verbally describe their ideas, 'designers' typically visualize their innovations in the form of hand-made drawings or even virtual 3-D renderings. For many designers, making their own renderings is much more than just a pure hobby; it is their intended career. Thus, they demonstrate impressive drawing and design skills and some of them even dream about becoming professional basketball footwear designers for one of the major brands. In order to achieve this goal, many study industrial design or go to art schools. Hence, the community is regarded as an ideal place to gain feedback from a knowledgeable audience, which in turn helps the designers to further improve their skills:

> Now, I begin to understand how important is to get inputs from this community (which is made of truly kicks lovers as I am) to improve my skills and refine my technique.

To increase the challenge and fun when making renderings, from time to time designers initiate so-called 'Designers' Roll Calls'. In these friendly competitions, a community member assigns to the designers a specific innovation task, such as 'design the basketball shoe for the year 2050', and then the designers of the community try to fulfil this task within the given deadline. The feedback and comments of the knowledgeable audience indicate the quality of contributions:

> Whoa […] I really think that ALL the submissions from you guys are (read: wow!!) there ain't never gonna be a shortage of creative talent in here.

An example illustrating the high skills of designers in online basketball communities is a Designers' Roll Call which took place in the Niketalk community in April 2003. The task was to draw the so-called 'Air Jordan XIX', an upcoming basketball shoe of which at that point no pictures had been revealed by the producing company. Despite the fact that the designers had only a few verbal clues to assist them (for example, it has a lace cover), some of the submissions shared very close similarities with the actual basketball shoe which was launched several months later (see Figure 8.4).

Maybe the most intriguing example which illustrates the high innovative and creative potential of community members was found in the archive of Niketalk: Jason Petrie, known under the username 'Alphaproject', continuously showcased his renderings in the Niketalk community and improved his skills through the competent feedback from other shoe enthusiasts. At that time one member, amazed by one of his designs, predicted:

User design   Company design

Figure 8.4   Comparison of the Air Jordan XIX made by user (left) and producing company (right)

Source: Niketalk, April 2004

> One day I will hold your first designed Nike sneaker in my hands, telling myself that this one is from Alpha, who had his beginning at Niketalk.

This came true. Alphaproject was discovered by Fila and now designs footwear at Nike (Kicksguide, 2003).

Interestingly, despite the high quality of their ideas, innovative members are not only willing to share their knowledge within their online communities. Rather, several examples could be found which indicate that user-innovators are also willing to collaborate with companies free of cost. On one occasion, a member of the Niketalk community claimed to work for Reebok and started a discussion on how Reebok could improve its basketball line. Although no rewards were offered, a very productive discussion unfolded, with more than 100 detailed replies within five days. Even when first doubts about the identity of the author arose, the discussion continued unaffected. It seemed that although no rewards were offered, the contribu tors felt sufficiently rewarded by the challenge of the task and their participation in an interesting discussion:

> I for one couldn't care less if the guy was really from Reebok or not. It's still an interesting discussion and a lot of the comments make for interesting reading.

Another example which illustrates that innovative members even share their designs with sporting goods companies and actively initiate contact is a design contest on a private user homepage dedicated to basketball shoes, called 'Kicksguide'. Each month, several community members submit their designs to the theme of each month. They hope that one of their designs may be elected 'Artist Series Shoe Design of the Year' and, as the winning design is submitted to various sporting goods companies, their creative and innovative talent may be recognized by a company and career opportunities consequently arise.

6. Discussion

Online gatherings of consumers, at least in the field of basketball shoes, represent a large pool of equipment-related knowledge. Basketball community members interact with like-minded people and engage in vivid discussions related to basketball equipment. Sharing their experiences and engaging in innovation activities is considered fun and perceived as a possibility to gain and show know-how. The exchange of basketball-related knowledge is seen as the main task of the community. Following Sawhney and Prandelli (2000), creating new knowledge means creating new relationships and sustaining the community itself. The process of deep and recurrent knowledge-sharing is considered to be the origin of every community. In the same vein, Hemetsberger (2001) remarks that task involvement combined with learning constitutes a self-sustaining system that helps to maintain the community.

Our findings show that at least a small number of community members are very knowledgeable and highly skilled, even creating their own virtual products with an impressively high quality and level of innovation. Hence, not only software development communities (Franke and von Hippel, 2003; Von Hippel and von Krogh, 2003) and offline user innovation communities (Franke and Shah, 2003; Shah, 2000), but also online consumer groups are highly innovative, despite the fact that the designers of virtual basketball shoes will never benefit from wearing their own creations. In contrast to lead user innovations, innovation creation in basketball communities is driven rather by excitement than by pure need (Urban and von Hippel, 1988).

At first, individual knowledge about basketball shoes is commonly shared and becomes collectively known (Nonaka and Konno, 1998). Important findings are archived and can be retrieved from anybody, at any time. Thus, knowledge stays vivid over time and can be passed on to new members (Descantis et al., 2004).

An interesting, so far unexplored, pattern of knowledge generation that could be identified is that of the so-called 'Designers' Roll Calls'. These friendly design competitions stimulate innovation creation and dissemination of the most complex knowledge. By posting pictures and animations of self-created shoe designs and concepts, the so-called 'designers' disclose not only their explicit but also their implicit knowledge. In the design of an innovative shoe, the consumer's implicit, non-verbally articulated knowledge about basketball equipment, such as values, feelings, perceptions of latest trends and design preferences, surfaces (Nonaka and Konno, 1998). Visual models help to transfer sticky knowledge to the community (Ogawa, 1998; Von Hippel, 1998, 1994). While only a few community members are capable of creating 'professional' shoe designs, many less-skilled members help to improve the innovation by giving their opinion, coming up with proposals for improvement or asking challenging questions. Other designers in turn may be inspired by the proposals of others and come up with even more radical innovations. Through the intense interactions, numerous contributions and countless loops of 'trial-and-error' experimentations, finally a new product results that is for superior than if it had been innovated by a single user. A sense of group efficacy emerges (Hemetsberger, 2001). 'The overall community can be seen as a dynamic system of adaptive learning that produces innovations from the ideas of community members' (Hienerth, 2004). Besides contributing their knowledge, another important function of less-skilled community members is to admire the designers, to show recognition and to take on the role of fans (Schouten and McAlexander, 1995).

In principle, community members are willing to share their knowledge and ideas when approached by a sports equipment manufacturer. Hence, the two main preconditions for successful virtual integration of community members into a company's innovation process – the community's innovative potential and willingness to participate – seem to be fulfilled.

While this study provides first insights into joint-knowledge creation within online consumer groups and supplies much plausible evidence that online consumer groups are a promising source of innovation, further research is required to come up with more generalizable and quantifiable results. Based on our findings, it would be interesting to examine whether other online communities centring around physical consumer goods other than basketball footwear, for example, mobile phones, cameras or skies, demonstrate similar patterns of knowledge creation and innovative potential. In addition, a quantitative study on what innovative communities expect from companies when sharing their knowledge with them is long overdue. A variety of conceptual and empirical studies is needed to explore the virtual integration of communities into a company's innovation process in full detail.

7. Managerial implications and outlook

In all of the five observed consumer online communities, very knowledgeable members can be met who are able to think of creative ways to modify existing or innovate new basketball footwear. In addition, these members seem to be willing to collaborate with producers and could provide valuable contributions such as information, knowledge and assistance to various tasks of a company's innovation process (Dahan and Hauser, 2002b; Nambisan, 2002). The question arises how producers could access community members' product-related knowledge and integrate this knowledge in their new product development processes.

For specific innovation tasks, a company could provide special interaction equipment like toolkits (Von Hippel and Katz, 2002) or virtual customer tools (Dahan and Hauser, 2002b) that facilitate participation and transfer of community members' know-how. Selected communities may serve as pools of qualified consumers that are invited to participate via postings and banners (Füller et al., 2004). For example, new, customizable cushioning technologies could become a topic for a specific virtual community integration project. The community members could be asked via posts and banners to contribute to the design of such a new cushioning technology. To support the knowledge transfer, community members could be provided with a user-based design tool (Dahan and Hauser, 2002b) that facilitates the knowledge transfer.

In contrast to the punctual integration of community members for specific tasks, a company could aim to benefit from the ongoing knowledge exchange and innovation activities within online communities. Obviously, continuously monitoring the communication of thousands of community members for innovative ideas represents a high commitment in terms of time and cost. Hence, community members with new ideas should become active themselves and contact the company of their choice. This could be realized by installing a permanent link on basketball community websites such as Niketalk to directly connect community members with the innovation team of the company of their choice. The community itself could take on a central position, as it could activate the link in cases where its community members think that a certain innovation should be introduced to and discussed with a company. Of course, issues regarding intellectual property and gratifications have to be clarified before a company decides to collaborate with communities. With their 'community of creation' concept Sawhney and Prandelli (2000) have suggested a potential governance model. For effective and efficient interaction with online communities, knowledge and skills are required. Not every company may have those skills yet, especially if it is difficult to reach the right consumers or to create a certain context of interaction. Under such conditions, Sawhney et al. (2003) note that it may be advisable to rely on 'innomediaries', third-party actors who facilitate the knowledge transfer and are specialized in the virtual dialogue with communities.

References

Almanac (2004) http://www.c-i-a.com/pr0904.htm, accessed 5 November.

Andersen, P. H. (1999) 'Organizing International Technological Collaboration in Subcontractor Relationships: An Investigation of the Knowledge-Stickiness Problem', *Research Policy*, 28, 625–42.

Armstrong, A. and J. Hagel (1996) 'The Real Value of On-line Communities', *Harvard Business Review*, 4(3), 134–41.

Arnould, E. and M. Wallendorf (1994) 'Market-Oriented Ethnography: Interpretation Building and Marketing Strategy Formulation', *Journal of Marketing Research*, 31(4), 484–504.

Bagozzi, R. and U. Dholakia (2002) 'Intentional Social Action in Virtual Communities', *Journal of Interactive Marketing*, 16(2), 2–21.

Barrett, M., S. Cappleman, G. Shoib and G. Walsham (2004) 'Learning in Knowledge Communities: Managing Technology and Context', *European Management Journal*, 22(1), 1–11.

Brown, J. S. and P. Duguid (2000) 'The Social Life of Information', *Harvard Business Review*, 78(6), 194–199.

Brown, J. S. and P. Duguid (1991) 'Organizational Learning and Communities-Of-Practice: Toward a Unified View of Working, Learning, and Innovating', *Organization Science*, 2(1), 40–57.

Brown, J. S. and P. Duguid (2001) 'Knowledge and Organization: A Social-Practice Perspective', *Organization Science*, 12(2), 198–213.

Butler, B., L. Sproull and S. Kiesler (2002) 'Community Effort in Online Groups: Who Does The Work and Why?', forthcoming in S. Weisband and L. Atwater (eds), *Leadership at a Distance* (NJ: Lawrence Erlbaum Publishers Inc.)

Carayannis, E. (1998) 'The Strategic Management of Technological Learning in Project/Program Management: The Role of Extranets, Intranets and Intelligent Agents in Knowledge Generation, Diffusion and Leveraging', *Technovation*, 18(11), 697–703.

Chesbrough, H. (2003) 'The Era of Open Innovation', *MIT Sloan Management Review*, Spring, 35–41.

Cohen, W. and D. Levinthal (1990) 'Absorptive Capacity: A New Perspective on Learning and Innovation', *Administrative Science Quarterly*, 35, 128–52.

Dahan, E. and J. Hauser (2002a) 'Managing a Dispersed Product Development Process', in B. Weitz and R. Wensley (eds), *Handbook of Marketing* (Thousand Oaks, CA: Sage Publications), MIT SLOAN working paper.

Dahan, E. and J. Hauser (2002b) 'The Virtual Customer', *Journal of Product Innovation Management*, 19(5), 332–53.

Dahan, E. and V. Srinivasan (2000) 'The Predictive Power of Internet-Based Product Concept Testing using Visual Depiction and Animation', *Journal of Product Innovation Management*, 17, 99–109.

Davenport, T. H. and L. Prusak (1998) *Working Knowledge: How Organizations Manage what they Know* (Boston, MA: Harvard Business School Press).

Descantis, G., A.-L. Fayard, M. Roach and L. Jiang (2004) 'Learning in Online Forums', *European Management Journal*, 22(5), 565–77.

Franke, N. and E. von Hippel (2003) 'Satisfying Heterogeneous User Needs via Innovation Toolkits: The Case of Apache Security Software', *Research Policy*, 32(7), 1199–215.

Franke, N. and S. Shah (2003) 'How Communities Support Innovative Activities: An Exploration of Assistance and Sharing Among Innovative Users of Sporting Equipment', *Research Policy*, 32(1), 157–78.

Füller, J., M. Bartl, H. Mühlbacher and H. Ernst (2004) 'Community Based Innovation – A Method to Utilize the Innovative Potential of Online Communities', in 37th Hawaii International Conference on System Sciences (Hawaii: Big Island)

Garud, R. (1997) 'The Distinction between Know-How, Know-What, and Know-Why', in A. Huff and J. Welsh (eds), *Advances in Strategic Management* (Greenwich, CT: JAI Press), pp. 81–101.

Glaser, B. and A. Strauss (1967) *The Discovery of Grounded Theory* (New York: Aldine de Gruyter).

Hagel III, J. and A. Armstrong (1997) Net Gain: Expanding Markets through Virtual Communities (Boston, MA: HBS Press).

Hemetsberger, A. (2001) 'Fostering Cooperation on the Internet: Social Exchange Processes in Innovative Virtual Consumer Communities', *Advances in Consumer Research*, 29, 354–6.

Hemetsberger, A. and R. Pieters (2001) 'When Consumers Produce on the Internet: An Inquiry into Motivational Sources of Contribution to Joint-Innovation', in C. Derbaix et al. (eds), edited proceedings of Fourth International Research Seminar on Marketing Communications and Consumer Behavior, La Londe, Leopold-Franzens-Universität Innsbruck.

Hemetsberger, A. and C. Reinhardt (2004) 'Sharing and Creating Knowledge in Open-Source Communities – the Case of KDE', Fifth European Conference on Organizational Knowledge, Learning, and Capabilities, Innsbruck.

Hienerth, C. (2004) 'Impediments to the Transfer of Knowledge in Innovative Communities', in E. Carayannis and D. Campbell, (eds), *Knowledge Creation, Diffusion and Use in Innovation Networks & Clusters: A Comparative Systems Approach Across the U.S., Europe and Asia* (forthcoming, 2005) (Greenwood Publishing Books).

Kambil, A., B. B. Friesen and A. Sundaram (1999) 'Co-Creation: A New Source of Value', *Outlook Magazine*, 3(2), 23–29.

Kettanurak, V., K. Ramamurthy and W. D. Haseman (2001) 'User Attitude as a Mediator of Learning Performance Improvement in an Interactive Multimedia Environment: An Empirical Investigation of the Degree of Interactivity and Learning Styles', *International Journal of Human–Computer Studies*, 54, 541–83.

Kicksguide (2003) http://www.kicksguide.com/articles/featured/alphaproject.asp Accessed: 1 December, 2003.

Kozinets, R. (1999) 'E-Tribalized Marketing?: The Strategic Implications of Virtual Communities of Consumption', *European Management Journal*, 17(3), 252–64.

Kozinets, R. (2002) 'The Field Behind the Screen: Using Netnography for Marketing Research in Online Communications', *Journal of Marketing Research*, 39(1), 61–72.

Lengnick-Hall, C. A. (1996) 'Customer Contributions to Quality: A Different View of the Customer-Oriented Firm', *Academy of Management Review*, 21(3), 791–824.

Leonard-Barton, D. (1996) *Wellsprings of Knowledge: Building and Sustaining the Sources of Innovation* (Boston, MA: Harvard Business School Press).

Levi-Strauss, C. (1966) *The Savage Mind* (Chicago: Chicago University Press).

McAlexander, J., J. Schouten and H. Koenig (2002) 'Building Brand Community', *Journal of Marketing*, 66(1), 38–54.

McWilliam, G. (2000) 'Building Strong Brands through Online Communities', *Sloan Management Review*, 41(13),

Muniz, A. and T. O'Guinn (2001) 'Brand Community', *Journal of Consumer Research*, 27, 412–32.

Nambisan, S. (2002) 'Designing Virtual Customer Environments for New Product Development: Toward a Theory', *Academy of Management Review*, 27(3), 392–413.

Nemiro, Jill E. (2002) 'The Creative Process in Virtual Teams', *Creativity Research Journal*, 14(1), 69–83.

Nonaka, I and N. Konno (1998) 'The Concept of "Ba": Building a Foundation for Knowledge Creation', *California Management Review*, 40(3), 40–54.

Nonaka, I., P. Reinmoeller and D. Senoo (2000) 'Integrated IT Systems to Capitalize on Market Knowledge', *in Knowledge Creation – A Source of Value*, von G., Krogh I. Nonaka and T. Nishiguchi (eds), (London and New York: Macmillian Press).

Nonnecke, B., J. Preece and D. Andrews (2004) 'What Lurkers and Posters Think of Each Other', in *Proccedings of the 37th Hawaii International Conference on System Science* (Hawaii: Big Island).

Ogawa, S. (1998) 'Does Sticky Information Affect the Locus of Innovation?: Evidence from the Japanese Convenience-Store Industry', *Research Policy*, 26, 777–90.

Prahalad, C. and V. Ramaswamy (2000) 'Co-opting Customer Competence', *Harvard Business Review*, January/February, 79–87.

Prahalad, C. and V. Ramaswamy (2004) *The Future of Competition: Co-Creating Unique Value with Customers* (Boston, MA: Harvard Business School Press).

Sawhney, M. and E. Prandelli (2000) 'Communities of Creation: Managing Distributed Innovation in Turbulent Markets', *California Management Review*, 42(4), 24–54.

Sawhney, M., E. Prandelli and G. Verona (2003) 'The Power of Innomediation', *MIT Sloan Management Review*, 44(2), 77–82.

Schouten, J. and J. McAlexander (1995) 'Subcultures of Consumption: An Ethnography of the New Bikers', *Journal of Consumer Research*, 22, 43–61.

Shah, S. (2000) 'Sources and Patterns of Innovation in a Consumer Products Field: Innovations in Sporting Equipment', working paper #4105, MIT.

Szulanski, G. (1996) 'Exploring Internal Stickiness: Impediments to the Transfer of Best Practice within the Firm', *Strategic Management Journal*, 17 (Winter, Special Issue), 27–43.

Teece, D., G. Pisano and A. Shuen (1997) 'Dynamic Capabilities and Strategic Management', *Strategic Management Journal*, 18, 509–33.

Tyre, M. and E. von Hippel (1997) 'The Situated Nature of Adaptive Learning in Organizations', *Organization Science*, 8(1), 71–83.

Urban, G. and J. Hauser (2004) '"Listening In" to Find and Explore New Combinations of Customer Needs', *Journal of Marketing*, 68 (April), 72–87.

Urban, G. L. and E. von Hippel (1988) 'Lead User Analyses for the Development of New Industrial Products', *Management Science*, 34(5), 569–82.

Vandenbosch, M. and N. Dawar (2002) 'Beyond Better Products: Capturing Value in Customer Interactions', *MIT Sloan Management Review*, 43(4), 35–42.

von Hippel, E. (1994) '"Sticky Information" and the Locus of Problem Solving: Implications for Innovation', *Management Science*, 40(4), 429–39.

von Hippel, E. (1998) 'Economics of Product Development by Users: The Impact of "Sticky" Local Information', *Management Science*, 44(5), 629–44.

von Hippel, E. (2002) 'Horizontal Innovation Networks – By and For Users', working paper, MIT Sloan School of Management.

von Hippel, E. and R. Katz (2002) 'Shifting Innovation to Users via Toolkits', *Management Science*, 48(7), 821–833.

von Hippel, E. (2005) Democratizing Innovation: Users Take Center Stage (MIT Press, forthcoming)

von Hippel, E. and G. von Krogh (2003) 'Open Source Software and the "Private–Collective" Innovation Model: Issues for Orgnaization Science', *Organization Science*, 14(2), 209–23.

Von Wartburg, Iwan (2002) 'Fallstudie Nike Shox', Universität Bern, working paper.

Wenger, E. (2000) 'Communities of Practice and Social Learning Systems', *Organization*, 7(2), 225–46.

Wenger, Etienne (2004) 'Knowledge Management as a Doughnut: Shaping your Knowledge Strategy through Communities of Practice', *Ivey Business Journal*, 68(3), 1–8.

9

Developing a Brokering Capacity within the Firm: The Enactment of Market Knowledge

Salvatore Vicari and Paola Cillo

Is market knowledge really useful to advance innovation and why are some companies better at using market knowledge to generate innovation than others? This paper addresses this issue conceptually, building on the assumption that it is distribution and usage of market knowledge which make the difference in innovative competition. We build on two different streams of research: market orientation and market knowledge, and knowledge brokering. We show why the emergence of internal market knowledge brokers may enhance the opportunity of innovation for organizations. We distinguish four different types of internal brokers. This distinction is related to the typology of knowledge to be transferred between two internal parties and the cognitive distance between these parties. Conclusions and implications are drawn on how companies should manage these figures of internal brokers in order to favour the distribution and the usage of market knowledge on the edge of innovation.

Introduction

Is market knowledge really useful to advance innovation and why are some companies better at using market knowledge to generate innovation than others? For many years, researchers and managers have focused their attention on the role of technological knowledge in the innovation process, somehow neglecting the role played by market knowledge (see Brown and Eisenhardt, 1995; Verona, 1999). Some researchers have tried recently to fill this gap and, recognizing the relevance of technological knowledge in underpinning product innovation, they have tried to consider both on a conceptual and empirical basis the impact that market knowledge might have on innovation (see Li and Calantone, 1998).

A number of scholars have recently challenged the idea that an important ingredient of innovation for companies might be their market knowledge, that is, the knowledge they have about their customers and competitors in the market (see Christensen and Bower, 1996). Indeed, their evidence shows that in some contexts paying too much attention to existing customers and competitors may lead some companies to lose their leadership. This result is attributed to the fact that the adoption of a certain mindset on the part of the company determines the replication of old frameworks in approaching the market.

In addition, companies tend to be inertial in the way they use and apply market knowledge to innovative purposes. More importantly, some studies have shown how in the relation between market knowledge and innovation the missing link lies in the processes of sharing and using the generated knowledge (Moorman, 1995). In the absence of *ad hoc* mechanisms enabling the sharing and use activities, companies are not able to leverage market knowledge to innovate.

Using this evidence, this chapter addresses the issue of how to deploy market knowledge to enhance organizational innovation. More specifically, we focus on the role played by knowledge brokers within the company to enable the exchange of complex market knowledge among groups with a high cognitive distance.

In order to focus on the ways market knowledge is implemented and used within the company by different organizational units, we integrate two streams of research.

First, studies on market orientation (for example, Narver and Slater, 1990; Kohli and Jaworski, 1990; Sinkula, 1994) and market knowledge (for example, Sinkula et al., 1997; Li and Calantone, 1998; Marinova, 2004) are considered to address the issue of how companies learn about customers, competitors and channel members in order to continuously sense and act on events and trends in present and prospective markets. These studies define the boundaries of the construct of market knowledge dealt with in this chapter.

Second, we consider the stream of research on knowledge-brokering in order to show how this capacity is fundamental to deploying the potential of market knowledge into organizational innovation.

From an academic perspective, this framework would facilitate a better understanding of the factors and mechanisms explaining the success of some companies compared to others in exploiting the power of market knowledge. We propose an integrated framework in which the nature of market knowledge is taken into consideration and, as a consequence, different mechanisms necessary to share and use market knowledge are defined. From the managerial point of view, the framework offers insights on how to manage market knowledge inside the company in order to exploit it for innovation purposes. We believe that the power of market knowledge resides in the ability of the organization to: (1) create a brokering capacity within the company; and (2) employ the mechanisms and tools coherent with the nature of the market knowledge to be produced, distributed and retrieved for innovation.

We postulate that a major role in this integration process is played by knowledge brokers acting inside the company and we define the characteristics and timing of action of these players with specific regard to the management of market knowledge in new product development projects. By definition, knowledge brokers integrate, recombine and transfer knowledge from one part to the other to foster innovation efforts of a specific node of the network (Hargadon and Sutton, 1997). We maintain that the same figures act also inside the organization with the final purpose of fine-tuning the efforts of exploration and exploitation strategies emerging at different levels. The recent literature developed on knowledge brokers – with particular regard to the interorganizational level – has, indeed, shown that the conditions for the emergence of these actors are: the presence of a structural hole between the two worlds that need to communicate, which implies the dispersion of knowledge that needs to be integrated; and the complexity of the knowledge to be transferred between the two parts (Hargadon and Sutton, 1997). Traditionally, a knowledge broker has taken the form of an innovation and design consultant company. We show that the main activities undertaken by these players do not change. Yet, their action is not 'one shot'; they intervene with specific timeframes and tasks for the goal they have to achieve.

The next section presents the chapter's conceptual underpinnings. The relationship between the typology of market knowledge to be integrated and distributed and the typology of internal brokers will be presented. Conclusions and implications for further research will be proposed in the last paragraphs.

Theoretical background

We rely on different streams of research in order to define the conceptual framework of market knowledge brokering within the company. We start by defining the content of this process, that is, market knowledge, and then we show how this knowledge may be manipulated within the company for innovative purposes.

In marketing literature, Glazer (1991, p. 2) defines market information in terms of 'data that have been organized or given structure – that is, placed in context – and endowed with meaning'. Similarly, the concept of market knowledge has been defined as 'organized and structured information about the market. Here organized means it is the result of systematic processing (as opposed to random picking), and structured implies that it is endowed with useful meaning (as opposed to discrete items of irrelevant data)' (Li and Calantone, 1998, p. 14). In terms of content, market knowledge, as described in market orientation literature, is relative not only to customers but also to competitors and other players working in different competitive environments (see Slater and Narver, 1995). The problem with these definitions of market knowledge is that they do not take into account the differences in the types of external knowledge to which organizations have access. Indeed, like technical knowledge, market knowledge has different dimensions, affecting the way it can be integrated and shared (see Polany, 1966; Winter, 1987; Zander and Kogut, 1995; Garud and Nayyar, 1994). In general, there are two explanations why there may be a transfer or an integration problem for complex knowledge: unwillingness and inability (Hansen, 1999). The inability problem is the one that appears focal in the analysis of the market knowledge integration process. Previous analyses of knowledge integration and transfer show that there are three dimensions of knowledge to consider relevant (Polany, 1962; Winter, 1987): its degree of articulation, complexity and independence. On the one hand, a low level of codification is close to the concept of tacitness, which implies that knowledge is difficult to articulate and can only be acquired through experience (see Nelson and Winter, 1982; Von Hippel, 1988; Nonaka and Takeuchi, 1995). The degree of complexity of knowledge depends on the amount of information necessary to describe it. Another dimension of knowledge, relevant for the purpose of this work, is the degree to which the knowledge is independent or part of a set of interdependent elements. Tacitness, interdependence and complexity are relevant dimensions of analysis in the process of absorption, transfer and integration of market knowledge. Indeed, these dimensions of knowledge tend to affect the ability of the organization to absorb and exploit a specific body of knowledge and require different mechanisms of integration (Hansen, 1999).

The definition of market knowledge we adopt in this chapter builds on the idea of knowledge used by Marinova (2004), who notes, 'market knowledge implies knowledge about customers and competitors' (p. 3). Yet, we extend this idea by operating a distinction between two levels of market knowledge. The first one is the knowledge that a company has about the actors in the market, that is, customers, trade and competitors (Day and Nedungadi, 1994). This knowledge represents the cognitive framework that a company uses, to understand the market and to take decisions, and resides inside the organization. For example, it has been empirically shown that customer knowledge development inside the organization may affect in a positive way new product performance (Joshi and Sharma, 2004). The second one is the knowledge that customers and trade have and that may be usefully deployed by companies through the enactment of specific tools for customer/trade knowledge-capturing. This second typology of knowledge resides in the interactions a company enables in the market, using different mechanisms to integrate customer and competitor knowledge into its knowledge base. By way of an example, mechanisms such as open platforms are put in place by software companies in order to use consumer knowledge to enhance the performance of a specific software program.

The knowledge asset developed by a company is the result of the integration of these two typologies of knowledge. The second type that is, customer and competitor knowledge, is more difficult to generate because of its tacit nature, but it comprises also the kind of knowledge that might represent a real source of competitive advantage because it enables the firm to satisfy expressed and latent needs and to foster its innovative activity while leveraging a high-potential knowledge that is its market network's knowledge (Jayachandran et al., 2004).

In order to establish a framework of how market knowledge, in both the configurations defined above, can be developed and used over time for innovative purposes, we will first consider the literature on market orientation that focuses on the processes underlying the ability of the organization to generate knowledge about customers, competitors and other players. Second, we will analyse the stream of research on knowledge brokering that has devoted a lot of attention to the processes that organizations can use to integrate knowledge. Finally, we will highlight the mechanisms and processes that companies may develop internally to distribute and use market knowledge over time. The relevant contribution of the streams of research considered for the analysis will be outlined in the next two sections.

Market orientation: Where and how market knowledge is created

A valuable contribution to the analysis of the main issue of this chapter comes from the scholars who, working in a marketing framework, have tried to address the question of which kinds of processes and capabilities drive market-oriented organizations (for example, Deshpande' and Webster, 1989; Kohli and Jaworski, 1990; Narver and Slater, 1990; Day, 1994a). The purpose of these works is twofold: on the one hand, they endeavour to identify the activities and processes of an organization that describe its market orientation; on the other, they seek to analyse the relationship between an organizational market orientation and an organization's innovativeness (for example, Slater and Narver, 1995; Hurley and Hult, 1998; Li and Calantone, 1998; Han et al., 1998). In these studies, the construct of market orientation is defined both in terms of processes and content of the market intelligence process. In particular, Kohli and Jaworski (1990) define market orientation as 'the organization wide generation of market intelligence pertaining to current and future customers needs, dissemination of the intelligence across departments, and organization wide responsiveness to it' (p. 6). In addition, Narver and Slater (1990) consider market orientation as a one-dimensional construct that comprises three different behavioural components: customer orientation, competitor orientation and inter-functional co-ordination. The first is the firm's understanding of the target market; the second is the firm's understanding of the capabilities of present and future competitors; lastly, inter-functional co-ordination is the co-ordinated use of the firm's resources and capabilities to create superior value for customers. The idea that results from the integration of these two perspectives is, first, that market orientation is an information-based construct, centred not only on customers, but also on competitors and players working in other industries. Indeed, there is a relevant difference between those firms that are customer-led and those that are market-oriented. 'Market-oriented businesses scan the market more broadly, have a longer-term focus, and are much more likely to be generative learners' (Slater and Narver, 1998, p. 1003). In addition, market orientation has a behavioural characterization. Indeed, the concept is related to the organizational information processes that affect an organization's market performance.

Recently, the impact of market orientation on organizational innovation has been investigated more deeply. The empirical evidence revealed controversial results with regard to this relationship. In Table 9.1 we depict the literature review on the relationship. The review shows that the results on the relationship between market orientation and innovation are inconsistent not only across studies that used the construct overall (for example, Atuahene-Gima, 1995; Hurley and Hult, 1998; Noble et al., 2002; Narver and Slater, 1994), but also in those analyses focused on the impact of each component of market orientation on innovation (for example, Christensen and Bower, 1996; Han et al., 1998; Voss and Voss, 2000).

Considering the absence of strong results supporting the relationship between market orientation and innovation, some researchers have challenged the idea that being market-oriented *per se* might represent the right path to follow. The empirical evidence to support this consideration has followed two different trajectories.

On the one side, there is a widespread conviction, empirically supported, that the generation of market knowledge in the absence of its sharing inside the company (Hoopes and Postrel, 1999, Marinova, 2004) and of its use (Moorman, 1995) does not affect innovation outcome. The focus on the upper part of the process, that is, the generation of market knowledge, is a necessary but not sufficient condition to produce new knowledge out of newly generated knowledge.

On the other side, a group of researchers have developed a more culture-oriented approach, based on the idea that companies may attain their market orientation in different ways. One approach, which could be referred to as proactive, relies on the use of the market, that is, the active production and interpretation of information about customers, competitors and the outside environment in general (see Rosa et al., 1999; Danneels, 2003). In a recent contribution, Narver and Slater (2004) explain that this approach is related to 'attempts to discover, to understand, and to satisfy the latent needs of the customers'. This process of generation and interpretation of the environment represents the main impulse of organizational decision-

Table 9.1 **Market orientation and innovation: A review of major studies**

Study	Major contribution of the study
	Positive relationship between market orientation and innovation
Slater and Narver (1994)	Market orientation – measured as customer orientation, competitor orientation, and inter-functional co-ordination – has a direct and positive impact on new product success.
Atuahene-Gima (1995)	Market orientation has a positive impact on new product performance, higher for incremental innovations.
Chandy and Tellis (1998)	Future-market focus has a direct impact on innovation.
Han, Kim and Srivastava (1998)	Overall, market orientation has a positive impact on administrative and technical innovation, which in turn affect organizational performance; customer orientation, in particular, has a positive impact on innovation.
Li and Calantone (1998)	Each of the three components of market knowledge competence – customer knowledge process, competitor knowledge process and marketing/R&D interface – has an impact on new product advantage and, through this, on organizational performance.
Lukas and Ferrell (2000)	Customer orientation is positively linked to new-to-the-world products, competitor orientation to me-too-products and inter-functional co-ordination to line extensions.
Slater, Narver and MacLachlan (2004)	Positive and significant relationship between proactive market orientation and new product success.

making and subsequent performance. On the other side, there are companies that can be defined as reactive in their approach towards market orientation. In this case, the information generated by the outside market is not acted upon and manipulated by the company; it is not deconstructed and reinterpreted to take decisions, but it represents the outside stimuli to which the company reacts (Slater and Narver, 1999). In this second approach, a learning experience is missing and this behaviour might have a negative impact on the company's innovative performance.

These approaches are different and might impact in a different way on organizational innovative outcome. Yet, both approaches emphasize market knowledge sharing and use as central processes to enhance organiza-

Table 9.1　Market orientation and innovation: A review of major studies
continued

Study	Major contribution of the study
	Negative or non-existent relationship between market orientation and innovation
Hurley and Hult (1998)	No evidence of market orientation as a predictor of a company's innovativeness.
Lukas and Ferrell (2000)	Absence of a relationship between market orientation and innovation.
Hult and Ketchen (2001)	The interaction between market orientation and innovativeness affects a company's performance.
Noble, Sinha and Kumar (2002)	No evidence of the relationship between market orientation and performance, nor of the mediational role of innovation.
Christensen and Bower (1996)	Customer orientation has a negative impact on disruptive innovation and organizational leadership in the market.
Han, Kim and Srivastava (1998)	No relationship between competitor orientation and inter-functional co-ordination and innovation.
Voss and Voss (2000)	Customer orientation, in the professional theatre industry, has a negative impact on financial performance because of the absence of breakthrough innovation.

tional innovative performance. For this reason, we integrate this stream of research with that on knowledge brokers to show how the brokering capacity might improve the market knowledge sharing process within the company.

Brokering capacity: How to integrate and recombine market knowledge over time

One major issue in managing market knowledge is related to the dynamics of knowledge, which is how to manage and use the knowledge produced in a certain period of time in different contexts and applications.

One of the methods of the supporting literature for approaching the issue of the integration and transfer of a complex kind of knowledge, such as market knowledge, is the social network theory (see Granovetter, 1973; Burt, 1992; Uzzi, 1996, 1997; McEvily and Zaheer, 1999) and the related approach based on the strength of ties perspective (see Granovetter, 1973;

Hansen, 1999; Uzzi, 1996; Ahuja, 2000). These two streams of research are primarily concerned with the relational bond between two or more social actors and the tightness of this relation as a means to share knowledge. They combine the network approach with the analysis of company resources and capacities (see Barney, 1991) and underline the role played by social, economic and professional relationships in explaining phenomena such as the formation of alliances (Gulati, 1999), the exchanges between companies (Uzzi, 1997), the acquisition of knowledge from outside sources (Hargadon and Sutton, 1997) or from different units within the same organization (Hansen, 1999). In particular, the concept put forward is that the network represents a resource and that a particular node can exploit and use the knowledge distributed in the network in its own process of value creation. The cornerstones of these two streams of research lie in the concepts of typology of ties – strong or weak – and the level of connectivity among the nodes of the network, taking into account the presence of structural holes in one actor's ego network (Burt, 1992; Ahuja, 2000).

As far as the typology of ties is concerned, the distinction between strong and weak is related to the fact that both have advantages or disadvantages. Researchers so far have reached a consensus on the fact that strong ties are considered as enhancing the opportunity for two social actors to share sensitive information with each other, while weak ties will provide access to non-redundant knowledge (Hansen, 1999). This idea is rooted in the work by Granovetter (1973) showing that, in the context of job research, an employment can be found more easily through acquaintances (that is, weak ties) than friends (that is, strong ties). The research presented in this study has reached a lot of applications in different contexts, such as the alliance and inter-organizational collaboration (Gulati, 1998; McEvily and Zaheer, 1999; Uzzi, 1997) and intra-organizational knowledge transfer (Hansen, 1999).

However, the advancement of the study into the field has shown how the perspective on the strength of ties needs to be integrated with considerations related to the structure of the network and to the level of connectivity that exists among the actors. The concept of connectivity refers to the structural holes theory developed by Burt (1992). According to this perspective, ties are redundant whether they lead to the same actors or not. 'Structural holes are gaps in information flows between alters linked to the same ego but not linked to each other' (Ahuja, 2000, p. 431). For these reasons, people on either side of the hole have access to different sets of information (Hargadon and Sutton, 1997). Figure 9.1 shows how networks B and C are connected through one of the nodes of the network A, covering a structural hole between B and C.

From the perspective of an actor aiming at accessing non-redundant knowledge, an ego network where partners have no links with each other

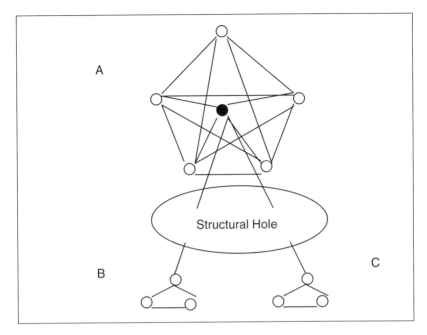

Figure 9.1   Where a structural hole emerges
Source: Adapted from Burt (1992)

has to be preferred to a network where partners are connected. In the first case, indeed, there is a major opportunity of accessing non-redundant knowledge. As shown by Hansen (1999), the interaction of partners through weak ties poses problems of time and speed of knowledge transfer, especially when the knowledge to be transferred – as in the case of market knowledge – is of a very complex nature.

The theory of knowledge brokering has been developed by Hargadon and Sutton (1997) speaking about the opportunities in high technological settings that companies might have by accessing a third party's technology through the action of specific players called technology brokers. The brokering activity is not based on a simple intermediation process, but involves four steps:

(1) access – filling the gap in the flow of technology between industries and between firms by occupying a central node or 'bridging' position between subgroups of a more extended network that do not interact with each other;

(2) acquisition – absorption of knowledge about a specific technology through intensive inter-industrial exposure and in-depth research;

(3) storage – memorizing the solutions in people, artifacts and procedures in the organization;
(4) retrieval – applying the stored and old technological solutions to create new solutions.

Recently the concept of technology brokering has been extended to that of knowledge brokering (Hargadon and Sutton, 2000; Sutton, 2002; Hargadon, 2003; Pawlowski and Robey, 2004; Verona Prandelli, and Sawnhey, 2005). In this broader view, knowledge brokers are defined as 'intermediaries ... between otherwise disconnected pools of ideas. They use their in-between vantage points to spot old ideas that can be used in new places, new ways and new combinations' (Hargadon and Sutton, 2000, p. 158).

The presence of these players helps to transfer complex knowledge between different parties not directly related, whose opportunities for interaction would be very rare and costly in the absence of such a broker. More important is that knowledge brokers create the opportunity for overcoming trade-offs between the strength of ties and the ease and speed of knowledge transfer, where weak ties imply access to non-redundant knowledge, but at a high cost, while strong ties enable an easier transfer of complex knowledge, but mostly give access to redundant knowledge (Granovetter, 1973; Hansen, 1999; Ahuja, 2000).

Recently, some studies have focused their attention on the role played by brokers within the company. These internal brokers have been defined as 'individuals who provide connections between communities of practice, transfer elements of one practice into another, enable coordination, and through these activities can create new opportunities for learning' (Wenger, 1998, p. 109). Similarly Brown and Duguid (1998) introduce knowledge brokers to indicate people participating in multiple communities and facilitating the transfer of knowledge among them.

Both these definitions assume that brokers do not act simply as agents or negotiators, but they manipulate knowledge before transferring it from one context to the other. More precisely, as emphasized by Pawlowski and Robey (2004, p. 649) they enact a 'process of translation [that] involves framing elements of one community's world view in terms of another community's world view'. The translation becomes a critical function of knowledge brokering for local knowledge to become comprehensible also to different units or communities within the company (Becky, 2003).

A model of brokering for the enactment of market knowledge

So far, we have introduced different streams of research to show: (1) the nature of market knowledge and the value that it might have, if fully explored, for innovative purposes; and (2) the importance of distributing market knowledge within the company especially among groups that do not share the same language and the same context of reference. Building on these two streams of research we aim at showing the reasons for the emergence of bridging roles, defined as internal market knowledge brokers, which enable market knowledge to be transferred from different groups within the company.

From the analysis we have drawn so far, there appear to be two major reasons for the emergence of bridging roles in the process of distribution and sharing of market knowledge.

First, the complexity of the innovative process within the company calls for a specialization of activities where those focused on the production of market knowledge are not necessarily those in charge of using it. Yet, notwithstanding these difficulties, the sharing and use of market knowledge is directly linked to the innovative performance of the organization. More specifically, the generation of market knowledge that is then not shared and used within the company represents a very costly but useless activity, as shown by a number of studies (for example, Moorman, 1995). This problem of developing synergies between exploration and exploitation strategies is not a new one in the management literature. To our knowledge, few studies so far have focused their attention on this topic (see Tushman and O'Reilly, 1997; Eisenhardt and Tabrizi, 1995; Kyriakopoulos and Moorman, 2004). Eisenhardt and Tabrizi (1995) suggest that firms might utilize experiential strategy while innovating. In this approach there is a mix of structure and uncertainty. Bierly and Chakrabarti (1996) suggest that firms with high levels of both radical and incremental learning produce a higher return on sales. More recently, Kyriakopoulos and Moorman (2004) show, through an extensive study of the Dutch packaging industry, how market orientation combines market exploitation and exploration strategies effectively by providing a unified frame of reference centred on customers' goals, by enabling market information flows inside the company and by integrating the two activities in line with dynamic environments. Specifically, this study shows the emergent need of a structured approach towards the development of synergies between the exploration and exploitation strategies. However, the path developed so far lacks the understanding of the mechanisms and processes related to the creation of synergies between the two strategies.

With specific reference to the kind of knowledge we are considering in this work, following Kyriakopoulos and Moorman (2004), on the one side, we define market knowledge exploitation strategies as those that imply a leverage on existing knowledge to refine marketing strategies, without exiting the existent path. More precisely, exploitation implies a company's moving along an existing learning curve, by leveraging its existent set of routines (March, 1991). On the other side, we define market knowledge exploration strategies as those that enact new approaches in the relationship with the market, by challenging existent convictions and routines of the organization. These strategies imply the development of new learning on the part of the organization and the definition of new routines and procedures related to how market knowledge is produced and used inside the organization. The brokering process, by enabling a richer flow of knowledge among exploration and exploitation units within the company, creates the opportunity for exploiting existent synergies between the two activities.

The second reason for the emergence of bridging roles in the process of distribution and sharing of market knowledge is that the market knowledge produced and distributed within the company is characterized by different levels of complexity.

As far as the problem of the type of knowledge is concerned, both codified/explicit and complex/tacit knowledge from the market are relevant. Some even claim that it is impossible to make a distinction between tacit and explicit knowledge, as there is always a tacit dimension even in codified knowledge (Nonaka et al., 2000). In particular, marketing researchers have been emphasizing the explicit dimension of market knowledge. In a sense, they have focused their attention on knowledge that is collected in customer databases, in customer satisfaction reports and in competitor benchmarking analyses (see Day, 1994b; Narver and Slater, 1990, 1994). However, a major part of market knowledge produced and transferred within the company is tacit, complex and often context-dependent. As highlighted before, these characteristics of market knowledge affect the opportunity of its transferral to and usage in a context that is different from the one in which it was created. Some researchers have rejected the idea of knowledge transfer models, which isolate knowledge from context and practice (see Brown and Duguid, 1991, pp. 47–8): 'Learners can in one way or another be seen to construct their understanding out of a wide range of materials that include ambient social and physical circumstances and the histories and social relations of the people involved. [...] Learning essentially involves becoming an insider. Learners do not receive or even construct abstract, "objective", individual knowledge; rather, they learn to function in a community.' So, one of the ways an organization can integrate tacit and complex knowledge, not easily learned when separated from the context in which it has been produced, is by becoming an insider within the context producing that knowledge.

The division of exploration and exploitation activities, on the one side, and the complex and often tacit nature of market knowledge to be transferred between different units, on the other, create the conditions for the emergence of a bridging role, such as the one we define as internal knowledge brokers. Internal knowledge brokers are those figures, individuals or teams, acting on market knowledge to enable the process of internal transfer between different groups or communities. Figure 9.2 illustrates the cornerstones of the market knowledge brokering process.

Figure 9.2   The role of internal knowledge brokers in enacting market knowledge

High	Knowledge Coder	Pure Knowledge Broker
Cognitive distance between the contexts	Selects the knowledge to be transferred and codifies it in a coherent language	Interpretation and manipulation of market knowledge e.g.: Villa Rosa - Barilla
	Information-Broker	**Integrated Knowledge Broker**
Low	Pure transfer of market information e.g.: Traditional boundary spanner	Becomes an internal component of the two parts that need to share knowledge e.g.: Diesel Creative Team, Diesel

Low   Complexity of market knowledge   High

Figure 9.3   Typologies of internal knowledge brokers

However, internal knowledge brokers might assume different configurations depending on the nature of the market knowledge transferred and on the cognitive distance between the contexts exchanging knowledge.

Figure 9.3 illustrates the different typologies of internal knowledge brokers distinguished on the manipulation of the market knowledge each one performs.

The simplest configuration is what we define as an information broker. This role is played by people within the company transferring market information between two different but very closely related contexts. This role is the one that, with higher probability, might be supported or substituted over time by technological devices, such as organizational intranet, enabling the knowledge to be shared and used by different actors and different branches within the same organization.

The knowledge coder is the configuration of broker that emerges whenever the two contexts that need to exchange knowledge are very distant from a cognitive point of view. This is, for example, the case of knowledge-sharing within the context of new product development projects. In these cases, indeed, the market knowledge generated by a market research unit or by those that have a direct contact with the market may be relevant also for the research and development activity that is evolving in other parts of the organization. When the languages and the cognitive frameworks of the different units are very distant, the only way market knowledge can be shared is by relying on the job of a third party able to code the information to be transferred in a way that is comprehensible for those that aim to use it.

The integrated knowledge broker emerges whenever the market knowledge to be transferred is very complex. This happens, for example, when the knowledge is generated by the interaction of a company with a community of customers in order to grasp new knowledge to be used in new product development processes. This type of knowledge is very contextual and difficult to share with other people within the company whe are not involved in the production of such knowledge. In this case the broker acts as internal actor in both the communities that need to share complex market knowledge. This is what happens, for example, in Diesel, a leading Italian company globally known in the casual wear industry. The company created the Diesel Creative Team, which operates as an integrated knowledge broker. Indeed, it is composed of six people from different backgrounds – marketing and distribution; communication; R&D; operation; and design – all contributing to various key phases in the collective development process. Their goal is to enable the process of market knowledge transfer from the designers' team to the marketing and communication function and to those in charge of the distribution of the product. In the fashion industry, indeed, the coherence of marketing activities with the themes developed into the collection is a key success factor and the only way to ensure this coherence is by leveraging the position of this team. In Burt's words, this covers a structural hole within the company and ensures the understanding of complex market knowledge by different communities that would be otherwise separated.

Finally, the pure knowledge broker emerges in those situations where there is a high cognitive distance between the two contexts and the knowledge to be transferred is highly complex. In this case, the broker acts as a solution-provider. Indeed, the only way to enable complex knowledge-sharing between highly distant contexts is to manipulate and package it in a way that is comprehensible for those who need it. The broker takes advantage of his position in the network to produce similar solution packages. We observed the presence of such brokers in very complex innovation-oriented organizations. In these cases, indeed, the need to pursue continuous innovation and the contribution of a different set of actors to this end pushes towards the adoption of key boundary roles. However, pure boundary spanners do not hold the competencies required to manipulate and repackage knowledge. An example of a pure knowledge broker is the case of Barilla, a leading Italian company in the food industry. Barilla has built over ten years a structure called Villa Rosa, which is dedicated to continuously monitoring customer trends and evolving habits through the direct involvement of consumers within the company's innovation process. This organizational team, physically separated from the rest of the company, represents a structure supporting the company's teams focused on new product development projects. It acts as a knowledge broker because it transfers *ad hoc* knowledge developed within Villa Rosa itself or within one of these projects on consumers. Market knowledge produced in one context is then repackaged and used to address the objectives of a different project.

Conclusions and implications for theory and practice

Recent studies developed in management have challenged the idea that close attention to customers' needs may positively affect a company's innovative performance. Christensen and Bower (1996), following the evidence of their study on the dynamics of innovation in the disk drive industry, conclude, 'the primary reason why such firms lose their positions of industry leadership when faced with certain types of technological change [is] because they listen too carefully to their customers' (p. 198). We depart from these empirical facts to show that the way market knowledge affects organizational innovative outcomes relies on the ability to share and use this knowledge within the company. This process, though, is not an easy one because, very often, market knowledge to be transferred has a complex nature and people sharing knowledge do not belong to the same cognitive contexts.

We propose that, in the presence of very complex market knowledge and the absence of a shared world and language, market knowledge sharing and usage may be enhanced by the presence of bridging roles, defined as internal knowledge brokers. We claim that there may be space for different configurations of knowledge brokers, but pure knowledge brokers emerge whenever market knowledge has a very complex and highly contextual nature. In this case, indeed, there is a real need for market knowledge to be manipulated and translated into a different language and the activities carried out by a knowledge broker may be fully deployed. As Pawlowski and Robey (2004, p. 666) emphasize, 'brokering is a critical element in facilitating convergence between shared systems and the practices they connect'. Market knowledge brokers foster the use of the knowledge produced of customers' knowledge and knowledge about the market developed by those in charge of it by translating and transferring it to those exploiting its value.

We believe that this stream of research sets the path for speculations on the opportunity of creating additional mechanisms, such as physical artifacts, that may enhance the use of market knowledge in organizational innovation projects. This topic has not been fully explored in the literature, especially for the case of integrating market knowledge both among people devoted to exploration strategy and those more focused on exploitation methods.

From a managerial point of view, our study contributes to the understanding of the mechanisms companies may adopt whenever they have a problem of sharing complex knowledge within the organization. So far companies have created interface roles, such as those we have defined as information brokers and knowledge coders. However, the most complex problems of market knowledge transfer that emerge in new product development activities are far from being solved. The pure knowledge broker and the integrated broker emerge as two relevant roles enabling the sharing of information. In this regard we think that companies should put major efforts into the creation of complex mechanisms to mend structural holes in key organizational processes in order to enable knowledge generated at a local level to flow to different areas, whenever and in whatever form it is needed.

Directions for future research

We began this chapter with a simple question: why are some companies able to use market knowledge where as others are not? Whether we speak of the design of a new computer or of new furniture, the integration of market knowledge is critical for competitive success, making a better understanding at a conceptual level an imperative.

This chapter has integrated different streams of research in order to identify from a conceptual point of view the approach companies might develop to foster market knowledge diffusion and use within the company. The first contribution of the chapter comprises its conceptual distinction between different approaches towards market knowledge creation within organizations. On the one side, there are companies proactive in developing market knowledge: they involve customers within their internal projects, enact the environment to produce information and make sense of it within the company. On the other side, there are companies adopting a reactive approach towards the market: they do not actively reproduce and interpret the information from the market.

Starting from this conceptual distinction, the chapter suggests how companies' performances strongly depend on the ability to use and integrate the market knowledge produced in and into its innovation activities. In particular, the chapter defines and articulates the role played by internal knowledge brokers to enable market knowledge diffusion and sharing to occur. We have shown via some examples how companies might exploit the power of market knowledge by creating *ad hoc* roles within the company to enhance the process of knowledge integration and how these roles depend also on the complexity of market knowledge to be transferred and on the cognitive distance among those who need it.

We believe that this study builds an important path into the conceptual development of knowledge management inside organizations in at least two major directions.

First, it moves the conceptual development of knowledge management from the problem of creation to examine transfer and use of the produced knowledge within the organization. Although other studies so far have paid attention to this issue (see Szulanski, 1996), the focus has been more on the organizational conditions that favour knowledge transfer within the company. However, we believe that there is space for a better understanding of the mechanisms and roles that an organization needs to create in order to enable knowledge sharing and use processes also among departments and teams that do not share the same cognitive world. This kind of analysis can be developed using qualitative case studies to better understand the emergent needs of interface roles enabling the sharing process to occur. As we have sustained previously, this issue is particularly important for those companies that need to integrate the efforts of different teams devoted to exploration and exploitation activities.

Second, the chapter emphasizes the growing importance of brokers to move knowledge not only among separated organizations, but also within the company. In doing so, it sets a rich research agenda on the knowledge management topic. Indeed, an interesting issue here is in the understanding of the different configurations and positions that can be played by these brokers within different organizational contexts. Particularly relevant appears their contribution in those contexts where a high level of integration is needed among teams of people focused on different tasks. In these cases, indeed, simple boundary spanners, or traditional interface roles, do not appear as appropriate to the task because there is a strong need for adaptation and manipulation of knowledge to make possible for one group of people to interpret and use knowledge produced by a different group. We believe that considerable effort could be exerted in this direction in order to better depict through comparative case studies the characteristics that brokers must have in order to make this knowledge-sharing process more fluid.

References

Ahuja, G. (2000) 'Collaboration Networks, Structural Holes, and Innovation: A Longitudinal Study', *Administrative Science Quarterly*, 45, 425–55.
Atuahene-Gima, K. (1995) 'An Exploratory Analysis of the Impact of Market Orientation on New Product Performance: A Contingency Approach', *Journal of Product Innovation Management*, 12(September), 275–93.

Barney, J. (1991) 'Firm Resources and Sustained Competitive Advantage', *Journal of Management*, 17, 99–120.

Becky, B. (2003) 'Sharing Meaning Across Occupational Communities: The Transformation of Understanding on a Production Floor', *Organization Science*, 14(3), 312–33.

Bierly, P. and A. Chakrabarti (1996) 'Generic Knowledge Strategies in the US Pharmaceutical Industry', *Strategic Management Journal*, 17, 123–35.

Brown, J. S. and P. Duguid (1991) 'Organizational Learning and Communities of Practice: Towards a Unified View of Working, Learning, and Innovation', *Organization Science*, 2(1), 40–57.

Brown, J. S. and P. Duguid (1998) 'Organizing Knowledge', *California Management Review*, 40(3), 90–111.

Brown, S. and K. M. Eisenhardt (1995) 'Product Development: Past Research, Present Findings, and Future Directions', *Academy of Management Review*, 20, 343–78.

Burt, R. S. (1992) *Structural Holes: The Social Structure of Competition* (Boston, MA: Harvard Business School Press).

Chandy, R. K. and G. J. Tellis (1998) 'Organizing for Radical Product Innovation: The Overlooked Role of Willingness to Cannibalize', *Journal of Marketing Research*, 34 (November), 474–87.

Christensen, C. M. and J. L. Bower (1996) 'Customer Power, Strategic Investment, and the Failure of Leading Firms', *Strategic Management Journal*, 17, 197–218.

Danneels, E. (2003) 'Tight–Loose Coupling with Customers: The Enactment of Customer Orientation', *Strategic Management Journal*, 24(June), 559–76.

Day, G. (1994a) 'The Capabilities of Market-Driven Organizations', *Journal of Marketing*, 58, 37–52.

Day, G. (1994b) 'Continuous Learning about the Market', *California Management Review*, 36(4), 9–31.

Day, G. and P. Nedungadi (1994) 'Managerial Representations of Competitive Advantage', *Journal of Marketing*, 58, 31–44.

Deshpande', R. and F. E. Webster (1989) 'Organizational Culture and Marketing: Defining the Research Agenda', *Journal of Marketing*, 53, 3–15.

Eisenhardt, K. M. and B. N. Tabrizi (1995) 'Accelerating Adaptive Processes: Product Innovation in the Global Computer Industry', *Administrative Science Quarterly*, 40, 84–110.

Garud, R. and P. R. Nayyar (1994) 'Transformative Capacity· Continual Structuring hy Intertemporal Technology Transfer', *Strategic Management Journal*, 15, 365–85.

Glazer, R. (1991) 'Marketing in an Information-Intensive Environment: Strategic Implications of Knowledge as an Asset', *Journal of Marketing*, 55, 1–19.

Granovetter M. (1973) 'The Strength of Weak Ties', *American Journal of Sociology*, 78(6), 1360–80.

Gulati, R. (1999) 'Network Location and Learning: The Influence of Network Resources and Firm Capabilities on Alliance Formation', *Strategic Management Journal*, 20(5), 397–420.

Han, J. K., N. Kim and R. K. Srivastava (1998) 'Market Orientation and Organizational Performance: Is Innovation a Missing Link?', *Journal of Marketing*, 62(October), 30–45.

Hansen, M. (1999) 'The Search-Transfer Problem: The Role of Weak Ties in Sharing Knowledge across Organization Subunits', *Administrative Science Quarterly*, 44, 82–111.

Hargadon, A. B. (2003) *How Breakthroughs Happen: The Surprising Truth about how Companies Innovate* (Cambridge, MA: Harvard Business School Press).

Hargadon, A. R., Sutton (1997) 'Technology Brokering and Innovation in a Product – Development Firm', *Administrative Science Quarterly*, 42, 716–749.

Hargadon, A. B. and R. Sutton (2000) 'Building an Innovation Factory', *Harvard Business Review*, May–June, 157–67.

Hoopes, D. and S. Postrel (1999) 'Shared Knowledge, "Glitches," and Product Development Performance', *Strategic Management Journal*, 20, 837–65.

Hult, G., M. Thomas and D. J. Ketchen Jr. (2001) 'Does Market Orientation Matter?: A Test of the Relationship Between Positional Advantage and Performance', *Strategic Management Journal*, 22(September), 899–906.

Hurley, R. F. and T. Hult (1998) 'Innovation, Market Orientation, and Organizational Learning: An Integration and Empirical Examination', *Journal of Marketing*, 62(July), 42–54.

Jayachandran, S., K. Hewett and P. Kaufman (2004) 'Customer Response Capability in a Sense-and-Respond Era: The Role of Customer Knowledge Process', *Journal of the Academy of Marketing Science*, 32(3), 219–33.

Joshi, A. W. and S. Sharma (2004) 'Customer Knowledge Development: Antecedents and Impact on New Product Performance', *Journal of Marketing*, 48(October), 47–59.

Kohli, A. K. and B. J. Jaworski (1990) 'Market Orientation: The Construct, Research Propositions, and Managerial Implications', *Journal of Marketing*, 54(April), 1–18.

Kyriakopoulos, K. and C. Moorman (2004) 'Tradeoffs in Marketing Exploitation and Exploration Strategies: The Overlooked Role of Market Orientation', *International Journal of Research in Marketing*, 21(3), 219–40.

Li, T. and R. J. Calantone. (1998) 'The Impact of Market-Knowledge Competence on New Product Advantage: Conceptualization and Empirical Examination', *Journal of Marketing*, 62(October), 13–29.

Lukas, B. A. and O. C. Ferrell (2000) 'The Effect of Market Orientation on Product Innovation', *Journal of the Academy of Marketing Science*, 28(2), 239–47.

March, J. G. (1991) 'Exploration and Exploitation in Organizational Learning', *Organization Science*, 2(1), 71–87.

Marinova, D. (2004) 'Actualizing Innovation Effort: The Impact of Market Knowledge Diffusion in a Dynamic System of Competition', *Journal of Marketing*, 68, 13–20.

McEvily, B. and A. Zaheer (1999) 'Bridging Ties: A Source of Firm Heterogeneity in Competitive Capabilities', *Strategic Management Journal*, 20, 1133–56.

Moorman, C. (1995) 'Organizational Market Information Processes: Cultural Antecedents and New Product Outcomes', *Journal of Marketing Research*, 32, 318–35.

Narver, J. C. and S. F. Slater (1990) 'The Effect of a Market Orientation on Business Profitability', *Journal of Marketing*, 54(October), 20–35.

Narver, J. C. and S. F. Slater (1994) 'Does Competitive Environment Moderate the Market Orientation Performance Relationship?', *Journal of Marketing*, 58, 46–55.

Narver, J., S. Slater and D. MacLachlan (2004) 'Responsive and Proactive Market Orientation and New Product Success', *Journal of Product Innovation Management*, 21(5), 368.

Nelson, R. R. and S. G. Winter (1982) *An Evolutionary Theory of Economic Change* (Cambridge, MA: Harvard University Press).

Noble, C. H., R. K. Sinha and A. Kumar (2002). 'Market Orientation and Alternative Strategic Orientations: A Longitudinal Assessment of Performance Implications', *Journal of Marketing*, 66(October), 25–39.

Nonaka, I. and H. Takeuchi (1995) *The Knowledge-Creating Company* (Oxford: Oxford University Press).

Nonaka, I., H. Takeuchi, R. Toyama and A. Nagata (2000) 'A Firm as a Knowledge-Creating Entity: A New Perspective on the Theory of the Firm', *Industrial and Corporate Change*, 9(1), 1–20.

Pawlowsli S. D. and D. Robey (2004) 'Bridging Users Organizations: Knowledge Brokering and the Work of Information Technology Professionals', *MIS Quarterly*, 28(4), 645–72.

Polany, M. (1966) *The Tacit Dimension* (New York: Anchor Day Books).

Rosa, J. A., J. F. Porac, J. Runser-Spanjol and M. S. Saxon (1999) 'Sociocognitive Dynamic in a Product Market', *Journal of Marketing*, 63(October), 64–77.

Sinkula, J. M. (1994) 'Market Information Processing and Organizational Learning', *Journal of Marketing*, 58, 35–45.

Sinkula, J. M, W. E. Baker and T. Noordewier (1997) 'A Framework for Market-Based Organizational Learning: Linking Values, Knowledge, and Behavior', *Journal of the Academy of Marketing Science*, 25, 305–18.

Slater, S. F. and J. C. Narver (1995) 'Market Orientation and the Learning Organization', *Journal of Marketing*, 59, 63–74.

Slater, S. F. and J. C. Narver (1998) 'Customer-Led and Market-Oriented: Let's Not Confuse The Two', *Strategic Management Journal*, 19, 1001–6.

Slater, S. F. and J. C. Narver (1999) 'Market Oriented Is Not Enough: Build a Learning Organization', in R. Deshpande' (ed), *Developing a Market Orientation* (Thousand Oaks, CA: Sage Publications), pp. 237–265.

Szulanski, G. (1996) 'Exploring Internal Stickiness: Tmpediments to the Transfer of Best Practice Within the Firm', *Strategic Management Journal*, 17, 27–43.

Sutton, R. (2002) 'Weird Ideas that Spark Innovation', *Sloan Management Review*, 43(2), 83–7.

Tushman, M. and T. O'Reilly, III (1997) *Winning through Innovation* (Cambridge, MA: Harvard Business School Press).

Uzzi, B. (1996) 'The Sources and Consequences of Embeddedness for the Economic Performance of Organizations: The Network Effect', *American Sociological Review*, 61, 674–98.

Uzzi, B. (1997) 'Social Structure and Competition in Interfirm Networks: The Paradox of Embeddedness', *Administrative Science Quarterly*, 42, 35–67.

Verona, G. (1999) 'A Resource-Based View of Product Development', *Academy of Management Review*, 24(1), 132–42.

Verona, G., E. Prandelli and M. Sawhney (2005) 'Innovation and Virtual Environments: Towards Virtual Knowledge Brokers', *Organization Studies*, forthcoming.

Von Hippel, E. (1988) *The Sources of Innovation* (Oxford: Oxford University Press).

Voss, G. B. and Z. G. Voss (2000) 'Strategic Orientation and Firm Performance in an Artistic Environment', *Journal of Marketing*, 64(January), 67–83.

Wenger, E. (1998) *Communities of Practices: Learning, Meaning, and Identity* (Cambridge: Cambridge University Press).

Winter, S. (1987) 'Knowledge and Competence as Strategic Assets', in D. J. Teece (ed), *The Competitive Challenge* (Cambridge, MA: Ballinger), pp. 159–84.

Zander, U. and B. Kogut (1995) 'Knowledge and the Speed of Transfer and Imitation of Organizational Capabilities: An Empirical Test', *Organization Science*, 6, 76–92.

10

Co-operation in a System of Distributed Cognition or How to Co-operate with Diverse Knowledge

Irma Bogenrieder

Since the importance of multifunctional teams for innovation has been recognized, there has been an ongoing discussion with regard to how diverse knowledge of the functional specialists should be combined and how co-operation should take place. In this chapter, I argue that a multifunctional team should be considered a distributed cognitive system. Such a distributed system should satisfy at least two requirements: shared location knowledge and developing a shared representation. The aim of this chapter is to conceptualize the processes whereby these requirements could be realized. These processes are described as joint speech acts. 'Speech Act Theory' conceptualizes language use as a type of social interaction. This theory is used to explain the development of location knowledge and shared interpretation.

Introduction

Multifunctional teams currently play an important role in innovative projects and innovation networks. Multifunctional teams in such innovative projects are characterized by the necessity of co-operation between diverse specialists, each with their own disciplinary knowledge and disciplinary background, in order to develop some innovative product or service. For realizing innovation, experts should combine their knowledge in a co-operative way. The advantage of diverse knowledge is stressed, as innovative product development requires the use of various expertise. Think, for example, about the development of an electronic scanning device for medical diagnosis. Co-operation between medical and computer technology experts is necessary in such a case. However, such diversity in knowledge is not only an advantage but also a problem. Diverse knowledge often implies that language and jargon are different. Experts also differ in their applied frames of reference (Boland and Tenkasi, 1995). Where experts differ in their knowledge, differences in life worlds could exist (Dougherty, 1990). In order to avoid a semantic jungle, I will refer to all these differences as differences in belief systems. These differences result in various specialists interpreting a problem or task in varied ways. Also, the criteria for the solution – sometimes called validation criteria – may be different between specialists. Differences between specialists in a multifunctional team, thus, cannot only be interpreted as cognitive differences in knowledge, they are more fundamental than that.

The question then arises, how can co-operation be achieved when experts differ in such a fundamental way? Is it realistic to assume that members in a multifunctional team already have some features in common *ex ante*? Shouldn't a common belief system better be conceptualized as the result of co-operative processes instead of assuming shared beliefs in advance? Tsoukas (1996) argues in this way.

In addition to this, there is another point of criticism. Do we really need general (that is, valid to the whole team) validation criteria? Or is it sufficient that specific members agree on shared validation criteria concerning a specific problem? In other words, how 'broad' and 'generalizable' do the validation criteria have to be? Furthermore, when specialists do not agree on validation criteria how can they co-ordinate their activities and co-operate in order to find an innovative solution? Co-ordination is generally understood as dealing with task dependencies that originate in specialization and division of labour (Grant, 1996; Crowston, 1997). In earlier writings, co-ordination is often understood as agreement on time, place and sequence of activities ('sequencing and scheduling activities' – Hoopes and Postrel, 1999). At the time of writing, this mechanistic concept of co-ordination is questioned. It is assumed that in order to co-ordinate complex and ambiguous tasks some shared meaning of the task and goal is necessary (Klimoski and Mohammed, 1994). Underlying these processes group members should have a common knowledge base, for example mutual understanding (Cramton, 2001), shared mental models (Klimosky and Mohammed, 1994) or a shared representation of the distribution of tasks (Weick and Roberts, 1993). For purposes of clarity, I shall call these newer insights 'co-operation'.

However, there are three problems concerning why these ideas about co-operation are not directly usable for multifunctional, innovative teams. First, in multifunctional teams a problem can only be solved by variance-seeking behaviour, with a portion of 'trial-and-error' during the 'solution' process. Second, agreement on a meaningful goal cannot be assumed as the goal does not (yet) exist at all (McGrath, 2001). And third, as already argued, mutual understanding and common validation criteria might not exist in advance. Thus, co-operation might be difficult as there is not (yet) a common interpretation of the task and goal; nevertheless, pure co-ordination is also falling short as there is not (yet) an overview of how activities should be scheduled and sequenced. The question thus remains of how to co-operate in a multifunctional team without having a common understanding of the problem and the goal and without common validation criteria.

In this chapter, it is argued that the causality should be exactly the other way round. Common understanding and validation criteria should be seen as a result of co-operation rather than a necessary condition.

The chapter proceeds as follows. First, I will introduce various notions of groups that have already dealt with this question. The most important notions of groups for multifunctional co-operation are epistemic community (Haas, 1992), transactive memory (Wegner et al., 1991), collective mind (Weick and Roberts, 1993) and distributed cognitive system (Hutchins, 1991). I discuss the requirements for co-operation as developed in these concepts. Several requirements can be identified. However, in the context of this chapter only one requirement – the development of a common representation of the distribution of work – will be discussed.

In this paper, I suggest that joint speech acts constitute the basic building block from which mutual or common knowledge is constructed from diverse knowledge. Also, roles and tasks are defined in terms of local interaction.

Requirements for cooperation in a multifunctional team

Recently, epistemic communities have been suggested as a form for innovative learning that makes use of the various specialists' belief systems. They are defined as

> a network of professionals with recognized expertise and competence in a particular domain and an authoritative claim to policy relevant knowledge within a domain or issue area […]. This network has (1) a shared set of normative and principled beliefs, which provide a value based rationale for the social action of community members; (2) shared causal beliefs, which are derived from their analysis of practices leading to a central set of problems in their domains and which then serve as the basis for elucidating the multiple linkages between possible actions and desired outcomes; (3) shared notions of validity – that is intersubjective, internally defined criteria for weighting and validating knowledge in the domain of their expertise; and (4) a common policy enterprise – that is a set of common practices associated with a set of problems to which professional competence is directed (Haas, 1992, p. 3)

This quotation nicely illustrates the assumption that is refuted earlier in the paper: members of an epistemic community already possess some criteria in common in order to co-operate. This assumption is understandable, as the notion of 'epistemic community' is often used in the context of geographical districts. Research has shown that people with some variation in knowledge, yet the same cognitive basis, easily find each other. Think, as an example, of a group of engineers required for the design of a textile machine. The ease of co-operation in such groups exists because they 'rely upon mutual understanding (which implies, at least, some common jargon if not a fully-developed language), a few procedural agreements about how to conduct research or design project activities, and some norms for the identification of what kind of knowledge ought to be shared, and with whom.' (Lissoni, 2001, p. 1482) Two main requirements for co-operation in an epistemic community can now be identified: first, common validation criteria or norms for conducting research; second, procedural agreement. In this chapter, I shall concentrate on the first requirement.

The notion of epistemic community makes clear that people should have some validation criteria in common. The advantages of knowledge specialization can be maintained to a certain degree as long as people agree on certain criteria. These agreements lie, in fact, outside a specialist's (content) domain. They describe how to evaluate and valuate others' contributions. Lissoni (2001) argues that agreement on these issues is easy as long as specialists rely on the same language. Thus, diversity in knowledge in an epistemic community is only moderately possible. Nevertheless, the notion of epistemic community allows for an important insight: there is no need to understand each other's knowledge in detail in order for co-operation to occur. Accepting a common validation criteria and a common procedure seems to be sufficient for enabling co-operation between specialists.

The notion of transactive memory (Wegner et al., 1985) stresses another aspect of multifunctional co-operation. The theory propagates that shared 'location knowledge' is necessary in order to make co-operation possible. 'Shared location knowledge' is described as knowledge of who knows what, which is shared by all members of a team. Closely related to location knowledge is the responsibility assigned to an individual to remember a certain item. Furthermore, 'a set of communication processes whereby two minds can work as one' (Wegner et al., 1985, p. 263) is necessary for making transactive memory effective. As individuals in a team possess detailed, specialized knowledge, shared location knowledge must be available to all team members in order to make knowledge usable. The individual as 'knowledge carrier', then, has the social responsibility to contribute when his knowledge is necessary. As intuitively attractive as this model might be, its authors do not provide any insight into how these communication processes take place. For example, does a transactive memory system need shared validation criteria? How is shared location knowledge established? What are the labels used in order to locate knowledge?

Although the theory of transactive memory supplies a poor description of the processes for locating knowledge and for co-operation, nevertheless, the theory makes clear again – as the model of epistemic community already had – that there is no need to fully understand others' knowledge for realizing co-operation. Furthermore, the theory stresses the possibility of a cognitive 'distribution of labour' as long as the various knowledge locations are connected to each other.

The model by Weick and Roberts (1993) of a 'collective mind' is a third theoretical insight when conceptualizing co-operation in a multifunctional team. Collective mind refers to the fact that people exhibit group behaviour without the existence of group norms or group pressure. Group performance in a collective mind is seen as the behavioural outcome when people act *as if* they were a group. More specifically: 'The second defining property of group performance is that when people act as if there are social forces, they construct their actions (contribute) while envisaging a social system of joint actions (represent), and interrelate that constructed action with the system that is envisaged (subordinate).' (Weick and Roberts, 1993, p. 363). The authors suggest heedful interrelating as a disposition for constructing a collective mind. The three processes of contributing, representing and subordinating are identified as the central processes for constructing a collective mind. Building up a shared representation is of great importance here. A shared representation is the cornerstone for an individual's contribution and subordination. 'There are group actions that are possible only when each participant has a representation that includes the actions of others and their relations. The respective actions converge relevantly, assist and supplement each other only when the joint situation is represented in each and when the representations are structurally similar.' (Asch in Weick and Roberts, 1993, p. 363).

The theory of collective mind suggests that people need a shared representation for co-operation in a quasi-group. Also, this theory acknowledges a cognitive 'distribution of labour'. Compared to the model of transactive memory, a representation is described not only as a set of knowledge locations. The function of a shared representation goes further. A shared representation determines and structures each individual member's behaviour. Contribution and subordination are relative to the shared representation. A shared representation offers an overview for the individual of how various activities relate to each other. The importance of common validation criteria for co-operation is not supported in the notion of collective mind. The function of a shared representation is comparable to the function of a procedural authority. Both offer an insightful structure on how members' activities are related to each other. Unfortunately, Weick and Roberts (1993) do not elaborate on how a shared representation may be developed.

Multifunctional teams as systems of distributed cognition

From the analysis above, two conclusions can be drawn. First, as all the above models and theories assume a mental 'distribution of labour', the view of a multifunctional team as a system of distributed cognition is conceivable. The characteristics of such a system are summarized by Hutchins and Klausen (1996):

(1) Access to information is distributed. Some people have more or different information than others.
(2) Storage of this information is also distributed in the system.

Second, in order to enable co-operation in a distributed cognitive system, such a system should satisfy some requirements. The various theoretical insights do not exactly overlap as far as the requirements are concerned. However, there are some common features which are considered necessary requirements for co-operation, including:

- shared location knowledge should be built up
- a shared representation and/or agreement on procedural authority should exist

Note that these features are not necessarily a complete list of requirements. For example, the social structure in a multifunctional team is not taken into account, nor are the 'social forces' as mentioned by Weick and Roberts (1993).

The analyses above, however, do not elaborate on how these requirements can be fulfilled. The processes for identifying shared location knowledge and for achieving a shared representation are not elaborated. How do these processes actually take place and which processes can be identified?

Hutchins and Klausen (1996) suggest intersubjective understanding or shared meaning of a situation or problem as the basic building block for co-operation. Intersubjective meaning is understood here as a distributed phenomenon. Intersubjective meaning implies that members construct shared knowledge about the distribution of knowledge in the sense of, 'I know that you know that I know that you know x' (Hutchins and Klausen, 1996). Hutchins and Klausen (1996) rely heavily on the notion of 'shared expectations' as a basis for developing intersubjective understanding. The case that is discussed by the authors is the crew on an airplane. The authors state in their analysis: 'Certainly, the pilots entered this situation with a considerable amount of shared prior knowledge about how things are supposed to go or how they typically go.' (Hutchins and Klausen, 1996) In fact, this case is similar to the characteristics of an epistemic community, where members can easily co-operate because of their common body of knowledge. However, the question raised in this chapter is, how can co-operation take place under circumstances where shared expectations do not (yet) exist. Shared expectations should therefore better be understood as an outcome of a communication process, not as an input.

In the following section, I suggest the notions of joint communicative acts, as developed by Clark (1996), and speech act theory as an explanation of how intersubjective meaning is constructed and how this leads to co-operation without some shared expectations in advance.

Intersubjective meaning of a situation and shared location knowledge

Assuming that a multifunctional team is considered as a distributed cognitive system suggests that intersubjective meaning should develop for a specific task or situation and on a local basis. Members should build up a shared or – better – intersubjective meaning simultaneously with insights into location knowledge. Intersubjective meaning is defined as: 'I know that you know that I know that you should respond.' (Hutchins and Klausen, 1996, p. 24) It should be clear from this definition that intersubjectivity consists of two parts: a shared understanding of the situation combined with shared knowledge about the distribution of knowledge. Intersubjective meaning is similar to what Cramton (2001) defines as mutual knowledge: 'In each case, mutual knowledge consists not only of the information itself but also the awareness that the other knows it.' (Cramton, 2001, p. 347) In other words, intersubjective understanding contains location knowledge and the sharing of that location knowledge which is the basic block of a representation in the sense of Weick and Roberts (1993). 'Mutual knowledge is knowledge that the communicating parties both share and know they share.' (Krauss and Fussell, 1990, p. 112)

The question is, how can intersubjective meaning be constructed given the diverse knowledge backgrounds of the participants and given the distributed nature of this knowledge? In a multifunctional team members do not know where knowledge is located – at least, not in the beginning. Hutchins and Klausen state, based on their research with pilots: 'In the course of their interaction, they use that shared knowledge as a resource to negotiate or construct a shared understanding of their particular situation.' (Hutchins and Klausen, 1996, p. 23) But what happens when reliance on a common body of knowledge is not available, as is the case in multifunctional teams?

Clark (1996) and Clark and Marshall (1981) formulate an answer to this question. They argue that communication exactly serves the purpose of building up mutual knowledge and intersubjective meaning. Clark (1996) insists that a speech act has to include a speaker and a hearer. Instead of just analysing the speech act of the speaker, the joint act between speaker and hearer should also be analysed.

It is within this (two-sided) communication that people try to establish a mutual belief that they understand each other well enough. The assumption of shared understanding *ex ante* is not necessary.

The claim is this: Every presentation enacts the collateral question 'Do you understand what I mean by this?' The very act of directing an utterance to a respondent is a signal that means 'Are you hearing, identifying, and understanding this now?' This is one goal of the presentation phase, and one goal of the acceptance phase is to take up that question. Respondents complete the joint project immediately when they answer or imply 'yes': they alter it when they initiate a repair sequence that implies 'no'. (Clark, 1996, p. 243)

Clark and Marshall (1981) argue that defining mutual knowledge is, from a logical point of view, an indefinite process; nevertheless, people are able to find mutual knowledge in seconds. Thus, they argue, mutual knowledge should be grounded in the shared belief that people have succeeded in understanding each other: 'The participants in a joint action try to establish the mutual belief that they have succeeded well enough for current purposes.' (Clark, 1996, p. 226) Clark and Wilkes-Gibbs (1986) argue that mutual belief is established through an acceptance process. This acceptance process makes the indefinite regress definite. The acceptance process is based on the principle of mutual responsibility in conversation, which says: 'The participants in a conversation try to establish, roughly by the initiation of each new contribution, the mutual belief that the listeners have understood what the speaker meant in the last utterance to a criterion sufficient for current purposes.' (Clark and Wilkes-Gibbs, 1986, p. 33) The authors assume that participants can achieve a common belief (that they have understood each other) through the course of the conversation. Mutual knowledge, as defined above, has now changed to the mutually accepted *belief* that intersubjective understanding is established. How co-operation takes place in a conversation makes participants accept the belief that intersubjective meaning has been established. A participant is obliged to interrupt the conversation when he believes that intersubjective meaning has not been successfully established, for example when he cannot accept that there is a mutual belief.

This conceptualization proves that the assumption is incorrect (see Cramton, 2001: 349) that 'there first must be mutual knowledge as a precondition for effective communication', as it is rather the other way round: by communicating intersubjective meaning is established in local communication. At the same time members learn and become aware of the (distributed) location of knowledge.

Weick and Roberts (1993) mention contribution within a representation as an important feature of a collective mind. This analysis suggests that both contributing and accepting another's contribution are also signals that make people believe that they have a shared understanding. The process of contributing is a constituent part of building up a representation. Furthermore, this analysis suggests that one of the most important contributions could be to signal that mutual belief is not yet established.

In addition to this communicative dynamics of how mutual knowledge is achieved, Clark (1996) also conceptualizes the reasons why a participant assumes that mutual knowledge is (not) achieved. The question, therefore, is: what makes somebody believe that there is mutual knowledge? Or, more accurately: what makes somebody accept the belief that mutual understanding is achieved? Both – theories of distributed cognition as linguistics – formulate as an answer that expectations about the other's behaviour establish the important hint as to whether mutual knowledge is achieved. When expectations are not met, the belief in mutual knowledge is weakened. Insights from speech act theory are used to explain how expectations towards another person arise. Note that it is assumed that members can achieve intersubjective meaning, but do not have to rely on a common body of language to do so.

Speech Act Theory and expectations as co-ordination devices

Speech Act Theory was first developed by Austin (1975). Speech act theory treats verbal utterances as a type of social interaction. 'Speech act makes a linguistic utterance, mainly by virtue of its meaning, the bearer of what would best be called a communicative sense. Notice, that a communicative sense belongs to the domain of social interaction and can in general be implemented in various ways, among which the use of verbal utterances is the most elaborate and often the most effective one.' (Bierwisch, 1980, p. 3)

Within speech act theory there lies the well-known distinction between illocutionary, perlocutionary and propositional acts when using language in context (Austin, 1975; Searle et al., 1980). Propositional or locutionary acts are about the true (false) representation of an utterance. They have a referential meaning. Furthermore, 'the illocutionary act [...] has a certain *force* in saying something; the perlocutionary act [...] is *the achieving of* certain *effects* by saying something' (Austin, 1975, p. 121). An illocutionary act pertains to the state of the speaker and his intentions. 'By performing an illocutionary act a speaker usually expresses also a certain psychological state relating to the propositional content. This psychological state is a function of the nature of the illocutionary force. Thus, for example, a speaker who promises to do something expresses his intention to do it. A speaker who orders expresses his desire that the hearer carries out a certain future action.' (Vanderveken, 1980, p. 256) The perlocutionary act concerns the speaker's desired effect on the hearer. The distinction between the illocutionary and perlocutionary acts is not always clear in the philosophical discussion. However, this difficulty is not essential here. In what follows, I shall make use especially of the illocutionary act; however, using it in this way may not be in line with the strict philosophical criteria.

What makes speech act theory interesting for explaining co-operation in a system of distributed cognition is the proposition that a speaker communicates not only propositions but also expectations with regard to the other's behaviour. Expectations on how to behave are expressed as illocutionary or perlocutionary acts. Thus, when the speaker and the hearer do not have the same knowledge or belief system, they nevertheless can communicate something beside: in the illocutionary act the speaker's intention towards his own behaviour and in the perlocutionary act the speaker's expectation of the intended effect on the hearer; expectations concerning the hearer's behaviour.

What matters here, is that speech act theory recognizes that an utterance has in addition to the locutionary act an element of social relatedness. An utterance is not only about the content but also about the expected behaviour between persons, for example between a speaker and a hearer or between myself as a speaker and myself as a hearer. 'The illocutionary point of an apology is to express to the hearer a regret or sorrow for a state of affairs. The illocutionary point of a promise is to commit the speaker to carry out a certain future course of action in the world of the utterance.' (Vanderveken, 1980, p. 253) Speech act theory thus recognizes that an utterance is directed towards somebody in a certain way and implies certain expectations, for example as a promise, as an order and so on. An utterance, thus, has in addition to the locutionary act the function of building up a particular relationship between hearer and speaker. The speaker wants to 'transfer' his intention to a hearer (note: we still do not know how the hearer might react to this intention). When communicating an intention in the illocutionary act, the speaker constructs a relationship between the speaker and the hearer and indicates his expectations. Hutchins and Klausen (1996) have stressed the co-ordinating function of expectations in a distributed cognitive system. However, they assume – similar to the notion of epistemic communities – that members should already have as a basis shared expectations. The line of reasoning based on speech act theory is the other way round. By making an utterance, a speaker not only explicates his message but also indicates his expectations (as in the case of the pilots in an aircraft). When the hearer goes along with these expectations the activities of speaker and hearer become co-ordinated. It was stated in the introduction that co-ordination defined as sequencing and scheduling activities is not usable in a multifunctional team. This is still true. Co-ordination of activities based on expectations does not need a planning approach. Co-ordination develops from the fulfilment of expectations. By repetition, a stable pattern of interactions can emerge which is similar to the development of a representation as described by Weick and Roberts (1993).

Critical reflection and conclusion

Multifunctional teams should combine diverse knowledge as it is brought in by team members in order to realize innovation. The problem is, however, that in such a team it is often unclear who has what knowledge and how to combine certain knowledge, especially when members differ in their belief systems. In order to find an answer, first, various notions of teams, communities and other types of groups are explored for identifying requirements for co-operation under the above-mentioned circumstances. In this exploration, a unified perspective could not be found. However, some common requirements could be identified, such as shared location knowledge and shared representation or – in another paradigm – agreement on a procedure.

The basic processes for co-operation are described on the basis of the model of joint acts and speech act theory. Joint acts enable the construction of intersubjective meaning. Intersubjective meaning is defined as: 'I know that you know that I know that you interpret situation x as ... (a certain issue)'. In this definition, two functions of intersubjective meaning are identified:

1. Shared location knowledge: participants become aware of the distribution of knowledge among members regarding a certain issue.
2. Establishment of a shared belief of understanding: participants agree on the belief that they understand each other.

When such intersubjective meaning is agreed upon, speech act theory claims that, as a next step, expectations for behaviour are formulated in communication. Expectations are considered an important device for co-ordinating activities and building up a representation. Whether there is 'real' mutual understanding cannot be guaranteed. The fulfilment of expectations is considered an important signal that intersubjective understanding has been achieved.

This elaboration leaves some unanswered questions. First, a multifunctional team is characterized as a system of distributed cognition. Hutchins and Klausen claim that 'cognitive labor is socially distributed' (Hutchins and Klausen, 1996, p. 19). The above analysis does not elaborate on the influence of social structure on the processes of constructing intersubjective meaning. Second, intersubjective meaning and expectations are described as the building blocks for developing a shared representation about the distribution of knowledge and about expected behaviour. It is currently unknown how locally developed intersubjective meaning is expanded into the larger system. Third, empirical work is necessary in order to test the claims and processes as described here. As a first step, hypotheses should be developed for testing.

References

Austin, J. L. (1975) *How to Do Things with Eords* (Oxford: Oxford University Press).
Bierwisch, M. (1980) 'Semantic Structure and Illocutionary Force', in J. R. Searle, F. Kiefer and M. Bierwisch (eds), *Speech Act Theory and Pragmatics* (Dordrecht: D. Reidel Publishing Company), pp. 1–35.
Boland, R. J. and R. V. Tenkasi (1995) 'Perspective Making and Perspective Taking in Communities of Knowing', *Organization Science*, 6(4), 350–72.
Clark, H. H. (1996) *Using Language* (Cambridge: Cambridge University Press).

Clark, H. H. and C. R. Marshall (1981) 'Definite Reference and Mutual Knowledge', in A. K. Joshi, B. L. Webber and I. A. Sag (eds), *Elements of Discourse Understanding* (Cambridge: Cambridge University Press), pp. 10–63.

Clark, H. H. and D. Wilkes-Gibbs (1986) 'Referring as a Collaborative Process', *Cognition*, 22, 1–39.

Cramton, C. D. (2001) 'The Mutual Knowledge Problem and its Consequences for Dispersed Collaboration', *Organization Science*, 12(3), 346–71.

Crowston, K. (1997) A Coordination Theory Approach to Organizational Process Design', *Organization Science*, 8(2), March–April, 157–175.

Dougherty, D. (1990) Understanding New Markets for New Product, Strategic Management Journal', *Special Issue: Corporate Entrepreneurship*, Summer, 11, 59–78.

Grant, R. M. (1996) 'Toward a Knowledge- Based Theory of the Firm', *Strategic Management Journal*, Winter Special Issue, 17, 109–122.

Haas, P. M. (1992) 'Introduction: Epistemic Communities and International Policy Coordination', *International Organization*, 46(1), 1–35.

Hoppes, D. G. and S. Postrel (1999) 'Shared Knowledge, "Glitches", and Product Development Performance', *Strategic Management Journal*, 20, 837–865.

Hutchins, E. (1991) 'Organizing Work by Adaptation', Organization Science, 2(1), 14–39.

Hutchins, E. (1999) *Cognition in the Wild* (Cambridge, MA: MIT Press).

Hutchins, E. and T. Klausen (1996) 'Distributed Cognition in an Airline Cockpit', in Y. Engestroem and D. Middleton (eds), *Cognition and Communication at Work* (Cambridge: Cambridge University Press), pp. 15–34.

Klimoski, R. and S. Mohammed (1994) 'Team Mental Model: Construct or Metaphor?', *Journal of Management*, 20(2), 403–37.

Krauss, R. M. and S. R. Fussell (1990) 'Mutual Knowledge and Communicative Effectiveness', in J. Galegher, R. E. Kraut and C. Egido (eds), *Intellectual Teamwork: Social and Technological Foundation of Cooperative Work* (Hillsdale, NJ: Lawrence Erlbaum), pp. 111–45.

Lissoni, F. (2001) 'Knowledge Codification and the Geography of Innovation: The Case of Brescia Mechanical Cluster', *Research Policy*, 30, 1479–500.

McGrath, R. G. (2001) 'Exploratoy Learning, Innovative Capacity', and Managerial Oversight, *Academy of Management Journal*, 44(1), 118–31.

Postrel, S. (2002) 'Islands of Shared Knowledge: Specialization and Mutual Understanding in Problem-Solving Teams', *Organization Science*, 13(3), 303–20

Searle, J. R., F. Kicfer and M. Bierwisch (1980) *Speech Act Theory and Pragmatics* (Dordrecht: D. Reidel Publishing Company).

Tsoukas, H. (1996) 'The Firm as a Distributed Knowledge System: A Constructionist Approach', *Strategic Managmenet Journal*, 17(Winter Special Issue), 11–25.

Vanderveken, D. (1980) 'Illocutionary Logic and Self-Defeating Speeach Acts', in J. R. Searle, F. Kiefer and M. Bierwisch (eds), *Speech Act Theory and Pragmatics* (Dordrecht: D. Reidel Publishing Company), pp. 247–72.

Wegner, D. M., Giuliano, T., Hertel, P. (1985) 'Cognitive Interdependence in Close Relationship', in W. Ickes (ed.) *Compatible and Incompatible Relationships* (New York: Springer), 253–276.

Wegner, D. M., R. Erber and P. Raymond (1991) 'Transactive Memory in Close Relationships', *Journal of Personality and Social Psychology*, 61(6), 923–29.

Weick, K. E. and K. H. Roberts (1993) 'Collective Mind in Organizations: Heedful Interrelating on Flight Decks', *Administrative Science Quarterly*, 38L, 357–81.

Part III

Managing the Knowledge-based Company

11

Bridging Leadership and Learning in Knowledge-based Organizations

Stefan Güldenberg and Heinz Konrath

This chapter examines how leadership influences learning in knowledge-based organizations. The pertinent literature suggests that leadership has a major impact on the learning capabilities of a corporation and its members. Consequently, organizations are increasingly viewing leadership as a source of competitive advantage. This is particularly true of high-tech and knowledge-based organizations that act in a complex and dynamic environment. Although there is a lack of empirical evidence of how exactly leadership influences learning in organizations, this chapter takes a modest step to further reduce the existing gap by pointing out how learning in organizations demands specific leadership requirements and how these leadership requirements can be achieved. We will propose a 'learning leadership model' that goes beyond the traditional understanding of leadership and can be used as a starting point for a holistic approach to leadership in knowledge-based organizations.

1. Introduction

One of the main challenges of knowledge management theory and practice is based on the deep assumptions we hold about leadership. Do we think leadership is a top–down or a bottom–up approach? Do we think leadership is a centralized function carried out by top management or is leadership distributed throughout the organization and independent from hierarchical positions? Do we think that great leadership needs a charismatic leader or can it be learned by everyone? Do we think leadership in knowledge-based organizations is all about knowing the right answer or about facilitating learning?

It is obvious that leadership has the potential to be both a great enabler and a great disabler of learning in organizations simultaneously (Senge, 1990). Nevertheless, the correlation between leadership, knowledge management and organizational learning has been largely neglected in research. Despite two studies (Driver, 2002; Ellinger and Bostrom, 2002) concentrating on different aspects of the interrelationship between leadership and learning, there is still a lack of empirical research in this area (see Crossan and Hulland, 2002; Easterby-Smith et al., 2000; Harvey and Denton, 1999; Miner and Mezias, 1996; Richter, 1998; Sadler, 2001).

This chapter takes another modest step to reduce this gap by showing how specific leadership requirements can be achieved in knowledge-based organizations. The approach taken in this chapter considers leadership in knowledge-based organizations from two perspectives: the individual and the organizational. Such an understanding not only refers to persons but also takes into account the capability to design effective organizational structures and to lead organizations strategically to achieve their goals. Therefore, this chapter addresses both organizational and individual contextual constraints of current leadership practices, taking into consideration organizational culture and strategy as well as individual capabilities.

2. Questioning the traditional concept of leadership

In recent literature, the concept of leadership has been moving gradually from centring on the individual to one centring on the organization:

2.1 Personalized leadership theories

These theories focus on the skills, behaviour, values and actions of the leader; company performance is primarily explained by the characteristics of top management (Finkelstein and Hambrick, 1990, 1996; Hambrick and Mason, 1984). Weber et al. (2001, p. 582) differentiate between two ways to assess and predict leadership performance. The first approach concentrates on characteristics that a successful leader should possess, such as charisma, self-trust and rhetorical ability, and then attempts to find people with these skills. The second approach evaluates leaders according to past performance, as in increasing company value or successfully turning a company around, and asserts that past performance is a good indicator of future performance. Charisma theory takes this one step further (see the early work by House, 1977; Conger and Kanungo, 1987; and, more recently, studies by Awamleh and Gardner, 1999; Hunt, 1999; Hunt et al., 1999; Shea and Howell, 1999). In this theory, a company's performance depends on the charisma of its leaders and their ability to motivate their employees.

Existing personalized leadership theories, however, do have several weaknesses (comparable criticism can be found in Hunt, 1999; Marion and Uhl-Bien, 2001). Their most significant is the assumption that the performance of companies can be traced exclusively back to the behaviour of certain individual persons, particularly the CEO:

> However, we also believe that, with some exceptions, existing approaches
> to the study of leadership remain heavily grounded in the premise that

leadership is interpersonal influence [...], and therefore focus primarily on leader attributes and follower emotions [...]. While this is certainly a critical aspect of leadership, it may not tell the full story. Moreover, this emphasis may be related to problems of reductionism and determinism [...] in the leadership field as a whole. Reductionism refers to research logic in which parts of a system are isolated and studied independently of the system from which they derive – the general idea is that, if one can understand the parts, one can draw conclusions about the whole. Determinism is the belief that all events are caused by preceding events and by knowing the preceding variables one can predict the future with certainty (Marion and Uhl-Bien, 2001, p. 391).

Underlying reductionism and determinism of existing leadership theories result in the following three assumptions of personalized leadership theories which need to be questioned:

1. Existing leadership theories often assume that specific leadership qualities are applicable to and successful in all organizations, independent of strategy and the structural context. These leadership qualities are often linked to the leader's personality and qualification. It is obvious that this leadership theory matches reality only if you assume either a very simplistic view of the world or a very high degree of abstraction (for example, the WICS model of leadership from Sternberg, 2003). Obviously, a person managing a bureaucratic company during a crisis needs to have a different set of capabilities than the founder or manager of a company in the high-tech sector during times of rapid expansion.
2. Existing leadership theories are further flawed as they do not consider the dynamic interrelationship between the individual, the leader and the organizational context as critical success factors of leadership. The configuration of the organization, especially the architecture of the management system (Mintzberg, 1979), can be taken as an example. Often, attention is paid only to the dynamic interrelationship between the leader and the follower. However, both leader and follower are acting in the structural context of an organization, which can be very heterogeneous regarding its hierarchical forms. In this context the principal-agent theory which deals with corporate governance architecture and its implications for management decisions is to be mentioned as a positive exception (Jensen and Meckling, 1978; Grossman and Hart, 1983). But the structuring of governance architecture is only a small task compared to the challenge of designing a leadership system which stimulates knowledge-creation and learning.
3. Finally, existing leadership approaches do not sufficiently consider the present and future challenges of organizational development. They are deeply embedded in a leader–follower model of the past, based on the

role of the leader as an omnipotent and omniscient hero. But the leadership model of the industrial age may no longer be appropriate for knowledge-based organizations acting in the knowledge-age: 'In the knowledge era, we will finally have to surrender the myth of leaders as isolated heroes commanding their organizations from on high. Top–down directives, even when they are implemented, reinforce an environment of fear, distrust, and internal competitiveness that reduces collaboration and cooperation. They foster compliance instead of commitment, yet only genuine commitment can bring about the courage, imagination, patience, and perseverance necessary in a knowledge-creating organization. For those reasons, leadership in the future will be distributed among diverse individuals and teams who share responsibility for creating the organization's future' (Senge, 1997, p. 32).

2.2   Organizational leadership theories

Such theories start with the points of criticism listed above and seek to extend the classical individual-centred and historical leadership approaches to include the organization, its current environment, culture, strategy and configuration. (See in particular the early work by Cyert and March, 1963; Mintzberg, 1979; more recently, approaches by Ghoshal and Bartlett, 1998; Hunt, 1991; Nonaka and Toyama, 2002; Schneider, 2002; Senge, 1999; Witt, 1998; Zaccaro and Klimoski, 2001). Gilley and Maycunich (2000, p. 100) define leadership as 'a process of making decisions regarding how to interact with employees to motivate them, then translating those decisions into actions'. In this sense the primary purpose of leadership is to motivate others to take actions to accomplish predetermined goals. Senge (1999, p. 16) views leadership as 'the capacity of a human community to shape its future, and specifically to sustain the significant processes of change required to do so'. According to Nonaka and Toyama (2002, p. 1005), leadership in a knowledge-creating company contains the following roles: creating a knowledge vision; building, connecting and managing the learning context ('ba'); maintaining creative routines; and constructing an effective incentive system. Leadership in the context of this research is not limited to senior executive leaders, but is seen as a requirement and an attitude *on all levels* of an organization.

From these points of criticism, we can therefore derive that, within the leadership theory, a contextual consideration is absolutely necessary to arrive at scientifically valuable statements. This comprises both the spatial context (organization, strategy and environment) and the temporal context (development stage of the organization). We consider particularly important the integration of the individual business leader into the entire leadership and governance system of the organization. In the next section we shall discuss the theoretical underpinnings of our empirical study.

3. Leadership and learning in the context of knowledge-based organizations

In accordance with Zack (2003), we understand the term *knowledge-based organization* to be concerned not with what the organization sells but by what the organization *does* and how it is *organized*. Therefore, the main characteristics of a knowledge-based organization cannot in the first place be found in their intangible and knowledge-intensive products and services, but rather in their underlying knowledge-based structure, strategy and processes. This includes among others the following actions (Zack, 2003, pp. 70f.):

- define the organization's mission in terms of knowledge;
- define the organization's industry and position within it in terms of knowledge;
- formulate strategy with knowledge in mind;
- implement knowledge management processes and structures that directly support the company's strategic knowledge requirements;
- transform the company into a learning organization; and
- treat the cost of learning as an investment, not an expense.

Following the organizational learning approach of Argyris and Schön (1978) Schein (1985) and Senge (1990), we assume that there is an important interrelationship between the organizational level and the individual level. This means that individual leaders (their skills, behaviour, values and actions) impact organizational leadership capabilities (the organizational culture, infrastructure and learning ability) and vice versa. This interrelationship can be seen as the seed for organizational change, which consequently forms the basis for organizational learning. The feedback process (organizational leadership impacts the individual) initiates a learning process on the individual level (see also Nonaka and Takeuchi, 1995, p. 13). The stronger the alignment between individual and organization, the better the organization will be able to learn. Therefore we attempt to integrate both leadership dimensions, the individual and the organizational.

3.1 Individual leadership in knowledge-based organizations

Organizational learning starts at the individual level. In a knowledge-based organization, *training and learning* are basic parts of corporate strategy and individual objectives. Senge (1990, pp. 139f.) considers personal mastery, that is, the capacity to produce results by mastering the underlying principles, a form of motivation. According to Osterloh and Frey (2000), money, power and status symbols are not the only motivators for people. Instead, people will be committed because they want to learn in order to perform well and to be recognized as people. Therefore, leadership should be responsible for facilitating individual learning. This not only increases the knowledge base of the individual and the consequent support of organizational learning; it also leads to a higher level of commitment and loyalty.

In our qualitative study, we will further address to what extent *soft skills*, such as communication, system thinking, the ability to create an environment of trust and to develop and share visions, support leadership in knowledge-based organizations. We will also examine how critical are hard or *technical skills*, that is, educational background, for effective leadership. In this context, the term 'technical skills' refers to the theoretical and practical capacity to perform any given task (product familiarity, sales experience and accounting knowledge).

How does *interpersonal networking and communication* impact the organizational learning process? Depending on the organizational culture, networking can be seen, at one extreme, as unproductive time or, at the other, as prerequisite to eliminating learning barriers and facilitating knowledge sharing. We will analyse how a culture that supports horizontal, vertical and diagonal networking and communication can facilitate the organizational learning process.

3.2 Organizational leadership in knowledge-based organizations

First, organizational leadership is about *shared leadership*. At the beginning of the twenty-first century, Western corporate culture is still struggling to form groups or teams representing organizations (internally as well as externally). Tradition requires having one person at the top. Leadership in a knowledge-based organization shifts from traditional 'one-at-the-top' leaders to a community of leaders. Such a community consists of executive leaders, networking leaders and local line leaders (Senge, 1997, p. 32). By acting as a leadership community, such individuals ensure alignment across all organizational functional areas as well as at the highest strategic degree. The alignment on the organizational and individual levels depends on the ability of individual leaders to create shared mental models and shared values. In such a model, the whole system of organizational leadership, not the individual leader, is accountable for the well-being of an organization.

In our study we will discuss to what extent *support from executive leaders* (Senge, 1997), that is, those living the values as role models on the highest organizational level, is required to achieve alignment between the individual and organizational levels. Additionally, we address the importance of executive sponsorship in practice and its impact on major change initiatives and organizational learning.

We will also examine the importance of strategic attention for organizational learning. *Strategic attention of learning* refers to the extent to which individual and organizational learning are an integrated part of strategic management and control systems (Simons, 1994). Learning organizations are based on a vision that is documented and shared with all members of the organization. Strategic goals and measures are clearly communicated. Artifacts and values (Schein, 1985) that focus on innovation, and are supported by a learning strategy, facilitate organizational knowledge creation. Furthermore, the linkage and alignment of the learning strategy to other strategies of the organization are crucial for the innovation process (Slocum et al., 1994). Such alignment can be achieved through objective-setting and performance-monitoring.

4.   Leadership and learning: Views of practice

In support of this chapter, we have carried out a study to obtain input on key topics related to leadership and learning from managers and leaders in a knowledge-based industry. A total of 125 managers and leaders from various companies participated in our survey, with 86 participants representing the IT/telecommunications industry. In addition, input from 39 selected managers or leaders from other knowledge-based industries was used to validate the feedback received from representatives of the IT/telecommunications industry.

To perform the survey, a web-based tool was chosen. The questionnaire consisted of 30 questions, of which eight served a statistical purpose (age, gender, geographic area of origin, company location, line of business, number of employees, function and level).[1] Of the 22 non-statistical questions, 21 were closed questions, offering the possibility to add individual comments if required and relevant. One question requested text input. Participants were chosen to achieve a wide variety of individual functions, managerial level, age and geographic territory. Prior to the official launch, a test run was made using three individuals to verify how the questionnaire was perceived with respect to clarity and time required for completion, along with the technical functionality, integrity and ease of use of the survey tool. All responses were kept anonymous, that is, feedback was not analysed on the individual level. The total number of responses of 125 represents a rate of 69 per cent.

We have used the opinions received to identify common issues that appear to be crucial for knowledge creation and knowledge sharing. By linking the information received to existing theory, we present a model that reflects future leadership requirements in knowledge-based organizations.

4.1   Individual leadership

A total of 97 per cent of responses confirm that continuous learning is a key requirement for the success of an organization. There is a high level of agreement across all industries and functions. Among respondents, as age and management seniority level increase, there is a tendency to view the importance of learning as slightly lower. On the other hand, in 39 per cent of the organizations in our survey, individuals spend an average of fewer than five days per year on training and learning (including all kinds of training and learning such as technical, managerial, language, systems, preparation for the job and so on), followed by 31 per cent reporting between five and ten days. These results can be interpreted as contrary to the consensus on the question regarding the importance of learning for organizational success.

A total of 98 per cent of all respondents agree/strongly agree that the ability to motivate others is a key leadership requirement, while 97 per cent express the same opinion on communication and networking, 96 per cent on creating an environment of trust and self-motivation and 95 per cent on developing and sharing visions. The importance of these soft skills for effective leadership is underscored by a comparatively low rating on hard skills, since only 59 per cent of respondents consider technical skills, that is educational background, as critical for effective leadership. Unlike input on soft skills, which shows a high degree of consistency, feedback on hard or technical skills varies depending on area of origin, location of headquarters, function, management level and company size.

A total of 74 per cent of all respondents agree, and 16 per cent strongly agree, that personal reputation of success versus failure impacts performance as much as compensation. Further examination shows that the impact of personal reputation on motivation increases with age (78 per cent of respondents less than 30 years old; 89 per cent of those between 31 and 40; 92 per cent of those between 41 and 50; and 95 per cent of those older than 51). While responses are consistent across company sizes and functions, responses of agree and strongly agree increase with level of management (79 per cent for lower management, 91 per cent for middle management and 94 per cent for top management).

A total of 97 per cent of all respondents of our leadership survey view communication and networking as key requirements for effective leadership. Concerning time spent for networking, a vast majority, 79 per cent of responses, indicates lack of time as the number one reason preventing networking. According to the results of the survey, 54 per cent of the participating managers spend up to 10 per cent of their working time on networking. Only 19 per cent of all participants indicate that they spend more than 20 per cent of their working time on networking. The age analysis shows that networking time increases with age. In this regard, responses are consistent across all management levels. The only exception is middle management, where, compared to lower and upper management, twice as many respondents indicate more working time spent networking. According to the survey, industry itself does not impact the networking culture of an organization. Concerning company size, feedback does not indicate a clear pattern, leading to the conclusion that company size does not automatically enable a networking culture. In this regard, responses are consistent across all functions (with the exception that HR/training/education spend the most time networking), showing that networking does not depend on functions. In the categories of headquarters, industry, function or company size, the survey feedback is consistent, that is, lack of time is the critical issue preventing networking. Only 19 per cent of respondents say they spend the right amount of time networking. In summary, we conclude that networking does not receive a high priority. Besides lack of time (equivalent to lack of priority), networking, in many cases, is considered unproductive. The importance of networking for innovation is obviously being ignored.

4.2 Organizational leadership

A total of 57 per cent of respondents agree, and a further 18 per cent strongly agree, that shared leadership, that is, a leadership team, is more effective than a single individual leader. Closer analysis of this positive response of 75 per cent on the question of shared leadership reveals the following details:

- Gender, geographic area of origin, geographic location of headquarters, line of business, company size and function do not affect the view of shared leadership.
- With increasing age, positive feedback on effectiveness of shared leadership gradually decreases (younger than 30 years, 80 per cent; 31 to 50, 77 per cent; older than 50, 63 per cent). With increasingly senior level of management, positive feedback on effectiveness on shared leadership gradually decreases (lower management, 85 per cent; middle management, 75 per cent; top management, 71 per cent).

A total of 87 per cent of the responses indicate that top management initiates organizational changes; 4 per cent say middle management, 5 per cent cite an internal work force combined of various management levels, and 4 per cent say external agents/consultants. A similar distribution is seen among all industries and company sizes in this survey.

A total of 78 per cent of the responses in the survey indicate lack of time as the main roadblock to organizational learning, followed by lack of budget (42 per cent), lack of sense of urgency (27 per cent), too much internal focus (27 per cent), lack of top management support (26 per cent), and lack of leadership (24 per cent). Results show a high degree of consistency across age, gender, function, industry and management level. Lack of time, as the main barrier for learning, can be interpreted as lack of priority, showing that there are no tools and processes in place to foster training and learning at the individual level. The feedback also indicates that in almost half of the companies investment in learning does not have high priority. The organizational learning process, like any other goal of an organization, requires enthusiasm and proper prioritization at all levels.

5.   The 'Learning Leadership Model' – practical implications

Based on the characteristics of individual and organizational leadership as described in section two, the roles of learning and leadership in knowledge-based organizations revealed in section three and the analyses of our survey in section four, practical implications that support organizational learning will now be proposed. The resulting 'Learning Leadership Model' adds an additional dimension to traditional leadership functions. It refers to a much broader leadership definition than traditional leadership and is not limited to top management. The main criteria that differentiate learning leadership from traditional leadership are *self leadership* and *shared leadership*. In a knowledge-based organization, learning leadership will be distributed and take place on all levels of the organization (Nonaka and Toyama, 2002).

5.1   Cultivating self-leadership as a necessary requirement at the individual level

Learning starts at the individual level, and the participants of our survey have almost unanimously (97 per cent) confirmed that continuous learning is a key requirement for the success of an organization. At the same time, it has been indicated that the average yearly time spent on training and learning is very low (70 per cent spend less than ten days). The main role of leadership in a learning organization is to create an environment of constant learning on all levels of the organization (individual, group and organization). Davis and Botkin (1995, pp. 41f.) identify four steps of learning: from data to information to knowledge to wisdom. In this definition, data are considered as ways of expressing things. An arrangement of data into meaningful patterns is considered information. Knowledge is the application and productive use of information and wisdom is the discerning use of knowledge. In these four steps to wisdom, training is understood as instruction and mastery at a given level, whereas learning is the movement from one level to the next. In this context, an important role of leaders in a learning organization is to put the right focus on learning, that is, on the process, not only on training. Closely linked to learning is unlearning. Unlike forgetting, unlearning is the result of an intentional process (Hedberg, 1981). At the individual level, the replacement of old knowledge by new knowledge results in unlearning. In an organization, unlearning avoids the maintenance of different versions of knowledge in different parts of an organization. Organizational unlearning avoids duplication and increases efficiency by eliminating knowledge that is not needed any more. The fact that the half-life period of knowledge is continually shortening is a result of unlearning due to more new knowledge being available. In a learning organization, training, learning and unlearning are integrated into the objectives of each member. The objectives are linked into the organizational strategy and support the necessary focus for execution on the individual level, thus forming the base for organizational learning. Self-leadership requires that each individual takes accountability for developing his or her own training and learning plans. Self-leadership also means *cultivating soft skills and social intelligence.* Merriam-Webster's Collegiate Dictionary defines 'social' as follows: 'involving allies or confederates'; 'relating to human society, the interaction of the individual and the group, or the welfare of human beings as members of society'; 'tending to form cooperative and interdependent relationships with others of one's kind'. The same source refers to 'intelligence' as 'the ability to learn or understand or to deal with new or trying situations'; 'the skilled use of reason'; 'the ability to apply knowledge to manipulate one's environment [...]'; 'the act of understanding'. In combination with Senge's (1990) identifying system thinking as the main leadership skill in support of organizational learning, social intelligence can be seen as the ability to communicate and to act based on a systemic view; to make this view transparent to all members of an organization; and to support learning on the individual as well as on the organizational level. The ultimate goal of leadership based on social intelligence is to generate this leadership behaviour across the entire organization. Leadership is not restricted to a selected group of high performing individuals or executives. It becomes a key requirement for each individual, team or group within an organization, independently from management level and organizational structure. It applies to each individual, whether heading a huge team or being a single supporter. The function of self-leadership in contrast to the traditional understanding of leadership is to produce more leaders, not more followers. Self-leadership is developing people to the point that they surpass their superiors. Followers are transformed into leaders. In this context it can be stated that soft skills, which support organizational knowledge creation, knowledge sharing and organizational learning (initiating motivation, communication and networking, creating an environment of trust, self-motivation, developing and sharing a vision), are more critical for effective leadership in learning organizations than hard skills, which can be considered as a minimum leadership requirement, depending on industry, business strategy and function – a view supported by more than 95 per cent of the survey respondents.

Communication has to be considered a key self-leadership requirement in learning organizations. The ultimate goal of self-leadership is to create an environment that fosters and facilitates communication and networking across the entire organization (vertical, horizontal, diagonal) and beyond.

It requires a significant mind shift that eliminates existing mental models with respect to leadership and accountability. The way in which members of an organization communicate with each other and with individuals or groups outside the organization impacts its culture and vice versa. Everything an individual in an organization is doing results in communication, whether through speaking, writing, acting, gesture and even by doing nothing. Communication sends signals to others that can be interpreted in various ways. The more an individual is aware of the importance of such signals and the more he or she ensures that they are interpreted in the desired way, the more effective this individual will become as a leader, independently from whether they occupy a traditional leadership position (Drucker, 1999). Feedback received from the survey confirms that 90 per cent of managers across various countries, industries, company cultures and management levels agree/strongly agree that personal reputation impacts performance as much as compensation. To create a moral bond among individuals, this attitude has to be leveraged, that is, it has to be brought from the individual level (reputation and pride for oneself) to the group level. Such a shift can be supported by the networking structure of an organization, as well as its cultural elements (communication, praises, rewards). Our view on the importance of communication and networking is shared by 97 per cent of all survey respondents. Nevertheless, the survey discloses that there is not enough networking due to lack of time. The future of knowledge management will depend partially on the willingness to prioritize knowledge activities such as learning, where the output may not be immediately measurable.

5.2   Cultivating shared leadership as a necessary requirement at the organizational level

At the organizational level, alignment and a common understanding across all organizational functions is a precondition for knowledge sharing and organizational learning. Shared leadership, that is, a leadership team instead of one individual leader at the top, facilitates this alignment through a common language, vision and strategy, and increases the effectiveness of the organizational learning process (75 per cent of responses received in the survey confirm this assumption). The vision has to clearly address both the present and future purpose of the organization and its goals. Shared leadership makes leaders more accessible and ensures alignment of the vision of an organization across all functions. Shared leadership creates an *identity* on the organizational level and strengthens the common bond across all functions (Kogut and Zander, 1996). It fosters the awareness of organizational reputation and highly leverages individual contributions to organizational performance. Shared leadership facilitates that the vision is communicated to, understood by and supported by all members of the organization and implies accountability across functional competence levels. Handy (1995, pp. 106f.) states that the leader(s) must live the vision, that is, if the leader(s) fail(s) to believe in the vision and to live it, credibility will suffer and the vision will fail. In the same context the leader(s) must remember that the vision is the work of others, that is, the vision will remain a dream without the work of others to make it reality.

A total of 78 per cent of the responses in the survey indicate lack of time as the main roadblock to organizational learning, followed by lack of budget (42 per cent), and lack of sense of urgency (27 per cent), which can be interpreted as lack of priority-setting. The organizational learning process requires enthusiasm and proper prioritization on all levels. Strategic thinking and planning identify the organizational priorities. Traditional strategic planning focuses mainly on financial goals that can be clearly measured, such as revenue growth, ROI or EVA, and strategy is communicated via budgets. People are seen as liabilities or expenses and are paid for their temporal presence. Consequently, time is money and organizational learning is often seen as (too) expensive. 'The top thinks and the local acts' is a typical expression of this situation. On the opposite side, leadership in learning organizations embeds intangibles as core parts of the strategy. Investment strategies in human, organizational and relational capital, even if there are no common defined measures available as yet, have to be made explicit in order to increase the knowledge base of the organization. People are seen as assets and are paid for their strategic performance. Strategic thinking and learning has to be shared throughout the entire organization. Each member has to verify existing processes within their own area of responsibility and align them to the overall strategy. The core question each individual has to raise is, 'how does the output of my work support the overall strategy of the organization?'

If shared strategic thinking and learning can be considered the engine of a change initiative, top management is the fuel. A total of 87 per cent of the respondents in our study indicate that top management initiates organizational changes and 26 per cent see the lack of top management support as the main barrier to organizational learning. Since change processes form the basis for knowledge creation and organizational learning, the efficiency of change management in an organization directly impacts its organizational learning process. Executive support can be provided in the form of a steering committee consisting of executive leaders. That steering committee not only offers escalation support to middle management responsible for the execution of a project (quick decisions in case of lack of consensus within the project team), but also sets the pace, ensures solid progress and can remove unexpected barriers beyond the authority level of the project team (for example, approval of additional budget). It is crucial that executive leaders communicate the purpose and the goal of changes throughout the entire organization to ensure full commitment to execution on all levels. Executive leaders need to act as role models, that is, live the values on the highest level of integrity. Operating with integrity forms a framework that helps members of the organization to navigate in times of uncertainty and ambiguity. Integrity builds trust, which is another precondition for knowledge-sharing. Unless individuals can believe that team or group performance will support their career development, they will continue to protect their knowledge against 'internal competition'. The perception that sharing knowledge is equal to losing knowledge will not be eliminated. Each individual contributes and impacts the culture of an organization. If it is required to change a certain culture (this is a complex and timely process), it is up to the leaders to initiate corrective actions (Schein, 1985).

5.3   The 'Learning Leadership Model': self-leadership and shared leadership combined

Figure 11.1 attempts to illustrate the impact of self-leadership and shared leadership on organizational learning in four stages of development.

Stage one indicates a *fragmented organization* with scarce or insufficient leadership. Individuals act in uncoordinated and isolated ways; there is no clear picture of how individual contribution impacts the overall performance of the organization. Learning (if any) exists only on the individual level, not on the organizational level; communication and networking are insufficient.

Stage two represents an organization with a traditional, hierarchical management. These organizations represent what De Geus terms *territorial organized companies* (De Geus, 1997, p. 138). Roles and responsibilities of all members are clearly defined by mandate. Each member knows where his or her own responsibilities start and end. Most of the members have a more or less clear picture of the goals of the organization but, due to a lack of communication, knowledge-sharing and innovation are prevented. The members of the organization could be described as preservers of their own territorial gardens.

Stage three reflects an organization that works with a high degree of self-leadership. A high degree of social intelligence in combination with reputation-based incentives and well-established communication and networking channels support knowledge transfer and organizational learning. The performance of the organization as a whole is higher than the sum of all individual performances would be. In a *relation-based organization* (Marshall, 2000, p. 81), the leadership structure reflects an emphasis on dialogue, exchange and interaction. Communication in the leadership team flows in all directions and is based on open dialogue and honest and candid discussions. However, organizational learning and knowledge creation remain limited to the internal system and do not make full use of external networking.

Stage four represents a *learning organization* with a high capacity for learning leadership. It is characterized by fully utilized self- and shared leadership to prevent knowledge barriers. Unlike in traditional organizations, learning organizations are involved in creating the future versus simply reacting to an existing environment (Senge, 1999). Alignment, a common language, executive support and a learning strategy create an environment of continuous learning and understanding of reality. In this highest stage learning leadership exists throughout the entire organization; there is no risk of an over-managed or under-led corporate culture (Kotter, 1996, p. 28).

| Stage 1 | Stage 2 | Stage 3 | Stage 4 |

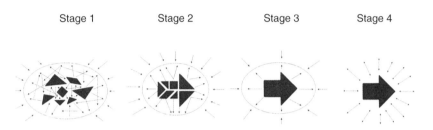

Figure 11.1   The 'Learning Leadership Model'

6. Conclusions

In the economy at the time of writing, the strategic importance of organizational learning and knowledge is on a steady rise. Innovation as a result of organizational learning and knowledge generation is increasingly becoming the driver for value creation and sustainable success in commercial enterprises. Knowledge-based organizations require specific leadership skills and behaviours (which we call 'learning leadership') to successfully create an environment that supports innovation strategies. Our study shows that learning leadership goes beyond traditional, hierarchical leadership. In such an organization leadership has to be seen as a capability, not as a position.

First, learning leadership is based on *self-leadership* at the individual level. The ability to lead oneself lies in constant learning and training inside a human community (the organization). Soft skills and social intelligence, in this regard, are more important than hard skills. An organizational culture that fosters horizontal, vertical and diagonal *communication, networking and personal reputation* increases the efficiency of knowledge-sharing and organizational learning.

Second, learning leadership is based on *shared leadership* at the organizational level. A shared vision and strategy facilitates alignment inside the organization and increases the effectiveness of the organizational learning process. Of course, organizational learning can take place without being linked to strategy, but this would increase the likelihood of less efficiency or failure. On the other hand, executive support is important. Although knowledge management is part of everyone's job, it is the role of executive leaders of a knowledge-based organization to make organizational learning an integrated part of the strategy.

Note

1 A copy of the questionnaire is available upon request from the authors.

References

Argyris, C. and D. A. Schön (1978) *Organizational Learning: A Theory of Action Perspective* (Reading, MA: Addison-Wesley).

Awamleh, R. and W. L. Gardner (1999) 'Perceptions of Leader Charisma and Effectiveness: The Effects of Vision Content, Delivery and Organizational Performance', *The Leadership Quarterly*, 10(3), 345–73.

Conger, J. A. and R. N. Kanungo (1987) 'Toward a Behavioral Theory of Charismatic Leadership in Organizational Settings', *Academy of Management Review*, 12(4), 637–47.

Crossan, M. and J. Hulland (2002) 'Leveraging Knowledge through Leadership of Organizational Learning', in C. W. Choo and N. Bontis (eds), *The Strategic Management of Intellectual Capital and Organizational Knowledge* (Oxford: Oxford University Press), pp. 711–23.

Cyert, R. M. and J. G. March (1963) *A Behavioral Theory of the Firm* (Englewood Cliffs, NJ: Prentice-Hall).

Davis, S. M. and J. W. Botkin (1995) *The Monster under the Bed* (New York: Touchstone).

De Geus, A. (1997) *The Living Company* (Boston, MA: Harvard Business School Press).

Driver, M. (2002) 'Learning and Leadership in Organizations: Toward Complementary Communities of Practice', *Management Learning*, 33(1), 99–127.

Drucker, P. (1999) 'Managing Oneself', *Harvard Business Review*, 77(2), 65–74.

Easterby-Smith, M., M. Crossan and D. Nicolini (2000) 'Organizational Learning: Debates Past, Present and Future', *Journal of Management Studies*, 37(6), 783–96.

Ellinger, A. D. and R. P. Bostrom (2002) 'An Examination of Managers' Beliefs about Their Roles as Facilitators of Learning', *Management Learning*, 33(2), 147–79.

Finkelstein, S. and D. C. Hambrick (1990) 'Top Management Team Tenure and Organizational Outcomes: The Moderating Role of Managerial Discretion', *Administrative Science Quarterly*, 35(3), 484–503.

Finkelstein, S. and D. C. Hambrick (1996) *Strategic Leadership: Top Executives and Their Effects on Organizations* (Minneapolis: West).

Ghoshal, S. and C. A. Bartlett (1998) *The Individualized Corporation: A Fundamentally New Approach to Management; Great Companies are Defined by Purpose, Process, and People* (London: Heinemann).

Gilley, J. W. and A. Maycunich (2000) *Beyond the Learning Organization: Creating a Culture of Continuous Growth and Development Through State-of-the-art Human Resource Practices* (Cambridge, MA: Perseus).

Grossman, S. J. and O. D. Hart (1983) 'Implicit Contracts under Asymmetric Information', The Quarterly Journal of Economics, 98(3), 123–56.

Hambrick, D. C. and P. A. Mason (1984) 'Upper Echelons: The Organization as a Reflection of its Top Managers', *The Academy of Management Review*, 9(4), 193–206.

Handy, C. (1995) The Age of Unreason: Thinking the Unlikely and Doing the Unreasonable (London: Arrow Books).

Harvey, C. and J. Denton (1999) 'To Come of Age: Antecedents of Organizational Learning', *Journal of Management Studies*, 37(6), 783–96.

Hedberg, B. (1981) 'How Organizations Learn and Unlearn', in P. C. Nystrom and W. H. Starbuck (eds), *Handbook of Organizational Design* (Oxford: Oxford University Press), pp. 3–27.

House, R. J. (1977) 'A 1976 Theory of Charismatic Leadership', in J. G. Hunt and L. L. Larson (eds), *Leadership: The Cutting Edge* (Carbondale, IL: Southern Illinois University Press), pp. 189–207.

Hunt, J. G. (1991) Leadership: A New Synthesis (Newbury Park, CA: Sage).

Hunt, J. G. (1999) 'Transformational/Charismatic Leadership's Transformation of the Field: An Historical Essay', *The Leadership Quarterly*, 10(2), 129–44.

Hunt, J. G., K. B. Boal and G. E. Dodge (1999) 'The Effects of Visionary and Crisis-Responsive Charisma on Followers: An Experimental Examination of Two Kinds of Charismatic Leadership', The Leadership Quarterly, 10(3), 423–48.

Jensen, M. C. and W. H. Meckling (1976) 'Theory of the Firm: Management Behavior, Agency Costs and Ownership Structure', Journal of Financial Economics, 3, 305–60.

Kogut, B. and U. Zander (1996) 'What Firms Do? Coordination, Identity, and Learning', *Organization Science*, 7(5), 502–18.

Kotter, J. P. (1996) *Leading Change* (Boston, MA: Harvard Business School Press).

Marion, R. and M. Uhl-Bien (2001) 'Leadership in Complex Organizations', The Leadership Quarterly, 12(4), 389–418.

Marshall, E. M. (2000) *Building Trust at the Speed of Change: The Power of the relationship-based Corporation* (New York: Amacom).

Miner, A. and S. Mezias (1996) 'Ugly Duckling No More: Pasts and Futures of Organizational Learning Research', *Organization Science*, 7(1), 88–99.

Mintzberg, H. (1979) *The Structuring of Organizations: A Synthesis of the Research* (Englewood Cliffs, NJ: Prentice-Hall).

Nonaka, I. and H. Takeuchi (1995) *The Knowledge-Creating Company: How Japanese Companies Create the Dynamics of Innovation* (New York: Oxford University Press).

Nonaka, I. and R. Toyama (2002) 'A Firm as a Dialectical Being: Towards a Dynamic Theory of a Firm', *Industrial and Corporate Change*, 11(5), 995–1009.

Osterloh, M. and B. S. Frey (2000) 'Motivation, Knowledge Transfer, and Organizational Forms', *Organization Science*, 11(5), 538–50.

Richter, I. (1998) 'Individual and Organizational Learning at the Executive Level: Towards a Research Agenda', *Management Learning*, 29(3), 299–316.

Sadler, P. (2001) 'Leadership and Organizational Learning', in M., Dierkes A., Berthoin Antal J. Child and M. Dierkes (eds), *Handbook of Organizational Learning and Knowledge* (Oxford: Oxford University Press), pp. 415–27.

Schein, E. H. (1985) *Organizational Culture and Leadership* (San Francisco, CA: Jossey-Bass).

Schneider, M. (2002) 'A Stakeholder Model of Organizational Leadership', *Organization Science*, 13(2), 209–20.

Senge, P. M. (1990) *The Fifth Discipline: The Art and Practice of the Learning Organization* (New York: Doubleday).

Senge, P. M. (1997) 'Communities of Leaders and Learners', *Harvard Business Review*, 75(5), 30–2.

Senge, P. M. (1999) 'The Leadership of Profound Change: Toward an Ecology of Leadership', in P. M. Senge A. Kleiner, C. Roberts, R. B. Ross, G. Roth and B. J.

Smith (eds), The Dance of Change: The Challenges of Sustaining Momentum in Learning Organizations (New York: Doubleday), pp. 10–21.

Shea C. M. and J. M. Howell (1999) 'Charismatic Leadership and Task Feedback: A Laboratory Study of Their Effects on Self-efficacy and Task Performance', *The Leadership Quarterly*, 10(3), 375–96.

Simons, R. (1994) 'How New Top Managers use Control Systems as Levers of Strategic Renewal', *Strategic Management Journal*, 15(3), 169–89.

Slocum, J. W., M. McGill and D. T. Lei (1994) 'The New Learning Strategy: Anytime, Anything, Anywhere', *Organizational Dynamics*, 23(2), 33–47.

Sternberg, R. J. (2003) 'WICS: A Model of Leadership in Organizations', *Academy of Management Learning and Education*, 2(4), 386–401.

Weber, R., C. Camerer, Y. Rottenstreich and M. Knez (2001) 'The Illusion of Leadership: Misattribution of Cause in Coordination Games', *Organization Science*, 12(5), 582–98.

Witt, U. (1998) 'Imagination and Leadership: The Neglected Dimension of an Evolutionary Theory of the Firm', *Journal of Economic Behavior and Organization*, 35(2), 161–77.

Zaccaro, S. J. and R. J. Klimoski (2001) *The Nature of Organizational Leadership: Understanding the Performance Imperatives Confronting Today's Leaders* (San Francisco, CA: John Wiley & Sons).

Zack, M. H. (2003) 'Rethinking the Knowledge-Based Organization', *MIT Sloan Management Review*, 44(4), 67–71.

12
Leadership and Strategy as Intangible Assets

Hans Hinterhuber and Christian Stadler

Intangible assets have an impact of up to 80 per cent on the economic value of a firm. In the twenty-first century competitive landscape intangible assets represent the key drivers for a firm's competitiveness. This chapter shows that leadership and strategy are the intangible assets which contribute most to competitive advantages.

Firms with charismatic leaders, effective strategies and efficient execution outperform comparable firms more during difficult economic conditions than during strong economic years. Leadership and strategy, however, are not the domain of a firm's top management team; in fact, they are more or less everyone's business. Suggestions are offered on how to better deploy leadership and strategy in the leadership company, whose core competency is the development of leadership skills on all levels of responsibility.

1. Introduction

> You can be invincible if you never get involved
> in a competition where to win is not in your power.
>
> Epictetus

The knowledge society is based on intangible assets; this proposition shows that the competitive advantages of firms have shifted from material to immaterial, from visible to invisible things. Intangible assets can account for up to 90 per cent of a company's economic value; 74 per cent of BP's and 82 per cent of 3M's value are attributed to intangible assets (Edvinson, 2004). Figure 12.1 illustrates the exponential impact of intangible assets on the economic value of a firm.

This chapter shows that leadership and strategy are the immaterial competences which contribute most to a company's value. The following story serves to define immaterial competences. A man intends to buy a painting from Nasreddin. Looking at the price of 10,000 dinars, the man hesitates,

The impact of intangible assets
on a company's value (%)

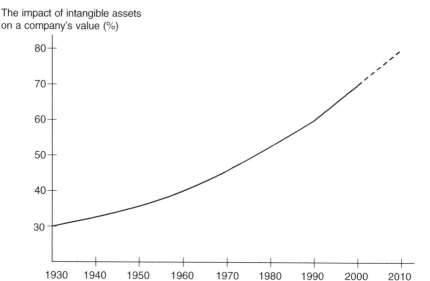

Figure 12.1   Intangible assets account for more than 70% of a company's value
Source: Edvinson, 2004; Baruch, 1999

considering the potential price increase of the painting. He inquires cautiously, 'May I return it, if my wife doesn't like it?' 'Certainly,' answers Nasreddin. A few days later, the man brings back the painting and explains, 'My wife thinks the painting doesn't fit in our home. Can you take it back?' 'Of course,' answers Nasreddin and, turning to his assistant, requests, 'Please give 12,000 dinars to this gentleman!' 'I paid only 10,000 dinars for the painting,' the man objects. 'I know,' says Nasreddin, 'but in the meantime the value of these paintings has increased.' The man reflects for a moment, then leaves the shop with the painting.

The story shows how immaterial competences, in this case a change of perspective, add value. The chapter analyses this in six parts.

First, we show that intangible assets and competences form the basis of competitive advantages.

Second, we discuss the empirical evidence, which emphasizes a direct and fundamental relationship between leadership and strategy and profitable growth.

Third, we define leadership along two dimensions: (1) discovering and exploiting new opportunities, and (2) inspiring people to work enthusiastically towards common goals.

Fourth, strategy is defined as the way foward from a firm's core competence to achieving its core task, that is, making the customer more competitive or increasing the quality of his or her life.

Fifth, we argue that the impact of leadership and strategy on the firm's performance is heightened under more difficult economic conditions.

Sixth, we conclude that the firm of the future will be the leadership company, whose core competences are represented by leadership and strategy at every level of the organization.

2. Intangible assets and immaterial capabilities as the key drivers of a firm's competitiveness

> Associate only with people who can make
> you better and allow those to follow you who
> you can improve. In this way, an interaction
> begins. We learn while we are teaching.
> Seneca

Figure 12.2 shows the key factors accounting for a company's value (Eustace, 2000):

- tangible assets (plant, machinery, inventory, cash and so on);

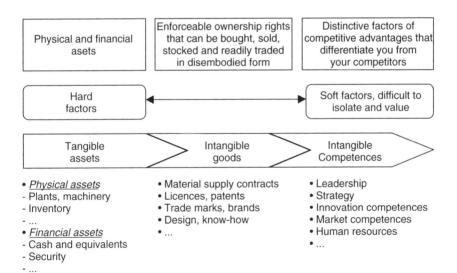

Figure 12.2   The assets base of the twenty-first-century firm

Source: Eustace, 2000

Figure 12.3   The link between financial performance and key drivers
Source: Maister, 2003

- intangible goods (material supply contracts, licences, patents, trade marks and so on);
- intangible competences (leadership, strategy, innovation and so on).

Intangible competences such as leadership and strategy are difficult to separate from the organizational context and the firm's management system in which they are embedded. Intangible competences require an environment in which they can grow. The resource-based view emphasizes the role of the firm for increasing its value, whereas Porter's industrial economics approach is based on industry attractiveness. Hamel and Prahalad (1994) argue that a firm can achieve challenging objectives, often beyond expectations, by using its dynamic capabilities and strategic resources, that is, its core competences, and thereby is able to offer its customers a superior added value. We focus on leadership and strategy techniques which differentiate high performing firms from low performing firms (Finkelstein and Hambrick, 1996; Fulmer and Goldsmith, 2002).

Figure 12.3 below is enlightening as it provides us with an overall perspective of the factors which account for the performance of a firm (Maister, 2003). Quality and customer relationships have a direct and immediate impact on a firm's financial performance. Satisfied employees are the sources for good quality and good customer relationships. The figure shows that the key drivers of value production are intangible assets and intangible competences. The better the leadership and strategic skills of the top management team, which shapes the key drivers, the better the performance of the firm.

3. Leadership and strategy as key drivers for profitable growth

> Strategy is the evolution of the originally
> guiding idea according to continuously
> changing circumstances.
>
> Helmuth von Moltke

Empirical studies show that the more turbulent a market, the more a company's success depends on the leadership behaviour of its top decision-makers and their teams. There is also a direct correlation between business success and the actions of leaders. This includes both the speed at which they act and the scope of action available to the decision-makers and their teams, provided that this flexibility is used in the best interest of the enterprise (Waldmann et al., 2001; Finkelstein and Hambrick, 1996). Leadership creates and expands the scope of action and increases the speed of response that enables an enterprise to attend proactively to strategic issues without creating a stressful and hectic atmosphere.

The attractiveness, profit and growth potential of a market are important, but they can only explain the success of an enterprise to a limited degree. The attractiveness of a market can be compared with the wind that fills the sails of a ship. The stronger the wind blows, the more swiftly and easily the ship reaches its destination. Neither leadership nor strategy can accomplish anything without wind, even if the sails are set perfectly. Leadership means finding out the direction the wind is blowing, taking into account a possible absence of wind and, through proactive behaviour, growing even stronger during a lull. There are always chances somewhere. Naturally, an entrepreneur is as happy about favourable market conditions as a sailor is about a good wind. Yet it is not the wind, but rather the sails that determine the course. These sails represent leadership and strategy.

In summary, this means that enterprises can be steered towards a successful future even when the market conditions are unattractive, that is, when the wind is weak, but this can happen only if the decision-makers in the company exercise good leadership and if the strategy is right. The more turbulent the markets are and the better the leaders utilize their field of action, that is, the favourable winds, the more important strategy and leadership become for entrepreneurial success. In the final analysis, it is leadership that makes the difference between enterprises, ultimately responsible for the success of some companies and the failure of others.

Figure 12.4 shows that in times where the average EBIT of the 500 Top European companies decreased by 27 per cent, 31 per cent of the firms were able to achieve profitable growth. According to Mercer Management Consulting, this can be attributed to superior leadership and strategic capabilities.

Similar results are evidenced in an analysis of Roland Berger (Bötzel et al., 2004): only 26 per cent of the world's largest companies, in a long-term

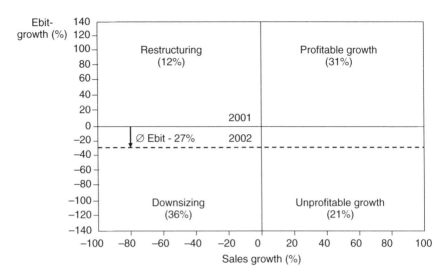

Figure 12.4   The comparative performance of the 500 largest European companies
Source: Mercer Management Consulting, Nötzli Breinlinger, 2003

perspective, combine an above average growth of sales and profit. All companies have access to the same management know-how and to more or less similar systems and processes. The analysis of Roland Berger explains the superior financial performance of the 26 per cent leading companies in terms of their demonstrating a better strategy, a better leadership behaviour at all organizational levels and a better use of resources. Human resources (CEO, SBU managers and board directors) account for 42 per cent, and competences (innovation capabilities, market know-how and processes) for 30 per cent of the profit and sales growth of high-performing companies; execution skills such as ERP and the business system account for 28 per cent of profitable growth.

In conclusion, the leadership and strategic capabilities of a firm on all organizational levels are more important than industry attractiveness. Industry attractiveness accounts for approximately 20 per cent of the economic value added to a company (Hitt et al. 2005).

3.1   Leadership

> Not everyone who tries hard will be able to
> hunt and kill a gazelle, but everyone who has
> succeeded in doing so has certainly tried hard.
> Annemarie Schimmel

Leadership comprises: (1) discovering and exploiting opportunities which others haven't seen, (2) inspiring people to work enthusiastically towards common goals and (3) being authentic.

Roughly speaking, this results in the following key elements (see Figure 12.5):

- vision;
- creating values and maintaining direction; and
- acting as a positive role model.

Thus, anyone who wants to lead must:

- be a *visionary*: he or she must stimulate the will to succeed by planting a vision in the hearts of his or her team, a vision that shows a direction, gives meaning and moves the enterprise towards results;
- achieve short-term results and *strengthen* the enterprise in the long run, that is, work towards long-term prosperity for all partners by *maintaining the direction and constantly ensuring that things stay on course*;
- act as a *role model* and show courage: setting an example and being willing to accept risks is the only way to communicate efficiently, inspire the team, provide a positive impetus and maintain momentum.

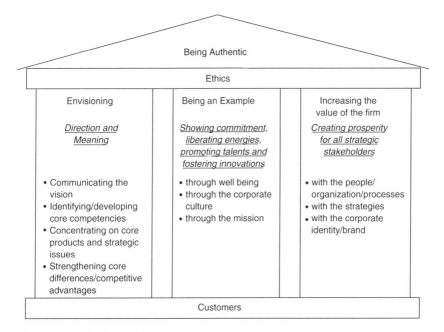

Figure 12.5   The leadership power house

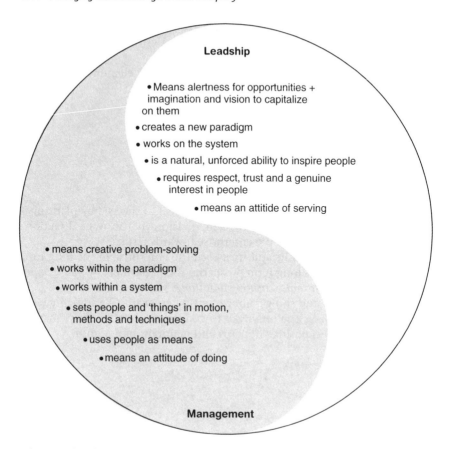

Figure 12.6   The unity of management and leadership

In contrast to leadership, *management* is creative problem-solving; in other words, optimizing something that already exists. There are numerous methods, instruments and attitudes that can help an enterprise to improve its competitive position and to achieve competitive advantages. Thus, management is much easier to learn than leadership.

Depending on the specific situation, leaders require both leadership and management skills (see Figure 12.6). Leadership and management complement each other like Yin and Yang; neither is possible without the other. That is why the frequently cited opposition of leadership and management does not make sense.

The ability to instil a vision into the hearts of staff is generally considered one of the prerequisites for leadership. A vision is not a goal; it is a projection of an 'ideal' that will become a concrete 'concept' at a later point of time. Thus, the first characteristic of leadership is the ability to set a direction that makes sense and leads to results. This requires rational thinking as well as intuition and emotion

Value for customers, the people working in the company and the other stakeholders can be created only if the direction is maintained. The second characteristic of leadership is therefore the ability to maintain direction. This means being in the driver's seat, leading the people in a company and stimulating and empowering them to invest their enthusiasm in common goals that lead towards the vision. Staying on the right course also means acknowledging the irrational element of leadership. It means that the leader must allow the people in a company to think and act independently during the implementation phase while still being in charge. This is the best way to ensure the optimum performance of individuals as well as allow for free development of the personal abilities of everyone involved. All of this is connected with the ability to work in teams and to be a team player. It is the leader's responsibility to focus the right people on the right tasks, to integrate and to help them to be even better than they themselves would believe possible. Thus, leadership means teamwork and networking.

Such leadership requires independent workers with commitment to a team effort as active individuals. They have to be able to make appropriate decisions, on their own initiative and independently but within the framework of the whole. Only then can they cope when – as is often the case – contingencies, risks or new opportunities threaten to alter the original plan.

The third leadership characteristic refers to the function of setting an example. Of key relevance here is to practise what we preach or, to use an American saying, to walk the talk. The only people who can communicate efficiently, stimulate others and set them in motion in a positive sense are those who act as a role model. They show commitment and courage, radiate enthusiasm, live ethical values, set energies free and support innovations. This is possible only if they are authentic.

3.2 Strategy

> Strategy is a system of expedients ad hoc.
> Helmuth von Moltke

The basic elements of competition do not change in the course of time. What changes is the speed at which information can be utilized worldwide or with which new competitors destroy existing competitive positions (Porter, 2002).

Strategy is the path from the core competence to the core task. The core task of each enterprise follows the vision and consists of making customers more successful or more competitive or increasing their quality of life and at the same time increasing the value of the company. 'A difficult, complicated or subtle thought', according to Walther Rathenau, 'is as unsuitable in business as it is in life. Every great business idea can be expressed in a sentence that a child can understand. Here, like everywhere else, the trick is simplicity.' The *core competence* is the totality of the dynamic capabilities, resources, processes, technologies and attitudes that ensure that the process of increasing the value of the enterprise is ongoing.

The core competence of the Austrian crystal group Swarovski consists of a comprehensive system of crystal-cutting technology, design, marketing and information technology as well as the ability to create attractions for customers (for example, through the 'Crystal Worlds' or the Collectors' Society). The core task is to impart joy through crystal. The core competence of the steel technology group Salzgitter AG is the production, processing and selling of steel; the core task is to increase the success of customers by ensuring an optimal supply of steel and steel components.

Strategy as the path from core competence to core task unites the *resource-based view* (core competence) with the *market-based view* (core task) of the enterprise. Thus it is not possible to develop a strategy unless both the core competence and core task are clearly defined.

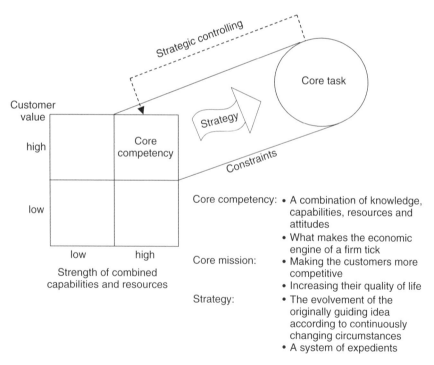

Figure 12.7   Strategy as the path from the firm's core competency to the fulfilment of its core task

The leading thought is the core competence, which has to be further developed to keep pace with ever-changing customer needs and competitive conditions. The central questions leading to a strategy concern not, 'How do we become number one in the market?', but, 'How do we make our customers the best in their markets?'

The objective of the strategy is to bring about a long-term, sustainable increase in the value of the enterprise; one that lies above the market average or at least above the capital costs.

According to Moltke, strategy is nothing more than the application of common sense. What he implies by this, as will be shown in the following, is *critical* common sense.

Strategy is a theory of practical action.

4. Leadership and strategy have a greater impact on company performance in a weak economy than in a strong economy

> The quality of your life depends
> on the quality of your thoughts.
> Marcus Aurelius

Flynn and Staw (2004) demonstrated in an archival study that firms with charismatic leaders outperformed comparable firms more during weak economic years than during strong economic years (see Figure 12.8). The relationship between leadership and economic conditions was also tested by the authors using the industry-specific measure of conditions facing the firm; the results demonstrated a significant interaction between leadership and industry-specific conditions. According to the findings of Flynn and

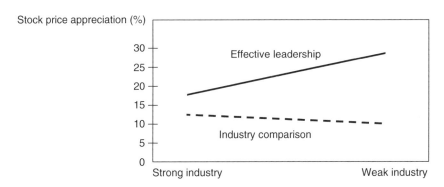

Figure 12.8 The impact of charismatic leadership and industry strength on stock price appreciation

Source: adapted from Flynn and Staw, 2004

Stock price appreciation

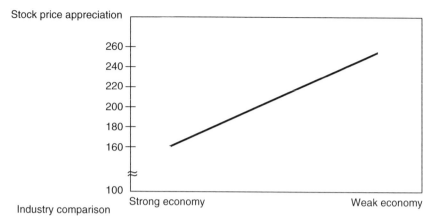

Industry comparison

Figure 12.9 The impact of leadership and economic conditions on stock price appreciation

Source: adapted from Flynn and Staw, 2004

Staw, when industry-specific conditions were weak, companies with charismatic leaders performed better than comparable firms (see Figure 12.9).

The following conclusions can be drawn:

1. Charismatic leadership and good strategies increase the attractiveness of a firm for its shareholders.
2. The more difficult the economic conditions, the more important leadership and strategy.
3. Top management teams create an environment and an organizational context in which managers can deploy their leadership skills.
4. A long-term outstanding leadership performance is the result of conscious and conscientious efforts of many engaged managers.
5. The strategically directed collective efforts make a great company (Whittington, 2002).

The analysis of elementary failures in strategic decision processes confirms these results (Finkelstein, 2003). Finkelstein, after studying 197 instances of business failure, identifies the reasons for the failures as follows:

1. Leaders make wrong strategic decisions not because they are incompetent or stupid, or both, but due to a wrong construction of reality.

2. Senior executives persist in a destructive path even when there is clear evidence that it isn't working.
3. Senior executives do not receive the information or are not able to filter it out of the superfluous and fallacious information not needed for strategic decision-making.
4. Unsuccessful leadership habits keep senior executives from correcting their mistakes.

5. The firm of the future is the leadership company

> By taking over a role you are not able
> to cope with, you not only discredit
> yourself, you also neglect another role
> that you could perform honorably.
> Epictetus

The *leadership company* is an enterprise whose core competence lies in the development of the *leadership* abilities of executive personnel and employees at all levels of responsibility. The *leadership company* promotes and develops a network of leaders. What takes the *leadership company* into the future is the staff's entrepreneurial thinking and acting in all areas of responsibility. The importance of this for the long-term and sustainable increase in the value of the company grows as the future becomes harder to plan and as things change faster and become more complex.

But how does an enterprise become a *leadership company*? The firms that are developing in this direction – for example, General Electric, Royal/Dutch Shell and Nestlé – proceed according to a two-step method (Tichy and Cohen, 1997):

1. Promotion of *leadership* competence at all levels of responsibilities, through targeted training and educational programmes. This makes all the members of the company more aware that *leadership* is more valuable than management.
2. It is the duty of every employee with leadership responsibility to educate and train others (education [Lat. e-ducere] is regarded as the development and instruction of what is already present; it places emphasis on reiteration – 'you educate people, you train dogs') and actively participate in matters of leadership. To succeed in this, he or she should use every meeting and every encounter with fellow staff members to pass on *'teachable points of view'* (Tichy and Cohen, 1997). 'Teachable points of view' are, for example:

- his or her personal experience in opening up new possibilities or in solving problems creatively;
- the values he or she lives by and exemplifies that are worthy of emulation;
- his or her experiences with customers and with colleagues who are proud of the company's products and services;
- his or her success in dealing innovatively with strategic issues; and
- situations he or she encounter that require personal courage, loyalty, careful consideration, flexibility and a strong desire to act.

Good leaders, according to the director of the 'Global Leadership' programme and book author Noel Tichy, are good story-tellers. If we set good examples, we will find imitators.

In the *leadership company*, leaders use clearly communicated, frequently repeated and plausible modes of behaviour to encourage their staff to:

- explore new opportunities and solve problems creatively, developing and implementing suitable concepts;
- exemplify the values that support the successful implementation of these concepts;
- radiate positive thinking and acting as well as enthusiasm and joy of living'
- make difficult decisions in situations when a consensus is not possible; and
- include the element of chance in their decisions in order to increase the room for entrepreneurial action.

Setting examples can occur on three levels (Varvelli and Varvelli, 2000):

1. on the *level of the pragmatic example*: expressing thanks, being courteous and punctual, radiating cheerfulness and enthusiasm, expressing oneself precisely, paying attention to things at the workplace and so on;
2. on the *level of professionalism:* the leader adopts a behaviour that exemplifies a consciously chosen, active, positive lifestyle. It is characterized by open and honest communication, a tolerance for errors, trust, a willingness to take responsibility and initiative. This type of example-setting forms the basis of the corporate culture and influences the personality of the members of the company;
3. on the *level of one's character and behaviour*: the leader's words correspond with his decisions and actions; he shows respect for others, respect for the achievements of predecessors, high esteem for the ability of others, ethical behaviour, courage, benevolence and other classic virtues. The person on this level who passes on 'teachable points of view' influences

the modes of behaviour of the employees and becomes a model of ethical and spiritual life. 'Those who have met persons who set this type of example will never forget them.' (Varvelli and Varvelli, 2000).

In the *leadership company* management executives are measured by the number of employees they have developed into leaders. The learning organization is a necessary condition for a *leadership company*, but that alone does not suffice. The sufficient condition is to create a *teaching organization* in which each person, regardless of his level of responsibility, shows others through his example how to make customers more successful and more competitive, how to outperform the competition and how to create value for all *key stakeholders*. The *leadership company*, to cite Tichy (2002), is a teaching organization: the more expertise an enterprise develops in teaching leadership, the longer and more sustainable its success will be.

Ultimately, this means that the *leadership company* lives and develops according to the leadership capabilities of executive personnel and employees at all levels of responsibility and how the leader and his team deal with them. The more freedom of action they have and the better and faster leaders discover and utilize new possibilities in the interests of internal and external network partners, the longer-lasting and stronger the leadership role and *performance* of the *leadership company* in the network will be.

The *leadership company* thrives on the values, standards and objectives that are exemplified from the top down, indicating a desirable direction, creating room for action and providing meaning. Leaders are a reliable reference point if they are modest (Stadler and Hinterhuber, 2005); make suggestions with 'teachable points of view' and offer examples; give others a feeling of security; and find time for personal talks. To summarize, the *leadership company* is not a combination of regulations, rules, processes or technologies. It is a community of people who are bound together by common values, who work on common projects, who are in constant evolution and who are a source of pride for everyone. They are essentially characterized by their attitude towards active and innovative learning and teaching, by their promotion of innovations and talent and by the way they open up new, value-adding possibilities within the framework of symbiotic internal and external networks.

In the competitive environment at the time of writing, the companies that will prevail are those that surpass their competitors in developing and utilizing the leadership capabilities of their management executives and employees to open up new possibilities or to avert poorly calculated risks.

The golden rule for building a leadership company is: select managers who are more capable than you are, use their talents and give them the chance to grow and to take responsibility. Senior executives will be measured and rewarded by what types of managers and co-workers they have employed and how many of them they have developed into true leaders.

6. Conclusion

> More powerful than fate is the will of men.
>
> Seneca

This chapter has shown that immaterial assets and competences form the basis for achieving sustainable competitive advantages in the twenty-first century. Leadership and strategy as intangible assets influence profitable growth more than industry attractiveness. The impact on company value of leadership and strategy is more relevant in a weak economy than in a strong economy. These findings give credibility to the argument that the firm of the future will be the leadership company. The core competency of the leadership company is the development of leadership skills at all levels of responsibility of the firm.

The higher the sum of leadership skills and strategic capabilities, the better a company functions. The better the firm works, the greater will be the benefit for all key stakeholders. The better the quality of the water, the happier the fish will be. The question is not whether to create a company consisting only of leaders, but how to develop more leaders than in today's firms.

References

Lev, Baruch (1999) 'Seeing is believing', *CFO Magazine*, February.

Bötzel, H., M. Reichl, O. Conze, H. V. Daniels, Ch. Kleppel and Ch. Seeliger (2004) *Zum Wachstum führen* (München: Roland Berger Strategy Consultants).

Edvinson, L. (2004) 'The New Knowledge Landscape', in S. Crainer and D. Dearlove (eds), *Financial Times Handbook of Management*, (London: McGraw Hill), pp. 19–23.

Eustace, C. (2000) 'The Intangible Economy: Impact and Policy Issues', report of the European High Level Expert Group on the intangible economy, European Commission, Brussels.

Finkelstein, S. (2003) *Why Smart Executives Fail* (New York: Portfolio).

Finkelstein, S. and D. Hambrick (1996) *Strategic Leadership: Top Executives and their Effects on Organizations*, (St. Paul, Minneapolis: West Pub Co.).

Flynn, F. J. and B. M. Staw (2004) 'Lend Me Your Wallets: The Effect of Charismatic Leadership on External Support for an Organization', *Strategic Management*, 25(4), 309–30.

Fulmer, R. M. and M. Goldsmith (2002) 'Future Leadership Development', in S. Chowdhury, (ed.), *Management 21C*, (London: Prentice Hall), pp. 172–85.

Hamel, G. and C. K. Prahalad (1994) *Competing for the Future* (Boston: Harvard Business School Press).

Hinterhuber, H. H. (2005) *Leadership. Strategisches Denken systematisch schulen von Sokrates bis Jack Welch*, 4. Aufl. (Frankfurt, A.M.: Frankfurter Allgemeine Buch).

Hinterhuber, H. H. and E. Krauthammer (2005) *Leadership – mehr als Management*, 4. Aufl. (Wiesbaden: Gabler Verlag).

Hitt, M. A., J. S. Black and L. W. Porter (2005) *Management*, (New York: Pearson Prentice Hall).

Hitt, M. A., R. D. Ireland and R. E. Hoskisson (2005) *Strategic Management. Competitiveness and Globalization*, 5. Aufl. (Cincinnati: South-Western Pula).

Krauthammer, E. and H. H. Hinterhuber (2005) *Wettbewerbsvorteil Einzigartigkeit* (Berlin: Gabler Verlag).

Maister, D. (2003) *Practice What You Preach: What Managers Must Do to Create a High-Achievement Culture* (New York: Free Press).

Nötzli Breinlinger, Ursula (2003) 'Die Konjunkturflaute als Herausforderung', *Das Wachstum der Unternehmen unter der Lupe*. NZZ 11.1, p. 21

Porter, M. E. (1985) *Competitive Strategy: Techniques for Analyzing Industries and Competitors* (Boston: Free Press).

Porter, M. E. (2002) 'An interview with Michael Porter', interviewed by N. Argyres and A. M. McGahan in *Academy of Management Executive*, 16(2), pp. 43–52.

Stadler, C. (2004) *Unternehmenskultur bei Royal Dutch/Shell, Siemens und DaimlerChrysler* (Stuttgart: Frauz Steiner Verlag).

Stadler, C. and H. H. Hinterhuber (2005) 'Shell, Siemens and DaimlerChrysler: Leading Change in Companies with Strong Values', *Long Range Planning*, forthcoming.

Standfield, K. (2002) *Intangible Management* (Amsterdam: Academic Press).

Tichy, N. M. (2002) *The Cycle of Leadership: How Great Leaders Teach Their Companies to Win* (New York: Harper Business).

Tichy, N. M. and E. Cohen (1997) *The Leadership Engine: How Winning Companies Build Leaders at Every Level* (New York: Harper Business).

Varvelli, R. and M. L. Varvelli (2000) *Lavorare positivo* (Milan: IL sole-24 ore Libri).

Waldman, D. A., G. G. Ramirez, R. J. House and P. Puranam (2001) 'Does Leadership Matter? CEO Leadership Attributes and Profitability under Conditions of Perceived Environmental Uncertainty', *The Academy of Management*, 44(1), 134–43.

Welch, J. and J. A. Byrne (2001) *Jack. Straight from the Gut* (New York: Warner Books).

Whittington, R. (2002) *What is Strategy – and does it matter?* 2nd ed. (London: Routledge).

13

Intellectual Capital: Measurement Approaches as Prerequisite for Management?

Manfred Bornemann

Introduction

Knowledge as a resource of special attributes increasingly attracts management attention. After some initiatives to learn more about knowledge management, usually one or more of the following questions emerges to become top priority for decision-makers:

- What precisely is our knowledge base?
- What is the value of this knowledge base?
- How can we visualize and describe the knowledge base?
- Is the knowledge base utilized according to our strategic priorities?
- How can we use knowledge better?

The last decade up to the time of writing has brought a huge variety of approaches all trying to answer these questions. In the organizational framework, which shall provide the basis for the following discussion, at least three major approaches to dealing with the phenomenon of knowledge can be differentiated, all of which contain differences in scale and scope of addressing the questions listed above:

1 The discussion of *intellectual property rights* comes from the legal domain and seeks to define clear guidelines for the possession and utilization of knowledge. This is a highly controversial topic, with major differences not only within the philosophical sphere but, as a consequence, within national legislation. Protection of 'products of the mind' on one side and free access and use of these values on the other side are extreme points with alternative consequences for the future development of economies as well as organizations.

2 As soon as one can claim the intellectual property on a sound basis, managerial accountants enter the stage in order to attribute some financial value to the *intangible assets*[1] of an organization. There are various,

highly regulated approaches to assessing monetary value, but most experts agree on the high context-dependence, lacking of precision and, as a consequence, relatively low validity of these valuations.

3 Unaffected by the precise euro or dollar figure that is associated with knowledge, a third perspective focuses on *intellectual capital*. This rather managerial approach focuses on the value creation capacity of assets, which are regularly differentiated into human, structural and relational categories. There is a large body of literature available that covers this topic.[2] One of the major problems of the IC management perspective relates to the alignment of resources and their strategic use: there is a lot of knowledge and IC available but it is not yet effectively allocated to the most urgent tasks, where its marginal contribution is the highest.

As a consequence of this third perspective, professionals from various backgrounds have developed concepts that support the *decision support function* and the *reporting function* for intellectual capital. IC reports (ICR) originated in Scandinavia[3] but quickly conquered other regions,[4] until today in 2005 ICR is a topic in most advanced economies. However, there are still great efforts necessary to transfer ICR concepts originating from the consulting and the academic world to business organizations.

Current challenges in intellectual capital reporting

The *status quo* of ICR is ambiguous and viewed differently by various authors. There is a problem of *differentiated IC terminology*, which is used in a manner 'relatively similar' but 'not quite the same'. An example provides the term 'structural capital', which sometimes refers to the 'internal structure'[5] of an organization and its past experiences, and includes brands. Sometimes the same term is separated from another dimension of 'relational capital' or 'external structure'. In the following, IC is defined as a composition of human, structural and relational capital.

This definition follows the tradition of both Edvinsson and Malone (1997) and Stewart (1997), which is one of the most widely used in the business context. However, as the topic of ICR emerged from managerial and consulting backgrounds, there are several almost identical approaches available which are copyrighted by different organizations. This does not exactly support the development of a generally accepted terminology and most likely will not change in the very near future.

Additionally, there are *several competing managerial concepts* from other functional origins available which have not yet been integrated into a comprehensive or holistic management model. This is not because nobody has tried,[6] but because sometimes competing paradigms prevent successful fusion.

Concepts that influence ICR

The very successful *EFQM model* thrives to improve organizational excellence and quality for many decades. It is very precise and technology-oriented. Strict documentation of processes should allow transferring production lines into other contextual or geographical areas. Many terms from IC are compatible with, if not identical to, EFQM terms as some methodologies have the same roots. However, on the application level the mental model of an engineer is not the same as that of a manager who should optimize intellectual capital. The first expects rather linear and predictable patterns, while the latter has to deal with dynamic and sometimes non-linear patterns.

Another concept used to deal with the intangible is supported by *ERP systems*. The classic business process is modelled according to cost structures, which are supplemented by additional categories for the 'knowledge parts'. These frequently time-based approaches allow complementing the classic value creation processes with in-time data about some carefully modelled knowledge-intense processes. However, large parts of the corporate knowledge map remain uncharted because of cost-benefit reasons: it is too expensive to keep track.

The much younger concept of *balanced score cards* (*BSC*) intends to communicate and enforce corporate strategy. Again, several issues of both objects of reference and methodology are strikingly similar, but the management philosophy differs fundamentally: the aim of the Kaplan and Norton (1992) BSC is to enforce a strategy top-down by communicating very clear targets which are imperative and frequently linked to incentives. In their upgraded publication in 2002, the successful authors explicitly try to apply their model to intangibles, but fail to recognize the difference in management approach. It is hard to merge top-down strategy with decentralized approaches such as ICR.

Most *IC management concepts* concede tremendous influence to employees. If not all, at least a relevant proportion of employees is seen as crucial for the value-adding capacity of an organization.[7] Hence it seems imperative to align the countless individual decision-making processes into an overall value-adding process. Local experts need to know about their peers, about their position in the value chain and about interdependencies as well as consequences of deviations from their own input. In the words of IC grandfather Leif Edvinsson (2001), people need new and more adequate 'bearing points' in the organization to 'navigate' their development processes. Only a comprehensive understanding ensures effective integration of original contributions. Therefore, it is a 'bottom up–top down' approach, where targets are the result of constant negotiation processes which in turn lead to a unique new product or service.

These concepts led to the development of many prototype models in Denmark and a little later in Austria, followed by Germany, which have only minor differences and could be defined as follows.[8] An intellectual capital statement is an instrument to assess and to develop the intellectual capital of an organization. It shows how organizational goals (strategy) are linked to the business processes (value chain), the intellectual capital and the business success of an organization, using indicators to visualize these elements. An intellectual capital statement describes the results of know-ledge-based activities within an organization.[9] System theory and construct-ivism provide the conceptual background for most ICR approaches. One model will be briefly discussed later, as there are some more challenges to be covered in the first instance.

Dichotomies of ICR

The dual usability of ICR for internal and external communication, as well as its decision support function, is the reason for several dichotomies that seem to exclude each other. The elements of the following list were identified in the course of developing and implementing the IC Report of ARC[10] and have not lost their relevance:

- The choice of *methodology of ICR* (indicator-based versus monetary and process versus structure) has a consequence in the compatibility with existing reports, for example in financial accounting, and hence in the management of IC within organizations.
- The *target group* (stakeholder/shareholder, institutions) of the report sub-stantially impacts the *level of disclosure* of data. Internal use for decision support meets higher transparency requirements than external com-munication intended for strategic positioning.
- The *extent of decision support* (internal management versus external authorities, investors, stakeholders) competes with *reduction of complex-ity*, which is needed for more general discussion.
- The *time perspective* (backward versus forward).
- The *validity of data* and availability of standards is one of the most con-verse issues.

As long as there is no clear definition of the functions that an ICR should provide, these issues will be hard to resolve. However, this is seen as one of the key benefits for ICR and integrated management of IC, as it is sufficiently powerful from more than one perspective.

Regarding the future of ICR, it will be necessary to address the issues and to decide what actually should be a priority and what should not. Aside from the methodology discussion, which was already covered above, the *definition of the target group* seems to have the most impact on ICR. In most business situations, this should be no problem at all. Reviewing the change in perspectives of financial accounting during the first years of this millennium, a general trend in transparency might help to overcome the innovation-killing climate of caution.

Management of Intellectual Capital

Edvinsson came up with some steps to use ICR for managing IC, when he suggested:[11]

1. understanding those parts of the ICR that show the capability for value creation and value extraction;
2. leveraging this value by the interaction and cross-fertilization of idle capabilities;
3. focusing on the flow and exchange, the 'transparency', of competencies in the organization by creating a buffer of knowledge, from which stakeholders can pick out what they need to be more productive;
4. capitalizing on this process by releasing, codifying, recycling and exchanging its components.

The third step in this rather cyclical approach is crucial to understanding the *paradigm shift*. Only if others know what the individual, the team and – on an aggregated level – the organization 'knows', concerning what their contribution for value creation could be can collaboration and exchange of IC be initiated. This is the first step in order to 'cultivate' IC in the organizational context.

There are several shifts in the corporate environment which affect the management of IC:

- *Diversification into small legal units* to improve risk management: particularly organizations in highly innovative domains tend to spin off legal entities for further development of promising ideas to prevent endangering the sponsoring company in case of failure.
- *Integration of value chains* to realize cost advantages while keeping legal independence: this allows for fast reorientation and re-formation particularly in highly innovative industries with short product life cycles Knowledge-intensive organizations regularly find application of their services in so far unknown markets.
- *Blurring organizational boundaries* in joint innovation and development processes: this is particularly relevant for very small organizations that associate with others in projects that involve limited time and are poorly defined.
- *Challenges to align teams* and small groups with independent and autonomous agendas to an overall strategy while avoiding local optima.

ICR can contribute to overcoming the challenges of these changes in the business environment, as it provides shared context and a shared language. One model that focuses on this management challenge while providing an excellent framework for communication is made available by the German Guideline for IC Statements, which will be briefly discussed below.

The model of AKWB

Six steps to approaching an ICR

AKWB is an international team of researchers dedicated to advancing the conceptual framework of ICR on theoretical and empirical levels.[12] It was asked by the German Ministry for Economics and Labour to develop a set of guidelines for intellectual capital reporting for small and medium-sized organizations. ICR, according to the German Guideline for ICR, is drafted in six steps including four milestones.[13]

Milestone I is the intellectual capital statement in its simplest form. As shown by Figure 13.1, three steps lead to the first result. The first step is to *identify drivers of IC* contributing to the achievement of the strategic priorities and to *self-assess the current degree* of available quantity and quality as well as systematic management of IC relative to the strategic requirements. This is performed by members of the organization from all hierarchical and functional levels. The target group of Milestone I is the management of the organization which can extract measures for improvement on the basis of the results.

Milestone II targets the same group, but supports the self-evaluation with indicators. Using facts and indicators from either already existing management information systems or various reports, *defining and measuring new indicators for IC* allows measuring changes independently from the employee's self-evaluation. The collection and assessment of indicators supports the later internal or external communication.

Milestone III provides a *document of the organization's intellectual capital*. It is adjusted towards a specific (external and/or internal) target group and describes the most important information attractively and in a structured

Six Steps Towards an Intellectual Capital Statement

| How? Management | Milestone IV |
| How much? Indicators | Milestone II |

How? Management — Milestone IV
Who? Communication — Milestone III
How much? Indicators — Milestone II
How good? Evaluation — Milestone I
What? Intellectual Capital
What for? Initial Situation

Figure 13.1   Approaches to an intellectual capital report[18]

form. The most important added value of this document is providing the context in which the organization's IC is to be seen. It helps to interpret the data and serves to create shared mental models which determine the resultant decision-making.

Milestone IV delivers a full intellectual capital statement which aims to monitor the organization and to support decision-making. It integrates among other things a *comprehensive cause-and-effect analysis* to shed some light into the so far 'black box' of the intellectual capital value creation process. This provides information with regard to where to optimally invest in order to improve the overall performance of the organization according to strategic requirements.

Benefits for developing ICRs

Organizations which have implemented an ICR report that a number of beneficial aspects can be expected:

- The joint development of the ICR across hierarchical levels *improves the general understanding* of how the enterprise actually works and *how IC contributes to value creation*. Management receives feedback related to the application of IC from operative business and employees gain an impression of the challenges faced by management. This leads to improved co-ordination of joint goals and future tasks such as decentralized decision-making.
- Developing a language for knowledge and IC and defining factors of IC with a strong strategic impact make it possible to *promote constructive discussions about IC* and to avoid misunderstandings that otherwise could lead to loss in productivity.
- Concentrating on a small set of influencing factors and knowledge of their contribution to the strategic priorities supports *focused learning and change* activities.
- Discussing the influential factors of IC in operational teams creates synergies and makes for an *innovative atmosphere*.
- Concentrating on customers and knowledge of their needs sustains a better *orientation towards added value and competitive advantages*.

The future of intellectual capital reporting

What is the future of IC Reporting? Is there any future at all? These questions are hard to answer in times of fading managements and shortening life cycles of concepts. However, there are a few encouraging developments that suggest there is a future for ICR, at least for the fundamental idea though maybe not for the terms currently in use. The model of AKWB briefly discussed above is being implemented in several organizations, but it is almost impossible to monitor the exact number of successful projects.

So far, more than 50 multipliers were trained in two-day seminars to spread the idea all over German-speaking areas, to a lesser extent internationally. The aim is to create as many prototypes and experiences as possible in order to learn more about usability and limits of this approach and its mutations.

Parallel to this approach, several other are being created by consultants and researchers, sometimes by business organizations, and certainly these will contribute to the variety of models. Particularly relevant to mention are initiatives sponsored by the European Unions Research Programme[14] and activities within OECD communities.[15]

With all necessary caution, a few predictions about the development of the topic of ICR could be made, referring to:

- valuation according to strategic requirements;
- relating ICR and ICM to daily operations;
- specialization of ICR;
- regional aspects of ICR; and
- conceptual development of IC models.

These will be discussed in varying degrees of detail in the next paragraphs.

Valuation according to strategic requirements

In order to gain relevance as a management instrument, IC Reports need to *provide strategic orientation*. ICR will have to answer the following questions:

- What are the strategic priorities?
- What are the relevant driving forces (of IC) to accomplish the strategy?
- Where does an intervention make most economic sense?
- Did we improve or worsen relative to the last period?

Currently, there is no absolute measure for IC available. From the management perspective, this is no problem at all, as usually a clearly defined strategy provides the yardstick for most of the daily operations. It makes sense to relate the *status quo* of IC to strategic requirements. However, there are a few challenges to master:

- *Reduction of complexity* while not becoming trivial: at the end of a business day, one question is most relevant, that is, am I in trouble or am I okay? Hence, evaluation of IC relative to the strategic priorities could provide an answer that is sufficiently simple while still focusing on the overall big picture.
- *Improvement of transparency*: as interdependence between organizational parts increases, demand for transparency and additional relevant data arises particularly within an organization. However, there are limits to

transparency, as soon as competitors are involved. Right now, the culture to share strengths and weaknesses is not established, and most likely this will not change soon. However, once means and instruments for providing transparency are available, the strategic option to actually share this insight with carefully selected partners gains relevance. It provides the path for new strategic alliances.

• *Creation of new strategic context-based images*: the bottleneck of transferring knowledge and aligning mental models is regularly routed in communication. Some decades ago, Boston Consulting Group (BCG) created their famous portfolio approach to map an organization's products relative to market volumes and marginal earnings. This revolutionized the perspective of most people involved in the marketing context. Today in 2005, we face similar challenges in the domain of knowledge and intellectual capital. New maps are required to visualize the strategic impact of IC.

Relating ICR and ICM to daily operations

The greatest challenges in managing the daily operations of an organization are to *create a shared context* and to *align the mental models* of interdependence of the people involved in the value creation process.

The future of ICR will depend on its ability to meet both challenges in a sufficient percentage of people. This seems of higher priority than coming up with a 'precise' euro or dollar value for IC, as the figure itself, stripped of its context and meaning, is neutral. But people need to decide. They need to allocate time and resources for a huge variety of tasks, all of them competing for attention, maybe the only scarce element in the business context. If there is no guideline, no framework or mental model as to how all these many individual parameters interact with and influence each other, an individual will not be able to distinguish the really important from the arbitrary and, as a consequence, act randomly. This is obviously an exaggeration, as there are many models available, but which is the one that we would like to apply in *our* organization? Which is the one that makes the difference in productivity?

A further challenge is to integrate highly autonomous teams with very specific knowledge bases and little common ground into new innovative groups which share specific models, but frequently lack a uniting mental model which could offer orientation for the decision-making processes. The joint development of an ICR could provide a commonly shared perspective and thus contribute to organizational development. It offers a chance to reflect the daily operations in the context of IC and strategic development.

Specialization of ICR

As discussed above, defining a target group is crucial for the actual design of an ICR and its future development. According to discussions in various contexts, there is demand for specialized reports depending on the specific needs of interest groups. Each will have individual strengths and weaknesses and aim to target different audiences.

Research and development

The focus here will be the 'know what', and it will deliver most likely aggregate data on specific content which is relevant in the scientific community. Two missions might attract attention:

1 reporting on genuine research in the business context to create awareness about the R&D function;
2 legitimizing the use of funds as suggested by the Austrian law that encourages universities to report on what they did to further develop their intangibles.[16]

Financial institutions

The discussion related to financial valuations for IC will not end in the immediate future, as the desire to relate intellectual capital to just one simple key indicator will not fade. However, financial markets and investors will, as they have throughout history, eagerly absorb public and non-public data about the knowledge base of organizations and factor them in to the market prize according to their expectations. As a consequence, structured delivery of data related to IC stocks and the intended future application will contribute to a more efficient market in the future.

In the context of Basel II, financial institutions will most likely use data about IC for external risk assessment. The hypothesis is not that an ICR in itself will contribute to cheaper interest rates, but that an organization that is aware of its IC and manages it accordingly will most likely deliver profitable results.

In the context of start-up funding, there is regularly no financial record available. An ICR could make all the difference and maybe deliver the data required for funding.

Integrated value chains and networks of excellence

As the need for fast ramp up of production capacities for new applications increases, new network organizations might emerge. They are not (yet) legally united, but might wish to share data about their intangible assets in a structured manner in order to better integrate their value chains. The first requirement of an ICR, a shared language, might support to develop a joint value proposition. Later it might contribute to improved business efficiency. A joint ICR allows organizations to:

- develop and communicate their shared vision and strategic priorities;
- better align their value-adding abilities; and

- develop the trust and credibility needed to attract the attention of a much larger potential customer, who otherwise might not even consider this consortium a supplier.

On a more general level, the differentiation of knowledge and derived application will require new *channels of communication*. ICR could provide just that for small groups, even individuals, who might find advantages in using a reporting structure that is similar to current ICRs. This communication function relates to one of the most widely used applications of ICR.

ICR for marketing purposes

The customers are regularly at the centre of organizational communication. Various instruments are designed to impress them and to develop good relations. One interesting path of development for ICRs is to further improve these relations by inviting customers into the development process of an ICR. Performed regularly, this added perspective offers invaluable feedback for all members of the organization, as the customer represents 'the truth of the market'. His inputs need not necessarily be what others see as their 'reality', but offer an alternative view. Whatever it is, ignoring this perspective will soon lead to economic problems.

Regional aspects of ICR

Global business players and technology leaders need data to optimally allocate their investments. As some of them follow the hypothesis that investments in knowledge-intensive businesses are best supported in regions with high availability of knowledge in the form of IC, they might be eager to get support in the form of regional IRCs. So far, documents that provide data about regionally available IC are rare exceptions.[17] However, the formal structure of an ICR provides a solid framework to deliver exactly this kind of data and allows positioning a region strategically. By aligning already existing knowledge bases to an overall development strategy and complementing so far missing elements, ICR might become a powerful instrument for regional development.

Conceptual development of IC models

At the time of writing, we face fast progress in the field of indicators for IC. A few hundred *indicators* are available in various contexts, sometimes overlapping and not yet consolidated to an integrated set. However, this huge variety will be analysed by academic researchers for IC and eventually yield an economical list that serves as a menu for organizations interested in benchmarking of selected topics. These indicators need to fulfil the criteria of precise definition of both words and formula in order to be reliable, valid and hence comparable.

After substantial reliable empirical data is available, statistical analysis might come up with some rules of thumb that allow *contextual interpretation*. Right now, the implicitly assumed logic 'the more, the better', which is applicable to most financial indicators such as return on investment, earnings, sales and so on regularly does not fit with IC. There are some ranges in the spectrum of indicators that are associated with positive impact on the organization and others with negative. An example is 'investment into work force training', with no training at all considered obviously negative. There comes a favourable distribution of investments, which fades into an area that is obviously negatively impacting organizational performance. This is reached when all resources (time and money) are dedicated to learning and none remain for the actual value-adding processes.

Finally, an improved *conceptual model* of IC reporting might emerge and be useful for different applications and interest groups while still providing a comprehensive internal structure. It would have to interface with strategy, as this provides overall orientation for the utilization of IC. Most likely it will address value creation processes, as these provide the organizational backbone for most enterprises. Additionally it will need to refer to business results, as these are the ultimate motivation to engage in business. It seems likely that the currently established terminology will be used, even though there are some conflicts with established schools of thought, the most obvious concerning the meaning of 'capital' in the domain of accountants versus managers.

Some people advocate the application of 'objective' measures for knowledge and IC. Even though this idea seems very attractive, particularly from so-called 'market-driven' forces, who expect a simple measure to improve their profits, it is not likely to be accomplished in the near future. This challenge ultimately ends in philosophic models of constructivism and non-constructivism and so on. My own idea is, it just is not 'simple' to do profitable business, but will require digging into the context of a deal, relating it to a specific strategic setting, thinking(!) and reflecting, and finally deciding. There is no easy way out and therefore there is need for good business sense, factual knowledge of context and, sometimes, humour so as not to take business too seriously.

Notes

1   For reference, see the definition of intangible assets according to IAS 38, 1998.
2   For an early summary of the discussion related to the management of IC, see Bontis and Choo (2002).
3   Skandia (1995).
4   The European Union funded several research programmes in The Netherlands, Spain, the UK and others, resulting in several national initiatives. On a legal level the most advanced is Austria, where parts of the public university budgets

are allocated relative to IC performance. On the SME context, Germany successfully repositioned itself with a set of guidelines for ICR, after failing to recognize the development in the beginning.

5　See Sveiby, 1997a and Sveiby, 1997b.
6　The University of St Gallen is currently almost synonymous for 'integrated' approaches, thanks to a tradition of research and teaching of many decades. See Bleicher (2000).
7　One interesting exception is provided by Strassmann (1996), who assigns the value-adding capacity exclusively to the management of an organization.
8　Source: Intellectual Capital Statement, Made in Germany, Guideline. Ministry for Economics and Labour, Berlin 2004. The terms 'intellectual capital statement' and 'intellectual capital report' are used without distinction.
9　Bornemann and Leitner (2002).
10　Ibid.
11　Edvinsson and Malone, 1997, p. 59.
12　For more information, see www.akwissensbilanz.org
13　Source: Intellectual Capital Statement, Made in Germany, Guideline. Ministry for Economics and Labour, Berlin 2004.
14　MERITUM, MAGIC and PRISM are three influential projects aiming to develop measures for IC.
15　The *status quo* of the OECD discussion related to IC is documented here: http://www.oecd.org/document/39/0,2340,en_2649_33703_33725863_1_1_1_1,00.html
16　For Austrian law regarding the organization of universities, see UOG, 2002.
17　Examples: Israel's Edna Pasher published a national IC report in 1998 based on the Edvinsson–Skandia model. Croatia published a national IC report based on the VAIC method in 2002 based on data provided by Ante Pulic. The municipality of Munich provided a document covering a sound overview of their knowledge intensive industries in 2002. Oresund Science Region created an illustrated survey on its science institutions.

References

Bleicher, K. (2000) *Integriertes Management* (St. Gallen: Campus).
Bontis, N. and C. W. Choo (2002) *The Strategic Management of Intellectual Capital and Organizational Knowledge* (Oxford: Oxford University).
Bornemann, M. and K. H. Leitner (2002) 'Measuring and Reporting Intellectual Capital: The Case of a Research Technology Organisation', *Singapore Management Review* (Special Issue on Management of Knowledge and Intellectual Capital), 24(3), 7–20.
Bundesministerium für Wirtschaft und Arbeit (2004) *Intellectual Capital Statement, Made in Germany, Guideline*, Berlin.
Croatian Chamber of Economy, Intellectual Capital Association (2003) *Intellectual Capital. Efficiency on National and Company Level*, Zagreb.
Edvinsson, L. and M. Malone (1997) *Intellectual Capital*, p. 59.
Edvinsson, L. (2001) *Corporate Longitude* (New York: Harper Business).
Edvinsson, L. and M. Malone (1997) *Intellectual Capital* (New York: Harper Business).
IAS (1998) *Intangible Assets IAS 38* (London: International Accounting Standard).
Kaplan, R. S. and D. Norton (1996) *The Balanced Scorecard: Translating Strategy into Action* (Boston: Harvard Business School Press).

Landeshauptstadt München (2002) Referat für Arbeit und Wirtschaft: München, *Stadt des Wissens*, München.

Lev, B. (2001) Intangibles: *Management, Measurement and Reporting* (Washington, DC: Brookings Institution Press).

MERITUM Project (2001) Intellectual Capital Report, *Guidelines for Managing and Reporting on Intangibles*, Madrid.

UOG (2002) Bundesministerium für Bildung, Wissenschaft und Kultur (bm: bwk) Universitätsgesetz 2002. http://www.unigesetz.at

Pasher, E. (1999) *The Intellectual Capital of the State of Israel* (Herzlia Pituach: Kal Press).

Pulic, A. (1996) 'Der Informationskoeffizient als Wertschöpfungsmaß wissensintensiver Unternehmen', in U. Schneider, (ed.), *Wissensmanagement, Die Aktivierung des intellektuellen Kapitals* (Frankfurt: FAZ).

PRISM: www.euintangibles.net

Reinhardt, R. (2002) *Wissen als Ressource: Theoretische Grundlagen, Methoden und Instrumente der Erfassung von Wissen* (Frankfurt: Lang Verlag).

Republik Österreich (2002) UOG 2002, § 13 *Leistungsvereinbarung*, Bundesgesetzblatt für die Republik Österreich.

Skandia (1995) 'Visualizing Intellectual Capital in Skandia', supplement to Skandia's 1994 Annual Report, Stockholm.

Spath, D., K. Wagner and A. Slama (2002) *Bewertung von Wissenskapital. Wettbewerbsvorteile nutzen durch bewussten und zielgerichteten Einsatz von Wissen*, Abschlussbericht des EU Projekts MAGIC (Measuring and Accounting Intellectual Capital), Fraunhofer IRB Verlag, Stuttgart.

Stewart, T. A. (1997) *Intellectual Capital: The New Wealth of Organisations* (New York: Doubleday Currency).

Strassmann, P. (1996) *The Value of Computers, Information and Knowledge* (New Canaan: Strassmann http://www.strassmann.com/pubs/cik/cik-value.shtml).

Sveiby, K. E. (1997a) *The New Organisational Wealth, Managing and Measuring Knowledge-Based Assets* (San Fransisco, CA: Berrett-Koehler).

Sveiby, K. E. (1997b) 'The Intangible Assets Monitor', *Journal of Human Resource Costing & Accounting*, 2(1).

Index